I have nev … hat a tender and
moving st … ily going through
the arduo … rageous and godly
spirit mix … rous unexpected
twists and … usband. The story
of the ruby necklace brought tears to my eyes. What a confident expectation is exhibited as the power of Christ and His Gospel is shown through Courtney's suffering and death and coming resurrection.

Bruce McAllister,
Director of Ministry Relations,
Gospel Fellowship Association Missions,
Greenville, SC

This deeply personal glimpse into one family's pain and the overwhelming grace of God they experienced will increase your faith. Even in very bad circumstances, the Gospel is still good news. Jesus Christ gives a song in the midst of suffering. Second Corinthians 1:4 reminds us that the Lord *comforteth us in all our tribulation, that we may be able to comfort them which are in any trouble, by the comfort wherewith we ourselves are comforted of God.* As you read this moving story, you will hear the testimony of people who found true comfort and desire to share it with others. Our stories are all different, but God's grace is always the same.

Scott Pauley
Evangelist

The author has led us through his and his wife's difficult journey in battling her brain cancer. The scriptural faith of the family and friends as well as that of the author and his wife is inspiring, solid, and instructive. I have often seen families rely only on faith or only on medical science for direction when facing these challenges. This family followed medical care while maintaining strong faith in God's will and His total control. The result was in His timing and plan. God used this cancer and this family for good, which was the patient's desire.

M. Gildersleeve, MD
Retired Internist

From Email Recipients

Justin's emails ministered to me like a modern psalm. In the midst of suffering and sorrow Justin and Courtney didn't turn in on themselves, but rather out to others and up to God. Their example was a powerful reminder to look to Jesus in every circumstance, the only source of life and peace in this world.

—work colleague

During the illness of your beloved wife, I was in an emotional state of trying to trust God with my physical state due to almost dying from COVID.

Not too long after my illness, we learned of my firstborn son's diagnosis of failing organs and the soon projected loss of his sight. Reading your weekly updates on the condition of your wife allowed me to pray for her and appreciate the grace and mercy that embraced your family. I would check for the updates to read the hope and faith you'd share as it gave me hope. You see I, too, had to entrust my son to God. My heart felt the pain and sorrow that was potentially bound to take place, yet you and your wife had such amazing faith and trust in God's perfect plan for her life.

It was those written words of faith, trust, and reliance on our Almighty's perfect will for your wife that helped get me through the pain and sorrow that awaited me prior to her passing. My son was just forty-eight years old, but God in His sovereignty took him home because it was time for my son to stop suffering. That, dear friend, was my relief, my comfort, and the reminder of God's grace and sufficiency. I can't thank you and your beloved wife enough for the strength and encouragement that you both gave me as I knew inevitably God was going to take my son home. I just want to encourage you and say thank you for never giving up or failing to trust the Lord during your ordeal.

—a mother

This story is all about grace imparted and grace reflected. Our family watched God give Justin and Courtney grace for an unimaginable trial, and we watched them reflect His grace as they sent emails full of faith, hope, and love in the face of pain and death. As their emails were an excellent example to us, so will this book show you an example of accessing and reflecting God's amazing grace.

—missionary and Bible translator

After joining Justin and Courtney's email list, I experienced how people throughout the world were holding up this couple through both prayer and earthly deeds. To read these emails is to see a shining example of how God provides and cares for people who are afflicted but nonetheless choose to walk in His ways, even if He does not choose to remove their affliction here on earth.

—a former coworker of Justin's

I always found encouragement from your emails. In spite of the trials your family went through, your faith and trusting in God's will for your life shone through.

—homeschooling mom

I was inspired by Justin and Courtney's faith, courage, and bravery that was demonstrated through their email updates. The email updates challenged my faith, courage, and bravery in return. I'm looking forward to having them published so I may be encouraged again in the future and may share the inspiration with others.

—accountant

As a relative, we have all had an interest in the family and Courtney's health. The strength of you two to handle adversity is what impressed most. The way you and your entire family carried on, helping out, and hearing from you helped us go on at times when we did not feel like it. The example Courtney set is impossible to follow.

—one of Courtney's relatives

Courtney and Justin's journey through the diagnosis of cancer to the death of Courtney demonstrated how a Christian can journey with God steadfastly from beginning to "end" no matter how surprising the journey may be.

—missionary

The most important thing I learned through the emails was how Father God showed up again and again in your story, and how He will do the same for us if we ask Him. My faith grew!

—Justin's cousin

William Cowper wrote, "Sometimes a light surprises the Christian while he sings"—Justin and Courtney's journey is full of surprising light and heartening song. It is a window through which I was privileged to witness their peace in the midst of pain, and their courageous perseverance in seeking the good and perfect purposes of our loving heavenly Father. Publishing this story is part of their "for good" (Romans 8:28-29)—a precious legacy of hope.

—a longtime friend

Courtney and Justin's journey demonstrated their devotion and faith in their Savior throughout. Courtney endured a lot of uncertain medical journeys and changes in her physical life with grace. She was an inspiration to those around her and used herself to show God's grace. Many people wouldn't see it that way. And that's how she was with all the family, making us feel better. She has no idea how much she is missed, and how many lives around the world that she may have changed because of cancer. Although the outcome is not what we wanted, Justin and the family keep serving God and praising Him daily, something that Courtney would have wanted and expected.

—Courtney's sister

HE HELPED US *Sing*

Through Cancer with Christ

Justin Martin

bookVillages™

He Helped Us Sing: Through Cancer with Christ

www.bookvillages.com

All Scripture quotations are taken from the King James Version.

“I Trust in You” © 2019, Maegan Stewart, www.hisownministries.com.
“The Promise of God.” Words and Music by Mary Rose Jensen, © Garden Rose Music, http://gardenrosemusic.com. CCLI#3423291
Used by kind permission.

ISBN-13: 978-1-95756-602-3

Interior Design by Niddy Griddy Design, Inc.
Cover Design by Kristen King

LCCN: 2022922583

Printed in the United States of America

1 2 3 4 5 6 7 8 9 10 Printing/Year 27 26 25 24 23

Psalm 84:11

For the LORD God is a sun and shield:
the LORD will give grace and glory:
no good thing will he withhold
from them that walk uprightly.

To the Memory of
My Beloved Wife
Who Saw the Elijah Clouds,
But Even More
To the God
Who Sent Them to Us

Contents

Foreword 11

Acknowledgments 13

The Martin Family 15

Introduction 17

1. Cancer! 19

2. Incurable Glioblastoma 29

3. Courtney Writes a Letter 41

4. A Merry Heart: Grandma's Revenge! 53

5. "Keen to Try Some Sort of Operation" 61

6. "I Feel Pretty" 73

7. Home!: "The Lord Is All That Matters" 83

8. "The Comforting Presence Is Real" 91

9. "How Could We Be Anything but Thankful?" 101

10. "We'll Take It"—Twice! 109

11. Grace and Glory 123

12. Sometimes, Spectacles Need Adjustment 135

13. Farewell, Scotland; Hello, Colorado 143

14. Joy, and Then Disaster 153

15. Small Gifts and Better Days 165

16. Milestones 179

17. Heartaches, and More Heartaches 193

18. "This Is the Worst Possible Scenario" 207

19. Courtney's Clinical Trial 219

20. Platelets and Low Blood Pressure 229
21. Infection! 241
22. The Mountains Were Still There 253
23. A Bad Fall! 263
24. This Was Good, Too 275
25. So Thankful! 291
26. The Hardest Chapter 305
27. Well with Our Souls 317
28. Into the New Year 329
29. A Threefold Cord 341
30. Courtney's Farewell Service 351
31. No Good Thing Withheld 361
32. Elijah Clouds 373
Appendix A: Getting Right with God 379
Appendix B: Symptom List 385

Foreword

"Wherefore by their fruits ye shall know them."
(Matthew 7:20)

If you have picked up this book, it is probably for one of a couple reasons: you know of the family and want to read about their experience, or you are dealing with a similar struggle (or know someone that is). Regardless of the reason, you rightly want to know of the authenticity of not just the story, but the people in it.

I can say with utmost certainty that the story told, the spirit shown, and the attitudes expressed are real. They are *also* raw and relevant- something we all need. The author is personally sensitive and spiritually aware while dealing with these trials and is also always concerned for others.

You will read with a broken heart for the trials and tribulations, but also with a joyful heart to know the testimony of a faithful family and the effect on an unknown multitude.

I first met the author and his wife while they were living in Scotland, just before the diagnosis. It has been a privilege to get to know them and become their Pastor. To see in real life their desire "*to do right and honor the Lord*" as well as their "*need to be kind to others whatever they felt*" has been authentic and Christ honoring.

You will see their commitment to God and each other, their love for Christ, and their determination to set a right example of Him. This book will help you begin to understand our flawed view of self, to see that what we think we deserve is just our own self-centered view and not the Lord's. Glimpses of *their* heart will help you to stop, think, and assess *yours.*

This book will be of untold value to many. Through the words and example of the author and his wife, it will model and teach answers to many questions we all have (or will someday face). It points to principles in the Word of God that, as it lighted their way, can light yours also.

Pastor Jason Brockman
Colorado Springs Baptist Church

Acknowledgments

All six of our "kids" (and spouses). Their encouragement, suggestions, and editing contributions helped turn an idea into reality.

The doctors, nurses, physical therapists, technicians, and medical researchers. They did their best to give us more time and showed us so much kindness. I will always be grateful.

Our church in Scotland. They loved us for years and prayed for us throughout.

Pastor Jason and Mrs. Mendy Brockman, for their example and support through hard months. The congregation of Colorado Springs Baptist Church loved us and encouraged me in this project.

Mrs. Faenell (Finster) Bartlett, my high school English teacher. She taught me the rules, but "you can break the rules if there is a good reason and you are a good enough writer," and she tried to make me good enough.

Many people gave valuable feedback on the early chapters. Pam Congdon and Don Congdon were my first editors.

Lena Searcy (web page) and Kristen King (book cover) made good things happen despite my paucity of artistic ability and creativity.

Karen Pickering and others at Book Villages gave such invaluable counsel and help that I must almost call this "our book." We all wanted it to really be "God's book."

Finally, so many people prayed, encouraged, and gave to us in so many ways. I couldn't list them all, and many prefer anonymity. Their reward is with the Lord.

The Martin Family*

Justin and Courtney

Katherine

Robert (Manda): Winston, Daffodil, Duncan, and Miles

Marguerite (Edward): Neil and Charlotte

Rosa

Eric

Alyssa

Winston, Daffodil, Duncan, Neil, Charlotte, and Miles (collectively) are "The Cuteness Roarers."

My fellowworkers unto the kingdom of God, which have been a comfort unto me.
Colossians 4:11

If our kids had not faithfully and diligently joined in the work of the ministry in Scotland, our church would not have existed. All six of them had important roles and served the Lord.

* All names have been changed.

Introduction

We Didn't Expect It

On Thanksgiving Day, 26 November 2020, we were given a diagnosis no one ever wants to hear. My wife, Courtney, had a glioblastoma, an incurable tumour, already over five centimetres in diameter and obviously growing very rapidly, in the right frontal lobe of her brain.

We didn't expect anything like that. Courtney was relatively young (fifty-seven), healthy, active, and careful about nutrition. She was well adjusted, happy, and thankful. She was bringing nothing into her life (mentally, emotionally, or physically) that would contribute to significant health issues.

So began a fourteen-month roller-coaster ride of joys and sorrows, laughter and tears, hopes and sadness—and singing and singing. I expected an intense trial of faith. Instead, God gave a simple assurance (mentally *and* emotionally) that, "Whatever happens, this is going to be okay." My Bible calls it, "the peace of God, which passeth all understanding" (Philippians 4:7).

We began writing emails asking for prayer—and they circled the globe. We didn't anticipate that either. We were "nobodies," not famous (and didn't want to be). I pastored a very small church in Scotland's Central Belt. We wanted our town to know Jesus but didn't care if the wider world heard of us. As the children's song says, we were just trying to let our light shine, "you in your small corner, and I in mine." We'd never networked to become "known"—but our emails still traveled.

Passing months brought another surprise. We heard, "We should encourage you, and instead, you always encourage and challenge us." That wasn't our goal; we just wanted to tell of God's goodness to us. Near the end, a friend wrote, "These emails may communicate your greatest work of ministry." Pastors read them to churches. People passed them on—to six people, to ten people, to even more—because they thought they were valuable.

After Courtney reached Glory, friends suggested compiling the emails to encourage others in life's extremely difficult phases. While this book includes untold parts of the story, including some excerpts from my inbox, it primarily tells our story through those emails.

The emails are mostly "raw." I was tired, sometimes writing urgently, very much "in the moment," with no time or energy to edit or refine the writing style. I didn't even sign all of them. That is the reality of life with cancer, and I've left the emails mostly unedited to reflect that (torturing my poor editor!), though I corrected some grammar and spelling mistakes. I used British English in emails written from Scotland and in the chapters containing those emails. I used American English for US-based material. For privacy reasons, I changed all names (including ours) and edited some geographical and other details.

The content of the emails, however, is unchanged. The emotions, the struggles, the songs we sang, the things we got wrong (whether because we misunderstood or were misinformed), those all remain. What God allowed us to think and feel is part of the story of His work in us, and this is not a medical history but a spiritual history of our passage through these days. May it help readers through their own spiritual journeys through heartrending crises.

I wish I could cure glioblastoma and this world's other heart-wrenching ills. I can't even offer the peace we had—it's not mine to give. Perhaps, though, this book may help draw you a step closer to the God who fills hearts with peace beyond human understanding. There is no One better to have with you when your world turns upside down. He can help you sing too.

Chapter 1

Cancer!

"There's a Cyst on the Front of Your Brain"

With those words from the doctor, followed by, "We do think it is cancer," our world forever changed. Thus, I sent the first of many of what I came to call "Courtney Cancer" emails.

25 November 2020 (Wednesday p.m.)

Dear All

The CT scan shows a cyst on the front of Courtney's brain. They are almost certain it is cancerous. She will be in through the weekend while they run further tests and check for cancer elsewhere in her body that may have spread to the brain.

They are very optimistic that it is treatable, especially because Courtney is in such good physical condition. All those dog-walking miles during lockdown helped! :)

Courtney is now having balance troubles, they don't believe it is safe for her to come home, and by being in hospital, they said she will get tests very quickly. They said once they have ruled out infection, they can use steroids to temporarily shrink the tumour and her symptoms should be significantly improved.

They said she certainly would not be allowed to travel now, but that the steroids might give her space to make the move and have treatment in the US instead. In other words, we might be moving very, very quickly, if we end up going that route, or we might not be moving for some time to come. There are many things very much up in the air.

Courtney is in good spirits. We've not travelled this particular journey, but we've seen the Lord's goodness to us so many times. I trust we had a good testimony with the doctors and nurse, we told them we're ok and why.

I was listening to Alexander Scourby's Bible reading on the way to the hospital, in the Psalms. I knew the doctor would not have asked me to come in if it wasn't "bad" news, and I knew from the symptoms almost certainly what they would say. Psalms 42 & 43 came up. "Why art thou cast down, O my soul? and why art thou disquieted within me? hope thou in God: for I shall yet praise him, who is the health of my countenance, and my God." We get those words three times in those two Psalms to make sure that even the thickest among us don't miss it. I also got through Psalm 44 before I arrived.

After giving us the results, they let us sit together in a room for a while and talk. So I got out my phone and we listened to Psalm 45, the Psalm of the King's Marriage. A nice thing to have next on the playlist when you are with your wife at times like this. And then, next was Psalm 46, so we listened to Scourby on that one, too. "God is our refuge and strength, a very present help in trouble."

We're fine. The Lord never puts us on a path that doesn't have a good end and a lot of good along the way.

Thanks for your prayers, we'll keep you posted. For tonight, you might pray that my ear doesn't get too sore, I'm on the phone a lot this evening.

In Him
Justin

And so, our cancer journey began. We'd moved to Scotland from America in 1995 and had mixed results with the Scottish National Health Service, but we'd always heard they were excellent with cancer care. We were about to find out for ourselves.

We were "too young" for cancer to hit us, but cancer knows no age limits. We were "too healthy," "too fit," but cancer doesn't care. We were "too spiritual," "too good," according to some, but that's neither logical nor theo-logical—we were not "too good," and even if we had been, that is not how God works.

Sure, I was a pastor, but we were little different from many thousands serving the Lord in "wee" churches like ours in Scotland and around the world. Like many others I was an unpaid pastor—my computer software work put food on the table. Also like many others, we suddenly had to face a life-shaking crisis. There was nothing particularly special about us, but even if there had been, cancer can come whether you think you are special or not.

The doctor and nurses gave us a few minutes, and Courtney said, "Well, we'll see what the MRI says, I guess." I nodded, and said, "Okay?" and she said, "Yes, except for the headache."

I said, "I listened to Scourby reading the Bible coming in." Courtney smiled, and said, "Of course." I told her what I'd just heard, and we listened to Psalms 45 and 46 together. We prayed, kissed goodbye, and I left (due to COVID-19 restrictions, I knew the doctors would want me to leave quickly). I went home, called family, sent the previous email, and started calling friends.

The night before had been long and late, and I was exhausted. I prayed, lay down, and slept. I remember that I slept well and woke up refreshed. I really believed what I'd said in that email: "The Lord never puts us on a path that doesn't have a good end and a lot of good along the way." I still believe it.

Maybe Something Is Wrong

We had visited Utah in October to see our new granddaughter, Charlotte, returning on 1 November. Courtney had a sore back from the trip, which appeared to be feeding into tension headaches. I would massage her neck and back, and she would sleep but wake up sore again.

Scotland's COVID lockdown regimen through the spring and summer had been very strict, with Scots only allowed to leave their homes for exercise once a day. Rather than being stuck unmercifully at home, we made our one time a day count, walking two, three, even five miles off through the hills. When we returned from Utah, we kept up our walking.

My first clues of a problem, unrecognised at the time, came on 17 November. Courtney was reading on her iPad, and I asked a question. She looked up for a couple seconds and then looked down and started reading again, without answering. It wasn't something I particularly needed answered right away. I thought, *Wow, she must really be concentrating on that,* and decided not to disturb her again.

Later, we went for a walk, and Courtney lagged. I

stopped, waited, and asked, "Are you okay?" She said, "It's just my headache." We went home, I gave her a massage, and it eased. Neither of us thought anything more. We'd walked over two miles at a quick pace, so obviously there was nothing significantly wrong.

A couple days later she had other symptoms, but it all fit with just a very bad tension headache. But on Sunday the 22nd, Courtney started to have nausea, and that evening I took her to urgent care. They gave her something for nausea and for head pain. They said to follow up with our General Practitioner in three days if she wasn't better. We didn't last that long.

"You Need to Take Her to Hospital Now"

Monday, Courtney did better, but Tuesday morning a severe headache was accompanied by serious confusion/disorientation. I called the GP clinic to ask for an emergency appointment that day. About an hour later, the nurse called back.

She asked if Courtney knew the day, and she said, "It's Sunday." When asked her address, Courtney rattled it off, laughing at such silly, easy questions. I told her, "You are laughing, but you just said it's Sunday, and it's Tuesday." She said, "Didn't you preach this morning?" From then on, Courtney would struggle to know the day and recognise the passing of time.

At our midafternoon appointment, the doctor examined Courtney and said, "Please wait in the waiting room for a minute." A few minutes later she came back and said, "I'd like to talk to you, Mr Martin. Mrs Martin, you can wait here; it's okay."

In her office, she said, "I phoned the hospital and arranged a scan. You need to take her to hospital now." I said, "She's not coming home tonight," and she said,

"No." I said, "We're five minutes away, can I stop for a few things?" and she said, "No, I want her in hospital as quickly as possible."

Later, I was told that the urgency was to get steroid treatment started, because the doctor believed that brain swelling was causing the symptoms and might kill her or cause permanent brain damage soon.

A Long Night

At the hospital, due to COVID-19 restrictions, they didn't want to let me in. Because of Courtney's confusion and inability to describe her symptoms accurately, I finally got past the "COVID police," and by 4:00 p.m. we were on the ward. I was left in the ward's waiting room. At 5:30 p.m. the nurses called me, and I saw Courtney briefly. A nurse asked some questions Courtney had struggled to answer. I was sent back to wait for the doctor.

I didn't dare leave the waiting room, lest the COVID enforcers out there find me and make me leave. There was nothing to eat. At 7:00 and 9:30, the nurses touched base, but then it went silent.

I knew how many steps crossed the waiting room horizontally and vertically, and how many to walk it in a circle. I counted as I circled in each direction, to see if I had a different gait circling left or right. I shifted chairs to count steps from wall to wall. I proved that my Fitbit didn't always count the last step when you stopped at a wall. I memorised each sign in the room without trying.

My smartphone apps were Bible and communication. I read the Bible as I paced and communicated with our kids when I rested. I had no news, but I reported my step count, made dumb jokes about my hunger and all the things I was going to eat, and told them I'd read all of Isaiah, Jeremiah, and more. I wasn't getting much from reading except the comforting assurance of God's presence as the familiar words washed over me, but that was worth a lot.

I was determined to stay to see the doctor so I could explain Courtney's symptoms. This was silly; the scan would tell the story. I wasn't thinking of that, and even if I had, I wasn't leaving my wife in the hospital without talking to a doctor.

I didn't want to harass the very busy nurses, but finally after 1:00 a.m., I called the ward phone. The nurse said, "Oh, are you still here?" I thought, *No, I've starved to death; that's just my ghost out in your waiting room,* but instead said, "I was told to wait for the doctor."

She said, "Oh, I'm very, very sorry" (which made me glad I'd kept my snarky thought to myself!), "but the doctor won't be seeing you tonight. Your wife had some medication and is asleep. Please go home and get some sleep. The doctor will call you tomorrow. Someone should have told you." I said, "Okay, thank you." My evil sense of humour wanted to say, "You might want to check your carpet; I've worn a path in it." But I didn't . . .

On the way home I committed to thank the health-care workers, to make their job as easy as I could, even if they made mistakes, and treat them as I would if they had turned up at church last Sunday. My evil sense of humour must wait until I wrote a book later, or something. It was my first "cancer commitment," but not my last one.

Despite it being the middle of the night, Alyssa (our youngest daughter, the only one at home) made sure I had something to eat, and I crashed into bed. I slept immediately but not long, not knowing just how many "immediately but not long" sleeps were in my future.

Suddenly, the Crisis Is Now

I woke to a busy day, which was only interrupted in the late afternoon, not by a call from the doctor, but a nurse saying the doctor wanted to see me. I knew face-to-face meetings during a COVID lockdown meant bad news. I got in the car, turned on Alexander Scourby's Bible reading, and drove to the hospital (as described in the email starting this chapter).

As I read those early emails, I see now how little I understood. For example, the steroid wasn't to shrink the tumour; it was to shrink the swelling. I was entirely clueless, but I knew it was a crisis. I also knew, whatever else, that I had one responsibility—do right, and honour the Lord. I was sure He would bring us through, though I had no clue what shape "through" was going to take.

The next day was Thanksgiving Day, which we always observed though we were in Britain and not America, spending it with Robert (our second-born) who lived nearby with his wife, Manda, and their three kids: Winston, Daffodil, and Duncan (with their cousins, known as "The Cuteness Roarers"). After my late night Tuesday, and without Courtney's help, so much was unprepared that we decided to defer Thanksgiving dinner until Friday. My memory is blurry, but I think I worked some that Thanksgiving Day, since I wasn't allowed to visit Courtney and we weren't having our Thanksgiving dinner. Mostly, I was just waiting to hear from the hospital.

It didn't seem real that Courtney could have cancer, especially not a brain tumour. I suppose I was still hoping the MRI would tell a different story—but deep down, I knew it wouldn't. I should have researched the different types of brain tumours so I'd know what to ask the doctor, but I didn't even think of that. It wasn't real enough for me to do that, maybe. I suppose that's common when cancer hits—it just doesn't seem real.

Chapter 2

Incurable Glioblastoma

26 November 2020 (Thursday about midnight)

Dear All

Please do not communicate this more broadly until Friday afternoon because I've not yet been able to speak to everyone in our church.

In human terms, the prognosis is very poor. As I said just before my dad's Homegoing, "We're in miracle-only territory." The Lord could turn this, but the doctors certainly cannot.

The tumour is a glioblastoma. Average life expectancy is optimistically a year, but the doctor says Courtney's is very advanced and large. Because there were no symptoms two weeks ago and only minor ones a week ago, he thinks it is fast moving. I asked about bringing her home to care for her, but he says she is not well enough to move, which to be honest I knew. They are using steroids to reduce the swelling and fluid which should ease the symptoms, but he did not believe that would help enough for her to come home.

Dr Z is an excellent doctor, but this is not his specialty, and perhaps he was being overly cautious so as to not give false hope in someone else's area. But he is allowing not only me but also Alyssa, and Robert and Manda, to visit, which with COVID indicates how serious he considers the situation.

The cancer specialists will be deciding whether they think they can operate. If they can, they will hope to remove enough of the tumour to ease the pressure on the brain and reduce a lot of the symptoms, and hopefully she can then come home.

If our kids come home, they will have to quarantine for two weeks, including away from us (or we wouldn't be able to go into the hospital). Dr Z could not guarantee, if they did, that Courtney would be on his ward and that they would be able to see her. He recommended that they wait until we talk to the oncologist. If Courtney may get to come home after an operation, that would be by far the best time for them to come.

He was certainly not saying that they cannot operate, but obviously wanted to prepare me for that possibility, and also that if they cannot, that this could go very, very fast.

We are ok. My mom asked how our kids are, and I told her that they all processed it exactly the way they would. How can the same parents have six kids with such different personalities? But if you'd asked me in a scenario to predict how our kids would react to something like this, I'd have nailed it dead on. :) They all know, love, and trust the Lord, and it shows, in their different ways.

I do not believe Courtney understands the diagnosis. The pain has worsened so the pain medication is now affecting her significantly. I hope to be able to explain to her tomorrow between doses, she would want me to do that.

And I'm ok. I held together until I got out of the hospital, then cried all the way to the car. Then, I preached one of my sermons at myself, said, "You won't make anything better by getting in an accident, and what kind of pastor are you, anyway?" So I prayed and asked the Lord to give peace for the drive and for the phone calls to come, and amazingly, when you ask Him for something that He's promised, He gives it. :) The phone calls are hard and I'll cry more but I'm sure He'll give the grace to do whatever is needed. He doesn't abandon us in times like this, He's not that kind of God. And as I told Courtney's sisters this evening, if the Lord is taking her Home soon, she'll be happier there than married to me!

Another thing Mom said, "How quickly life changes." Yes, but for the Lord, this is no change at all, it was part of His plan all along. Perhaps He lets us see sometimes that we're in "miracle-only territory" to remind us of our total dependence on Him at all times, to purge our self-sufficiency.

If Courtney was here looking over my shoulder, she'd say, "You've said enough, quit preaching, leave it at that," and, "It's time for bed." She'd have a point. Blessings to you all.

In Him
Justin

When the call came, a nurse said, "Dr Z would like to see you at 5:00 this evening." He isn't an oncologist, so I thought, *Maybe it isn't cancer after all.* We had never met, but in pastoral hospital visits I'd encountered his reputation often, and I was glad Courtney was under his care.

They let me in to see Courtney, who seemed even more confused. She was on both painkillers and steroids. When the doctor came, he took me to another room. Courtney wanted to go, but he said, "It's best you stay here, Mrs Martin. We'll be back soon."

I got our daughter, Rosa, on the phone, and he said, "I tried to talk to your wife, but she couldn't process it, due to the pressure on her brain. The MRI shows an incurable brain tumour, called glioblastoma." It seemed to be very aggressive. If they could operate, life expectancy might be a year, but it was very large, and an operation might not be possible. He hoped high steroid doses would help, but the brain swelling was very dangerous.

I went back to Courtney's bed. Rosa was still on the line. We tried to speak to Courtney, but she was unable to respond, and I didn't even know if she heard. That really hit me. My beautiful, brilliantly intelligent wife, almost entirely normal just a week ago, couldn't even talk or understand that she had cancer. Rosa said through tears, "I love you, Mom," and said goodbye. I stayed with Courtney a couple more minutes, kissed her, and left.

Going back to the car, sobbing, I became aware of people going into the hospital. I felt so guilty—who, entering a hospital, wants to walk past someone crying his eyes out? They might have terrible things in their life, and seeing me bawling wouldn't help them. At the car I made my second "cancer commitment"—I needed to be kind to others, whatever I might be feeling.

I drove home and told Alyssa, then called the rest of our kids. I called Courtney's parents and sisters, and my mom. When Mom asked how our kids were, I told her, "Everyone's responding exactly how I'd expect."

Alyssa, our youngest and the only one at home, was extremely lazy about housework but now she was doing it all; she was upset but working like a hero.

Eric (the next youngest), serving the Lord in Eastern Europe, logically analysed his next move, ripped through the options to find the best one without a lot of back and forth, then asked me, "And how are *you*?" For all his pretence of being a Spock-like analytical logic machine, he has a tender heart.

Rosa, our Doctor of Physical Therapy, would shed loads of tears, but she professionally interrogated the doctor, then began making sure no siblings would make mistakes on passports and was busily working out how medical situations and scenarios fit into everyone's travel plans.

Marguerite, after some tears, competently got to work on getting ready to come, despite having a newborn and a toddler.

Robert, our second eldest, worked out in detail (and discussed in further detail) all the different scenarios, always with a view to "What's the right thing to do in this scenario?"

Katherine, our eldest, was, of course, saying (if not in so many words), "It is a crisis, so I must do something. You need help; I will come immediately."

I later learned that they had created their own WhatsApp group to talk about their parents behind our backs as they arranged this, that, and the other. We'd trained them to serve, and now they were conspiring to serve us.

27 November 2020 (Friday noon)

Last night, Courtney was not able to communicate or follow what I was saying. This morning, the steroids seem to have helped with the pressure on her brain and she was able to talk and understand and go look up her tumour on the Internet. She's now sent the link out to a lot of people. That, at least, is normal for her! :) She is at peace, as am I.

I'm not claiming to have slept last night—my mind spun all night with all the things we'd planned, all the things we thought we might do, all the things that will change, all the things I have to figure out how to do, how does that crazy washing machine work, how does one plan a menu and a shopping trip :), what should be bought regularly and from where, etc., etc. There's not many things I know how to do well, I've been able to live in glorious blissful ignorance.

Proverbs has 31 chapters, one for each day of the month, doubling up on the 30th this month. I got up and read today's (chapter 27). Verse 1. "Boast not thyself of to morrow; for thou knowest not what a day may bring forth." As I used to say playing chess, "Check and mate." All the plans I've made are in the rubbish bin and any I make now probably will go there, too.

The doctor is allowing us to visit, which perhaps with current restrictions says more about how concerned he is than anything else would. Our kids, if they travel, would have to quarantine for two weeks before seeing her. The doctor recommended that they wait until we get a treatment plan, which could possibly happen even today, but our eldest, Katherine, will arrive Sunday afternoon—her church paid for her flight and told her to come now.

> That's all for now, will let you know when I know more.
>
> In Him
> Justin

I slept not at all. My mind just bounced from one thing to another. Finally, early that morning, I gave up and got up. I went to get my breakfast, as I did every morning, and got my vitamins, as I did every morning. Suddenly, I stared at them and said, "Why? Who cares about vitamins? What's the point? What do you have to live for, anyway?" Almost as quickly, the answer came back, "To serve the Lord, ya numpty, just like before!"

I do not ever recommend calling someone "ya numpty." I had never done it before, but if you are calling yourself that, and you are being a numpty, it's probably okay. So quickly the Wicked One comes, so easily, so powerfully and unexpectedly, when we're weak. He wants to turn us into numpties who not only say things but also do things we shouldn't.

I took my vitamins, got my breakfast, opened my Bible to read while eating breakfast—and the very first verse was Proverbs 27:1—"Boast not thyself of to morrow." Or, the Justin Martin version, "Don't be a numpty." I'd spent all night ripping through our plans and boastings for tomorrows and tossing them in the rubbish. They were gone—it was no wonder Satan found an opening. He'd crept in, and it was my fault. I was the loser because I'd spent all night ripping up my spiritual defenses, and I was in checkmate. When spiritually checkmated, all you can do is acknowledge it to the Lord and ask for help.

I went into the hospital, and Courtney was awake and *alert*! She was almost acting like herself! The first thing she said was, "You tried to tell me something about cancer last night, but I was too tired." (*Aha! You* were *listening*, I thought.)

I told her, "Yes. It is cancer, a very bad kind of cancer." I explained what glioblastoma is, that they could never get it all, and that there is no cure. The best we could hope for, if they could operate, was maybe a year. She looked at me, smiled, and said, "Are you okay?" No, my world just got ripped apart and my heart is broken, but I said, "Yes, I'm okay. It's not what I wanted, but God is good. He knows better than us what is best."

I don't think we ever said to each other, "We're going to trust God," or, "We're going to honour God in this." There was no outward declaration, no lifting our hands to heaven to make our solemn vow. It was just settled. We knew it was to be. We had been through the crucible of so many things that we didn't have to say it. We were going to honour the Lord, no matter what. We both knew it.

I guess this was the third "cancer commitment," but we'd been taught by hard knocks to make it long before. Either we believed what I'd preached all my life or we didn't. It wasn't really a "cancer commitment," but a life commitment. I'd not always practiced it as fully as I should have, but I was determined to honour the Lord like never before.

I could preach, but I was never really sure if I was a good pastor, a good evangelist, a good shepherd of the Lord's flock. Sometimes it didn't seem so, but at least I was doing it, rather than sitting in a comfortable and lazy pew in a big church. I wasn't sure I was good at honouring the Lord either, but I was determined to be the best cancer spouse unto the Lord that I could be. He would have my honour and praise, no matter what. It wasn't a new commitment, but a sharpening and refocusing of an old, broader commitment. It was settled in my mind then and there.

Courtney got out her iPad, I got my phone, and we started reading on glioblastoma. A few minutes later, Dr Z walked in with several others on his rounds. I could see tension on his face as he said, "A movie?" I realised, "He thinks he needs to tell her." I smiled and said, "Researching glioblastoma." He seemed to relax, and I remembered, "Be kind to them! His job is really, really hard!"

I didn't realise that wee kindness was a huge first step in "honour the Lord," too. From then on, we were "different" and the whole ward was talking about us. Other families couldn't smile in the face of glioblastoma, but God gave us smiles to dispense to the staff. I'm convinced He gave them because we wanted to honour Him.

After a while, I went home so Courtney could sleep and I could be there for a rather hurried Thanksgiving dinner. I was thankful, but my heart wasn't in a feast. I doubt anyone's was, but we still wanted it to be special for Robert and Manda's Cuteness Roarers. After eating, I sent the previous email. My inbox was overflowing.

We were getting encouraging emails from all over.

From someone in our church

We are really shocked and saddened to hear the news of Courtney's diagnosis.

I sense from your email your tremendous fortitude, and pray that God would grant you His strength, peace and grace for the trials ahead. May you cling to the promise that "neither death, nor life, nor angels, nor principalities, nor powers, nor things present, nor things to come, nor height, nor depth, nor any other creature, [shall be] able to separate us from the love of God, which is in Christ Jesus our Lord."

We sat this morning with the children and prayed for Courtney, for you, for the children and grandchildren, and asked God for healing for Courtney, and for relief from pain.

From a pastor in Oregon, USA

I'm sorry about your wife. I don't have words. I know you know how to think about it and what to do.

From a pastor in Tennessee, USA

I am very sorry for not responding sooner. I have not been sure what to say. Still not certain, except to say that we are praying for you and the family. I will be sharing it with our church family. They remember Rosa being with us while she was in the area, so will want to pray as well.

It is such a blessing to know that you all do not have to face this trial alone. You all have the joy and presence of the Comforter and the knowledge that God is fully in control and inclines His ear to your cry.

We love you all!

And my reply (a day later)—

I'm not sure what to say either. :) I'm just stumbling along and faking as if I know what I'm doing. Don't feel bad for not responding, I have no time for anything right now.

Nine days ago Courtney and I walked the dog more than two miles, most of it at a brisk pace. Tonight, I had to bear at least half her weight to get her to the toilet. And then she quoted "Day by Day" and said today we've found what His kind heart is giving us.

She knows it's likely less than a year. She doesn't yet know it might be less than two months, I don't want to tell her that part until I know.

I passed all responses on to Courtney. Many were from dear friends. I knew she would find them encouraging. But I knew the email about not sleeping and not knowing how to use the washing machine would bother Courtney. She didn't need to worry about me. So painstakingly, in forwarding the replies, I stripped off that email so she wouldn't see that paragraph—or I thought I did. Later I learned that she had seen it. I had missed one (or more). She didn't say anything at the time, but I learned later. It wasn't my only mistake.

Later, Courtney would join me in composing the emails, but she wasn't capable of that at this point. It would be a long time after that mistake before I put anything in an email that would have bothered her.

27 November 2020 (Friday midnight)

Dear All

I'll have to keep this short.

We still have no treatment plan from the neurosurgeon/oncologist/etc. team. Normally that would not happen until Wednesday, Courtney's doctor is pushing hard for Monday.

She's now in a private room, we can visit anytime. The grandkids may also be allowed in, we're not sure, she specifically asked for that today.

Katherine's church (and employer, she works in their school) told her not to wait for the treatment plan and just come and paid for her ticket. She arrives Sunday. The doctor is trying to slash through the quarantine requirement so she can visit right away, we shall see.

More symptoms keep appearing.

Courtney was able to send her sisters a video message this morning, and reminded them that "whatever happens, God is good."

We've now been told that they will work with us to bring Courtney home to care for her here once treatment is determined but that she must stay there until then.

Thank you all for the messages. I have not responded, I am sorry, but they have been read and forwarded to Courtney. She is trying to read them all, too. Blessings to you.

In Him
Justin

The kindness of Katherine's church meant so much. They released her from weeks of teaching, paid her expensive airfare from the smaller local airport, and gave her sufficient money for any other travel expenses. It let her rent a car, which turned out to be a great help. God will surely bless them.

Now that Courtney was in a private room, we had more conversations privately with the nurses and other staff, and began to hear, "Your family is different." The peace God gives was getting attention. I don't think it would have been there if we hadn't been determined to honour Him. Our kids, when they came, followed that same lead, as we expected. This lasted throughout the rest of our life-with-cancer. God was throwing doors wide open for spiritual conversations that never would have happened otherwise.

Chapter 3

Courtney Writes a Letter

My email communication had become a disorganised disaster. I had a family list, a ministry people list, a work colleagues list, and just people who got stuff forwarded to them. It was all one huge mess. My company helped me out and set up a mailing list for me—this was the first letter using it. It didn't happen until Monday; there was no email over the weekend because I was just too busy.

30 November 2020 (Monday p.m.)

Dear All

Some receiving this may not know that Courtney was diagnosed with a brain tumour, an advanced glioblastoma, on Thursday, after only a few days of symptoms. It is progressing rapidly. If you have not heard this before, I deeply apologise for failing to reach you, my communications have been extremely fragmented.

If you know of anyone who might wish to have this, please pass it on. Here is the update today.

I got the diagnosis Thursday evening and was able to tell Courtney on Friday. Her balance is being affected, and on Saturday she began falling. That night, before I left, Courtney quoted me this from one of her favourite hymns:

> He whose heart is kind beyond all measure
> Gives unto each day what He deems best—
> Lovingly, its part of pain and pleasure
> Mingling toil with peace and rest.
>
> ["Day by Day" by Carolina Sandell Berg, 1865]

Then, she said, "Today, we've had what He kindly deemed best."

Tonight, for the first time, I saw her distressed. She wants to write a letter to you all about it—hopefully tomorrow I can send it in an update.

Communication:

I need to simplify my life in regard to this. Thus:

Tomorrow's will be the last direct email from me on Courtney's condition—after tomorrow's, you will need to sign up.

My company graciously set up a distribution list for me [link]. For further updates on Courtney's status, please:

A. Add [link] to your address book so it doesn't get spam filtered.

B. Send an email to Lisa at [link] requesting to be added.

C. Send Lisa love and kisses (someone else is getting my love and kisses). :)

I have set up the most basic blog ever [link]. To send Courtney a message, please add a comment to the post for the day, we'll plan a new post every day. If she is too tired to read them, we'll read them to her.

She will be too tired to respond, unfortunately. Please keep them short, concentration is hard sometimes.

I will soon have a mechanism for you to communicate to our family.

To communicate with me, please use [my email]. (Warning: I'm hundreds of emails behind, I sadly won't be able to respond to everyone who deserves a response.)

Courtney's Status:

There is still no treatment plan, probably coming Wednesday now.

Courtney has fallen four times, and now uses a Zimmer (a walker). (I still find this mind-boggling, 10 days ago we walked 2+ miles at a brisk pace.)

She knows she should not get out of bed without help but the part that makes that stick in the brain isn't functioning, and she keeps getting up. She is now being watched 24/7 when I'm not with her.

Speaking is hard at times but she communicates well, and understands. But some things get muddled and her WhatsApp communication with family and church members includes some hilarious non-sequiturs and glorious typos. :)

Pain is currently back under control.

We escorted her Zimmer up and down the hall multiple times today. She always wants to park it, go without it, and try some stairs. Negative to both!

Family News:

Katherine arrived safely on Sunday. Thank you to Bay City Baptist Church (John 13:35).

Eric arrives Friday.

Marguerite and Rosa both intend to plan their

journey after we learn treatment plans, it's more complicated for them.

The doctor is trying to bypass the two-week quarantine rule (after international travel) so they can visit their mom right away.

Finally, please pray for the nurses who sit in Courtney's room and listen to her music. If the Lord takes away your balance and your self-restraint so that you have to be watched, you might as well use it in His service, right?

In Him
Justin

Saturday morning, I was at the hospital when the Charge Nurse came in, asked how Courtney was, and said, "You had a fall last night." I said, "I didn't hear about *that*!" and she said, "I'm sorry, someone should have told you."

After she left, Courtney said, "I didn't fall. I spilled and sat down on the floor to clean it up. But I was tired and it was easiest to lie down beside it while I cleaned it up. And then I couldn't get up again, so I had to call for help until someone heard me and came."

That was typical. Courtney did not want to burden anyone, so she would try to handle things herself (and perhaps end up being more burdensome as a result, due to her limitations). She also was becoming obsessive-compulsive about lots of things: cleaning, her fingernails, etc. The tumour was attacking in various ways, and new symptoms were appearing daily.

She didn't fall, but Courtney's inability to get back up by herself indicated problems in the motor-control function of her brain. Twice Saturday and twice more Sunday she did fall. It was the falling that triggered her comment Saturday, "Today, we've had what He kindly deemed best." I walked out of the hospital shaking my head at her ability to view the loss of balance and independence in that light.

When I left, a nurse moved into Courtney's room for the night. They had tried a bed alarm, but even though it sounded, she was too quick and would get out of bed and fall before they could get there. I came back early Sunday to get her up and dressed, went to church to preach, and then went back to the hospital for the afternoon and evening.

Our neighbours had been almost banging our door down asking how they could help, and one picked up Katherine from the airport Sunday afternoon. It was so good to have her home. At Dr Z's request, she'd had a (negative) COVID test, and he allowed her into the hospital to see Courtney. I was never sure whether he was supposed to do that, but I chose not to enquire too closely.

Also on Sunday, Robert and Manda brought their Cuteness Roarers to the hospital. They weren't allowed in, but they could stand under Nana's window and wave, and I helped her to the window. She was desperately missing them.

The nurses watched Courtney all night again. On Monday, after being at the hospital all day, I wrote the previous update late at night. I was at the hospital early every morning now to help Courtney get cleaned up and dressed. On Tuesday, I took my computer as Courtney had asked. She had a project to do.

1 December 2020 (Tuesday p.m.)

Dear All

Please read the letter from Courtney, below. It was hard work (this kind of thing is slow and difficult for her right now) but very important to her. We worked on it for two hours this morning.

We are still waiting to hear what, if any, treatment will be possible. They are still watching Courtney 24/7. They are all very kind.

Here's Courtney:

Dear Friends and Family

By now you know about my cancer. It has happened so fast, but the Lord is with us and encouraging us. I want to ask two favours of you.

First, this song ("We're Going Home to Glory Soon") got real. Please, listen to it, it is short: https://www.youtube.com/watch?v=xL7rDeNYwDY. I so want to see you over there.

Second, can you join us, sometime this Sunday, in singing "Because He Lives"? If you don't know it, you can play this and sing along: https://www.youtube.com/watch?v=Sm2wLKZoGPY. I know people around the world are receiving this, and it would be an encouragement to know that we are singing it together, because it answers everything.

It hurts me when people blame God and say He hasn't been fair. I know people mean well and say it out of love and affection. But please don't say that, even to yourself. The song answers it.

I don't want people who care about me to be angry with God on my behalf. I love Him for everything He has done for me, and I want you to love Him, too.

What is fair? If God were fair, He wouldn't have sent Jesus to die, and rise again for me. If God were fair, I'd have "crossed that river" long ago, and I would be in Hell.

But God did send His Son for a sinner like me, and He "bled and died to buy my pardon." Now He lives and I will, too. I will be with Jesus who loves me so much, in Glory. I'm ok, I'm better than ok.

I want to be honest with you. I'm afraid of "life's final war with pain." But it doesn't matter if I'm a coward, the lights of Glory will still be there. They are there for me, not because of any good in me, but because He lives. Death will give way to victory, and I'm not going to lose that even if I'm afraid of the pain. Jesus guaranteed my victory. He lives, and so will I.

Isaiah 25:8 *He will swallow up death in victory; and the Lord GOD will wipe away tears from off all faces; and the rebuke of his people shall he take away from off all the earth: for the LORD hath spoken it.*

John 3:16 *For God so loved the world, that he gave his only begotten Son, that whosoever believeth in him should not perish, but have everlasting life.*

John 11:25 *Jesus said unto her, I am the resurrection, and the life: he that believeth in me, though he were dead, yet shall he live:*

John 11:26 *And whosoever liveth and believeth in me shall never die. Believest thou this?*

Do you believe that? I'm asking you if you do, but do you see that verse? Jesus asked it first. We believe it. That is what we count on. You can believe it, and

> if you do, we will see you over there. Please contact Justin if you need help in understanding.
>
> It appears I may not see many of you again unless it is "over there." That only has to be sad if you aren't going there. Please, come join us.
>
> Love,
> Courtney

Several people had said that it wasn't fair that Courtney had cancer. That was the first time she cried after the diagnosis—she found it very upsetting to hear people say God hadn't been fair to her. She wanted to make sure people didn't say it anymore.

Courtney asked me to make the letter available online, so people could look it up again. That greatly surprised me. Courtney was such a shy and private person, so to ask me to put something so intensely personal online was significantly out of character. In fact, to write it at all was amazing—or it would have been if Courtney hadn't made her own "cancer commitments."

- She wanted God to be honoured.
- She wanted people who loved her to honour Him, not to say that He wasn't fair.
- She said, "I don't want my cancer to be wasted. I want God to use it."

Later, she struggled with this—with regretting the letter. She'd written it for family and friends and didn't expect it to go around the world. Even so, it kept coming back to this: "I don't want my cancer to be wasted." Her letter was one thing God used repeatedly, one of the ways He kept her cancer from being wasted.

The letter did go right around the world as people passed it to friends and family. Why did people like it so much? I told Courtney I thought it must be this: her letter said what Christians hoped *they* would say in similar circumstances. All true Christians want to honour the Lord, even if their world turns upside down. We might wonder, though, if we really have the spiritual strength. Courtney's letter gave Christians a model for what to say if their time came—and a challenge to develop a relationship with God that would enable them to say it.

A few of the responses that came in that day alone:

From Alaska, USA

Courtney, your brothers and sisters at The Church of Thorne Bay (Alaska) are praying for you and your family. If He chooses not to heal you here on Earth, we pray He takes you softly with minimal pain.

From South Carolina, USA

We are praying for you and your family. Our entire church here in Greer, SC, are praying for the Lord to guide, strengthen, heal, and protect.

From the son of a former member of our church

Dear Courtney, we are sorry to hear this. I have fond memories of planting daffodils at the church in memory of my mum. We are grateful for all you did for her and she loved being part of your church. We all send our love.

From a pastor in Nova Scotia, Canada, a multi-decade friend

We were so shocked to hear the news. Be assured of our prayers for you and your family as you walk through this valley with the LORD. May you know your Shepherd's unsearchable riches, His unspeakable gift, the One whose love passeth knowledge, and who can do exceeding abundantly above all we ask or think.

We love you and are praying for all.

From a pastor in Lithuania

We are praying for you often—and for your family. We thank God for you and what He has done in His perfect will through you all. We have sweet memories of our visit with you.

From former members of our church

You are in our thoughts & hearts. Devastated by the news. Know that we love you and that we are all praying for you, Justin & the family. (Rom 8,28) And we know that all things work together for good to them that love God, to them who are the called according to his purpose.

From Northeast England

We are and will continue to pray for you, Justin and your family, and to trust the LORD that He will bring about His perfect plan for your life.

From a close family friend in Scotland's Central Belt

You and your family are continually in my thoughts, and I bring you before the Lord often. May His love, grace, comfort and peace surround each of you.

From friends and members of a nearby Gospel Hall in Scotland

Praying for you all very much.

"He can do exceedingly abundantly above what we ask or even think"

Praying you feel the peace that passes all understanding knowing the Lord is with you in this difficult trial and will carry you through.

"Be still and know that I am God"

From Texas, USA

Justin, I will kneel down so you can cry on my shoulder. I am crying and praying for strength and peace for you in this troubled time. Our whole family and church here in Austin are praying for Courtney, you, and the extended family that God would heal her directly. If He chooses otherwise—that He will grant us peace in His decisions that bring eternal glory to Him!

From Malaysia

Blessings Sister Courtney!

We around the world are praying for you and your full recovery.

May The LORD bless you and keep you; The LORD make His Face shine upon you, and be gracious to you; The LORD lift up His Countenance upon you, and give you peace.

From Georgia, USA

I am so very sad for this troubling circumstance which has come to your family. But at the same time exhilarated and strengthened by Courtney's remarkably faithful attitude.

Courtney didn't ever seem to understand how many lives she touched, or why. I suppose the only One who can keep track of that has it in hand—if there are rewards to be given, He has it covered. Dwight L. Moody talked about what God could do with someone fully consecrated to Him. We would never claim to be fully consecrated—but we did have our "cancer commitment" to honour Him, no matter what, in Courtney's cancer. That wee bit of consecration was enough for God to work in our lives and the lives of many others.

Jesus talked about what God could do with just a little faith, as little as a grain of mustard seed. We saw some of what God could do with a little determination to honour Him.

Chapter 4

A Merry Heart: Grandma's Revenge!

♪

2 December 2020 (Wednesday p.m.)

This is the last time I will spam your email inbox unless you request updates.

Treatment Plan:
It still doesn't exist (except in the Lord's plan). However, we had a hint today that this may be a good thing, that they have not entirely ruled out the possibility of an operation. If they are able to operate, it will take pressure off Courtney's brain and give other treatments a chance to help. So, we wait until tomorrow. Of course, only a miracle can cure this.

Current Condition:
Some things are a little worse, others are definitely improved. The steroids are reducing the swelling around the tumour and improving some of the symptoms. Courtney's balance is better—she no longer needs the Zimmer, now she can walk (assisted) with a crutch. There has been some discussion of what will

be needed for Courtney to come home—again, much depends on the treatment.

Humour:
Courtney kept me laughing all morning.

Proverbs 17:22 *A merry heart doeth good like a medicine: but a broken spirit drieth the bones.*

I'll tell you the story. We got Fitbits to help remind us to keep active. We might have even had some competition as to who got the most steps in—but I've had a significant advantage the last 12 days. When Courtney got her Zimmer and we started going up and down the hall, we discovered she was "getting ripped off"—the Fitbit wasn't counting her steps because she was holding the Zimmer and not swinging her arm. So, she started insisting we should just park the Zimmer at the side of the hall and take off. I was having none of it—she wasn't ready for that.

So last night, Courtney was in bed and not sleeping, and she started plotting her revenge, what she was going to do to pay me out for my evil refusal to let her park the Zimmer. She was going to jump off the bed in the middle of the night and make the alarm on her bed go off and startle me awake. That will teach him! She was going to go online and start buying dresses until I was bankrupt—if I complained, she would buy more! She was going to file a frivolous GDPR report against me! She had a whole list, I learned all about them this morning. I should have been taking notes, I could tell you more of them.

Then, she decided to play some silly Christmas

songs to while the time away, and what came up? "Grandma Got Run Over by a Reindeer." She told me that it was obviously because Grandpa had provoked Grandma, just like JUSTIN had provoked COURTNEY. (Not knowing the song, I'm not sure whether her "provoking" theory has any merit or is just self-serving.) And so the ultimate revenge—she's going to sneak out of the hospital, and get run over by a reindeer, and I will never dare provoke her again!

This afternoon, she was reading the messages sent to her, and she said, "These make me sound like I'm some paragon. I'm really just a normal person." She then raised the question of whether normal people threaten to get run over by a reindeer to get even with their husbands. :) I chose not to get into further trouble by venturing an opinion.

Family:

Eric arrives on Friday. For Marguerite and Edward, and Rosa, it is better to wait until we find out the treatment plan. We are praying this will be tomorrow.

Communication:

Thank you again to those who have sent messages to Courtney on her blog. She has read them over and over. They are deeply appreciated. These messages are public. To send private messages that our kids, their spouses, and I will see, but no one else, go to [link]. Your message will not be visible (after you post it) to you or anyone else, but It will be to us. If you would like a reply, please specifically say so. I can be reached privately at [my email]. Thank you for all the messages, they are appreciated even if we fail to respond.

> Forward any update to anyone who you think will want it or profit by it. But please do not post the email addresses in any public Internet forum.
>
> Thank you for all the encouragement, love, and prayers.
>
> In Him
> Justin

Later, I learned that Courtney was quite unhappy with me about the Zimmer. She was coping by joking about it, but it was bothering her. I explained that I was following orders, and the nurses backed me up. That helped a little, but it didn't stick. Even when she accepted that she had to keep using it, she'd still get upset with me. It wasn't logical, of course.

The tumour wasn't messing with Courtney's intelligence, but it did impair logical function and memory sometimes. She would forget that I was just following medical instructions. When reminded, it would come back and she'd be okay while she remembered, but it just wasn't "sticking" for her.

A lot of things didn't stick during this phase. She found it very difficult, because she'd always been so competent about everything.

The messages she was receiving really did make her sound like some sort of paragon. That was hard too. We knew we weren't anything special. I wanted to stand on a mountain and yell, "Haven't people read this verse? Luke 17:10 says, 'So likewise ye, when ye shall have done all those things which are commanded you, say, We are unprofitable servants: we have done that which was our duty to do.'" We wanted to honour God, and it seemed like people wanted to honour us instead.

The responses kept pouring in.

From Minnesota, USA
Courtney,

We've never met, but I work with Justin. His updates are very encouraging for my faith, seeing the Lord at work in your lives. I have been praying for you every day, both for a miracle healing and that God will shelter your heart and keep you strong and courageous.

From Virginia, USA
Praying for you, sis, from all the way in Virginia!

From Florida, USA, multi-decade friends
Courtney and Justin,

We were shocked to hear the news. We admire the strength in the Lord that you are both demonstrating. You are speaking to all of us who know you in ways you may not imagine.

Unless you instruct us differently, we are praying for a miracle. We love you and stand ready to do whatever we can to help. So please, ask if there is something we can do.

On Courtney's messages blog, from Lithuania
Thank you for giving me a good example of such genuine welcoming and kindness I've never seen before or since. God certainly was the emphasis. That week we visited you remains a very fond memory. Thank you so much. This year the following verse has been significant:

2 Corinthians 12:9-10
And he said unto me, My grace is sufficient for thee: for my strength is made perfect in weakness. Most gladly therefore will I rather glory in my infirmities, that the power of Christ may rest upon me. Therefore I take pleasure in infirmities,

in reproaches, in necessities, in persecutions, in distresses for Christ's sake: for when I am weak, then am I strong.

From a Christian we've never met, in Scotland

Hi Courtney. I've been really touched by your letter and testimony. It will be a glorious day, won't it? Praying for you and your family as God asks you to walk this path. He hasn't left you or forsaken you but [is] right there in the midst of your storm. Much love.

On Courtney's messages blog, from a pastor in Oregon, USA

It has been good to know you, albeit briefly in our short visit to your church and home in Scotland. We enjoyed and appreciated our time there. Your letter via email was a great testimony to the grace of our Lord. We are glad for the peace you feel. We look for that day too when there is no more pain. I am both sorrowful for you but also jealous that you will get to see Jesus face to face.

From Bangladesh

Our family has been reading your updates. I've been moved by your faith and the hope resonates deep with me.

In recent years, the verses from Hebrews 2 have become precious to me, where it speaks of Jesus Christ who died to break the power of the enemy and to "free those who all their lives were held in slavery by their fear of death." Death is only a door—our home is on the other side!

Our hearts are weeping with you and rejoicing with you. You and Justin and your family are in our prayers.

From Justin's mom in Louisiana, USA

Look up for your redemption draweth nigh! And He giveth more grace! Good morning! I love you, Courtney. We are comforted by God in music and His Word. Just to see Jesus face to face will be unimaginable. Praying that pain will be controlled.

On Courtney's messages blog, from Justin!
Surprise, it's me! Love you!

From Utah, USA
My heart is breaking for the family that is hurting from afar. You are all in God's hands and we pray His will be done. So thankful for His grace that is sufficient.

From Pennsylvania, USA
Our hearts are with you and the family. I'm praying for God's grace to be felt for all, but especially for you during this difficult time. We love you and are with you in spirit despite the many miles apart.

From South Africa
We are praying for you all from South Africa.

From Wyoming, USA
Dear Courtney, we were rehearsing for the umpteenth million time this past Thanksgiving of a dinner visit to your house in Greenville, SC, way back in the dark ages when you gave me the experience of eating Unsweetened Pumpkin Pie (for the first and LAST time). Wowzers, what a surprise! And we always laugh remembering it. Praying for you all, may God richly bless you my friends.

Only six days after the diagnosis, I'd heard from every continent except the penguins of Antarctica—and I almost expected to hear from them next.

On one of these days, I learned about the email

slipup mentioned in chapter 2. Soon after Katherine's arrival, Courtney tearfully told the girls, "I want you kids to know, I want your dad to marry again when I'm gone. He needs someone to take care of him, to cook, to do his laundry, to make sure he's not lonely." Alyssa assured her she would take care of cooking and laundry.

I didn't know until then that Courtney had seen my email, but I was expecting some such thing before long and was ready. I said I was too old and set in my ways to be a good husband for anyone else, and it wouldn't be fair to marry someone else. I had built my habits around what fit with her, and I didn't think I could change enough to be a good husband for anyone else.

Katherine said, "That is something God would have to do, and if God does it, we'll all be fine with it." Courtney later told me, "Katherine is really wise sometimes." She never made the remarriage suggestion again, but she did worry about me for a long time.

I became quite proficient (in my opinion!) at laundry, so at least Courtney didn't have to worry about that. Months later, I found an answer that really worked. I said if she could trust God for her eternal destiny, she should trust Him to care for me for ten years or so here on earth. She still worried, but less.

I still had to endure some of our kids occasionally making wisecracks about the "perfect" new wife for me. With their suggestions, God would indeed have had to do a miracle to get me to the altar!

My personal view was that if Courtney was gone, it would be time to "spend and be spent" (2 Corinthians 12:15) in the work of the Gospel, not to look for another wife. God could change that, of course, but as of the time of this writing, that view hasn't shifted at all.

Chapter 5

"Keen to Try Some Sort of Operation"

3 December 2020 (Thursday p.m.)

Thank you for the messages sent to Courtney. They mean a lot, and she reads and rereads them.

Thank you for spreading the word. It is all very kind. It is encouraging to receive messages of love and promises of prayer from around the world. We are not famous and it is amazing.

Exciting News!

Today, we learned the neurosurgeons in Edinburgh are "keen to try some sort of operation." I was told not to expect this. Previously, when I asked if we might be looking at months rather than weeks, the doctor could not honestly say that. Now, perhaps, the Lord is using this to give us more time. Lord willing, Courtney will be transferred to Western General in Edinburgh tomorrow.

These people have God-given skills and use technology developed by the God-given skills of others. The Lord, who turns the hearts of kings (Proverbs 21:1), has moved them to attempt that which seemed unlikely. That is a good thing and we are very thankful.

But to be clear, it is not a cure or a miracle.

Please pray for wisdom for us (James 1:5) in any treatment discussions.

Current Condition:
Little is changed today.

Courtney's Revenge:
For those who enjoyed Courtney's plotted revenges against me from yesterday's update, I have two more. :) She now intends to go into my wardrobe and throw out all my favourite clothes (this is ok, I've been pretending for years that her favourite things for me to wear are my favourites, too). She's now also threatening to make desserts for me for the rest of my life and leave the sugar out of all of them.

I am unmoved. I still won't help her walk down the hall without her crutch, though we are both glad she doesn't need to use the Zimmer for now!

Thought for Today:
Sunday, I preached on "Scattered Thoughts in a Crisis." This is one of those scattered thoughts:

God's love works differently from ours. Scripture:

John 11:5 *Now Jesus loved Martha, and her sister, and Lazarus.*

John 11:6 *When he had heard therefore that he was sick, he abode two days still in the same place where he was.*

Messengers just arrived to tell Jesus that Lazarus is sick. Verse 5 seems out of place—it says Jesus loved them and then He stayed two extra days. If He loved them, He would go right away, right? But Jesus waited two days. Why? I think I know, but we're not told. We learn later that when Jesus arrived, Lazarus had been dead four days. So if Jesus had left immediately, Lazarus would still have been dead two days before He arrived.

But He waited, allowing them to suffer two extra days of grief—and yet, He loved them. So there was something in this extra grief that was for their good, and thus loving. Conclusion: God sometimes allows grief for our own good.

We don't think that way. We think love involves preventing grief if we can. God sees farther than we do. He sees that grief can produce good in us and for us, and He sees far enough to let us experience it at times, when that is what we need. His love isn't like ours.

Family:
Eric arrives tomorrow. Marguerite and Edward, and Rosa, are waiting to find out the timing of the operation and expected recovery to determine the best time to come.

Thank you for all the encouragement, love, and prayers.

In Him
Justin

From one of our church members

I'm not very good at this sort of thing but just want you to know that you and Justin are in my prayers. Being human is easy to question things but being saved and understanding that God's plan is perfect gives me comfort when I don't know why things happen the way they do. I pray the LORD give you comfort, peace, and healing.

From southern Scotland

We are praying for you and your family.

Praying God will continue to give you strength!

From Michigan, USA

Courtney, what a depth of wisdom and wonderful letter you wrote. I am sorry to hear about your battle with cancer but can see from your letter, that Jesus is your focus and I am truly encouraged by that element and it has helped me deepen my faith with our almighty Lord.

4 December 2020 (Friday p.m.)

Thank you for your prayers and kind messages. This will be brief today.

Courtney did not go to Edinburgh today—almost certainly tomorrow.

We may not know what operation(s) they propose until next week.

Eric arrived safely, a neighbour kindly picked him up from the airport. Everyone wants to do SOMETHING, anything, to help. So many people have been so kind to us.

Courtney's condition is much the same today. She was more tired but her sleep was disturbed, in part because of the "thunder snow" that hit during the night—it was so loud the police had many calls about explosions and car alarms were set off in parts of Edinburgh. It sounded like an explosion to me too, and the crazy thought popped into my mind, *I wonder if that's the hospital blowing up.* I immediately banished it from my mind as absurd, and didn't even get out of bed to look toward the hospital—but that was the end of my night's sleep. :) The human mind is a funny thing sometimes.

We are very thankful for what God is doing in many lives through this.

Thank you again, and again, and again, for the messages sent to Courtney. They mean a lot, and she reads and rereads them, and asks me to read them to her, both the public and private messages. And thank you again for spreading the word. It means a lot to us and to our church to know other believers are with us.

Thought for Today:

1 Corinthians 15:19 *If in this life only we have hope in Christ, we are of all men most miserable.*

If you think that being a Christian is just to make you a better person in this life and have a happier life, you are doing it wrong. :) Our faith is anchored in a confident hope of another life beyond this one. It definitely does make us a better person in this life, if it is functioning at all. It gives us a peace and joy even in the trials and heartaches that others may not have—certainly, that's what the nurses tell us they are seeing, that we aren't like other families.

But it doesn't mean the heartaches won't come. Our peace and joy finds its substance in our faith in the life to come. If we weren't confident in that eternity, we would be destroyed by what we are experiencing. We would be living a lie, our faith would be pointless. But it isn't a lie, and if the tears come, we can smile through them. We know this world is not the end. Our hope is in this life, yes, but not only in this life.

In Him
Justin

5 December 2020 (Saturday p.m.)

Dear All

The hymnwriter: "He whose heart is kind beyond all measure, gives unto each day what He deems best."

Courtney: "Today we again learned what He deemed best for us today."

Courtney went to Edinburgh Royal Infirmary today. I assume that means the operation will be there rather than Western General (as I previously expected). She's on a new ward that has only been open two months. We still don't know what they have planned, or what the Lord has planned.

It was a harder day, Courtney felt weak and tired and couldn't walk. She seemed better by the time she left for Edinburgh. It may have just been disturbed sleep, there was more thunder in the night and the patient in the next room had a very bad night.

ERI is being much more strict about visiting due to COVID, and perhaps also because now they have hope they can do something to help—before, we were effectively on death watch.

Please pray for the doctors, nurses, and other staff from the ward we just left.

Worth Remembering:

1 Peter 5:8 *Be sober, be vigilant; because your adversary the devil, as a roaring lion, walketh about, seeking whom he may devour.*

In a crisis, the devil doesn't fight fair. He hits you at your most vulnerable in the worst possible way, dropping thoughts into your mind just when the crisis has identified your weak points. You'd better get close to the Lord while you have a chance so you have the resources to resist when he kicks you when you are down. Otherwise, the crisis multiplies. He wants to destroy you and he's stronger than you are.

Thank you again for your prayers and kind messages.

In Him
Justin

From Oregon, USA
First Baptist of Boardman in Oregon will be singing "Because He Lives" to close our service on Sunday. Praying for you all!

From Vermont, USA
We, at the Vershire Bible Church, sang "Because He Lives" during our morning worship service this morning. We love you all and have prayed for you regularly over the years. We are grateful for your witness and the work you have done and your testimony to the young people here in Vermont. We will continue to pray for all y'all and may even sing "Because He Lives" next week too!

6 December 2020 (Sunday p.m.)

Dear All

Courtney saw the scan of her tumour this morning—it's one thing to be told how large it is, another to see it. This ward is not close to as good as the one Courtney was in before at communication with us, we're going to be discussing that tomorrow.

When I finally got a nurse who would talk to me

tonight she said there may be a biopsy tomorrow or the next day.

Courtney told me today, "I'm tired of being an example," and, "These people who keep saying I'm strong don't understand." Then, she turned around and asked me to print up a couple hymns for the nurses because they seem to have a hard time understanding people who have faith. So she thought if they had these hymns, she could use them to explain why we trust God in the dark times. So much for not being an example, right? :)

She's right about not being strong, though. We're being told that, and we aren't. And God won't give His glory to anyone else. The strength is His, not ours—please, don't say we are strong. We've just been given access to the One who is strong—and that's enough. When people say we are strong, they are putting a burden on us to be strong that we cannot carry. This one is God's.

The two hymns are "Abide with Me" (written just weeks before the passing of the hymnwriter) and "The Promise of God" (our friend Mary Rose Jensen finished this hymn in time for her mother's funeral). It contains 15 direct promises from God's Word, strung together to form 3 verses. "Weeping may endure for a night, but joy cometh in the morning." Mary kindly permitted us to include this in our hymnbook.

1 The promise of God is of joy in the morning.
The promise of God is of peace in the night.
He forgives us our sins.
Now He calls us His children.
His yoke and His burden are light.

2 The promise of God is that He will not leave us.
The promise of God is that He never sleeps.
As He cares for His own,
Giving life in abundance,
Our God will supply all our needs.

3 The promise of God is that we'll live forever.
The promise of God is that Christ will appear.
Then we'll rise up with Him
To the place He's preparing
And sorrows will all disappear.

Words and Music: Mary Rose Jensen, b. 1958
© Garden Rose Music, http://gardenrosemusic.com.
CCLI#3423291 Used by kind permission.

You can see the music and the Scripture references here: http://www.gardenrosemusic.com/pdfs/ThePromiseOfGod.pdf.

Thank you again for your prayers and kind messages.

In Him
Justin

When I called Courtney after church, she sounded really down. She wouldn't say why but I finally pried it out of one of the nurses—she had seen her scan. It's one thing to be told it is five centimetres; it's another to see your own brain scan with a huge tumour.

When I spoke to Courtney on the phone later, she sounded herself again. She was focused on helping the nurses understand about faith and giving them some hymns. Our problems always look bigger if we dwell on them and smaller if we're thinking about other people.

7 December 2020 (Monday p.m.)

Dear All

I was able to see Courtney today. I was told to be at the Edinburgh Royal Infirmary at 2 so the doctor could discuss with us. Upon arrival, they took me to Courtney's room, but the doctor didn't come until after 5. This actually meant we had all afternoon together, so having him be late didn't matter to me! I also got to stay after he left for a while but it was sort of becoming obvious they didn't want me there, so I finally left.

I will not be able to see Courtney before her operation on Wednesday. I do not know when I will get to see her after the operation, either.

We received far better news than I expected. The doctor can't know until he operates but he is optimistic about removing 90% or more of the tumour, and optimistic that he can do so without significantly impacting brain function further than has already happened. He made no promises but he hopes some symptoms may improve, perhaps significantly.

Actually, he made no promises about anything. He was very clear that everything is guesses right now. I was glad for that, there was a genuine humility rather than an arrogant "I know all the answers" attitude.

He was very pleased with the doctors back home, he said it was a "good pickup" for them to catch this as early as they did. He said it is most likely that the tumour has only started a few weeks ago, but it is now 5 cm in diameter.

If the tumour has penetrated certain parts of the brain, he will not try to remove those parts of it. He said the standard treatment after an operation is chemotherapy and radiation therapy.

I told him that there will likely be thousands of people around the world praying for him on Wednesday, I hope you don't make me a liar! :) He said nothing that indicated whether he has any faith, but he seemed genuinely pleased to hear it.

There are so many people who have been so kind and genuinely helpful in small and big ways. We are very grateful.

Please pray for a good night's sleep for Courtney and me, we are both very tired. Thank you all.

In Him
Justin

Our surgeon's special interest was early diagnosis. He was intrigued that our GP had identified glioblastoma so quickly—it was amazing based on the symptoms at the time. A day's delay likely would have allowed so much brain damage that there would have been no operation, and Courtney might not have even survived until Christmas.

Our GP had saved Courtney's life, and the surgeon didn't understand how. Her insistence on an immediate scan allowed diagnosis, operation, and treatment. I think God had placed "glioblastoma" in her mind. He wasn't going to take Courtney Home yet—there were things still to do, so God helped the GP pick up on it.

From a pastor in South Carolina, USA

Our hearts ache for your wife and the family. Both of us will be praying for Courtney. It is a blessing to know that God's grace is both available and sufficient.

From Alaska, USA

Courtney, the Church of Thorne Bay sang "Because He Lives" this morning at your suggestion. Amazingly, it went right along with this morning's sermon. Funny how God coordinates music and message. We will be praying for you and the surgeons this week.

From California, USA

I appreciated your words in the update from Sunday: (1) that you are not strong; He is! (Oh, may we all remember that in whatever circumstance we find ourselves!) (2) Mary Rose's hymn! What a joyous blessing those words are! Amen and Amen!

Chapter 6

"I Feel Pretty"

♪

8 December 2020 (Tuesday p.m.)

Dear All

I didn't get to see Courtney at all today, and she's finding e-communication difficult right now. She's very sensitive right now to noises like beeps, rings, etc. It's very encouraging that she's having an operation, but all the pressure on her brain is still there, and that makes lots of things hard.

Courtney is first on the operations list for tomorrow, which means her operation starts sometime between 0800–0900 British Standard Time tomorrow morning. I may not hear anything until after lunch time. The surgeon is going to have more important things to do tomorrow morning than talk to me, and we know Courtney is in the Lord's hands, anyway.

I think Courtney and I are both running on empty right now. Of course, the Lord is there and He is sufficient, He'll provide all the strength we really need. I believe He often lets us feel our weakness to remind us that our strength is in Him and not in ourselves.

Edward and Marguerite, and Rosa, plan to travel soon.

In Him
Justin

From former members of our church

Justin, can you keep us updated on Courtney please? We are praying and thinking of you all during this time.

Courtney is one of the most Godly women I have ever had the pleasure of knowing. Her faith has always encouraged me but even more so now. Her strength and her love for God is truly beautiful [to] see during this very hard trying time. Please hug her for me.

From a pastor of a nearby church in Scotland

We don't know you, nor you us. However, our family is praying for yours regularly.

Justin, is there anything I can do to make the normal everyday things easier? Provide a meal for you and your family here. Just tell me the place and we'll have the takeaway delivered, or if you're ok with a home cooked meal, my wife would take care of that. Groceries—just let me know what is needed and when and I'll sort it out.

I was deeply touched by the above, but when I told Courtney, she was upset. "We're becoming takers rather than givers!" I told her that was easy for her to say, since she was just lying around while we did all the work! I hadn't asked for help, and you have to let people help if the Lord lays it on their heart. That silenced her, for a time anyway. :)

From Illinois, USA, a lady I'd known for more than three decades

"Running on empty" is good because that means that we have to get God to fill us up, and then He will do this, because you both are not able to do anything but trust Him.

We are praying that the doctors and everything associated with the surgery will go according to God's will.

From Colorado, USA

We are praying for you. May you know God's loving presence as you wait for the operation. And, if God so wills, may the tumor be drawn out whole, leaving no root behind. May the doctor feel God's skill and inspiration as he operates. And, we join you in prayer that in life or death Jesus will be glorified.

From Florida, USA

I just wanted you both to know, that I am earnestly praying and interceding for you both. I do not know you personally, but my heart is fiercely praying for you. You are the first thing on my mind when I wake in the morning, and I have wept for you in intercession. I know how priceless you are to the Father, and I trust in His perfect plan unfolding, that His promises are beautiful reminders of His love for us, and He is so beautifully in control.

I wrote back to a dear friend in South Carolina—

What a wonderful letter. It's amazing how God uses our weaknesses and griefs. I begin to process more and more, "Surely he hath borne our griefs . . ."

I am amazed at many things happening. I do not know all that God has done with this or all He will do, but I know He is good. Courtney has said several times, she does not want her cancer to be wasted. She is a very shy and private person. It is strange and uncomfortable for her to receive messages from people she doesn't even know saying how she is affecting them. But I think it is of God.

From a pastor in Northern Ireland we've never met
Dear Justin, just a little text to say I am praying for Courtney at this difficult time and I trust that the operation will go well today. May you know at this time the peace of God in a wonderful way. 2 Cor 12;9

From Bangladesh
Thinking of you and your family, and praying for rest tonight, and for a successful surgery and peace for all tomorrow. May the Almighty sustain you.

From Florida, USA
We are praying with you all tonight.

From Virginia, USA
Praying for you, Courtney. May God provide a deep level of comfort, peace, and strength as you head into this operation.

I love how Jesus said let not your heart be troubled, neither let it be afraid. Even though we walk through the valley of the shadow of death, we don't have anything to fear, because God is with us.

9 December 2020 (Wednesday a.m.)

"Off to the Operation"

Dear All

They've just come to take Courtney to the operating theatre. There have been no emergencies arise overnight, so she is still first on the list this morning.

I know many have spent much time in prayer. The Lord will surely bless you for this.

Courtney told me last night she is totally at peace about this. So am I, and I slept well. In human terms, we're in very good hands. In reality, we're in the Saviour's hand.

In Him
Justin

From a pastor near Edinburgh, Scotland

I know that you know people are praying, and so I hesitate to shoot you an email. But, just in case a lot of us were being silent, I wanted to give you a shout out.

I woke up thinking about your wife's surgery and praying for God to guide the surgeon's hand. I'm also praying for God's grace for both of you as you are apart today.

We'll keep praying.

My response—

Thank you. Blessings to you. People have not been silent. Incredible.

From Wyoming, USA

Peace and sleep are precious gifts in such times. Grateful. Praying. I woke up at about 12:30 a.m. and was mindful that they'd probably be prepping Courtney for the surgery. You are on our hearts.

9 December 2020 (Wednesday mid-afternoon)

"In the Recovery Room"

Dear All

I have just spoken to a nurse, and then to Courtney, in the recovery room. She is moving arms and legs, has had some water, and is speaking a little bit. The first thing she said is, "Can you come in?" but unfortunately that isn't allowed due to COVID. They are giving her painkillers for head pain, obviously.

The second thing she said was, "How much of the tumour did he get?" I don't have an answer yet. But she's obviously aware of why she was there and what is happening. I'll update you as I know more. We are grateful they were able to do this.

In Him
Justin

10 December 2020 (Thursday p.m.)

Dear All

I wish I could give you more information, but I still have not been able to talk to the doctor, and obviously am not allowed in. Here's what I do know.

Courtney appears to have come through the operation fine without any negative consequences or further loss of brain function.

She is still in the high dependency unit, still receiving a lot of painkillers, and being given blood thinners to prevent clots.

They still are watching her carefully for complications, some of which could be severe. But the nurse also told me she might be on schedule to come home in just days!

There was a lot of confusion, but she has grown

more and more lucid today, and I believe is now thinking more clearly than before the operation, despite (I think) being on more painkillers.

The physiotherapist was able to get her on her feet today.

The man next to her in the high dependency unit had a pulmonary embolism, and is in a lot of pain, and she's been asking me all about the things that helped when I had mine years ago (the answer is pretty much nothing helped except lots of painkillers, unfortunately, and even that didn't really do it).

She had another MRI today and she says they've told her it looks good (I don't know what that means).

Courtney is very, very impressed with the doctors and nurses. She also says they are overburdened and feels guilty about asking them for anything, at which I remind her she's just had a brain operation and she's not thinking clearly. :) I may pay for this later, of course!

It looks like Edward and Marguerite will be here Thursday, and Rosa the following Sunday.

Thank you again for all your prayers. It is only two weeks ago that a doctor told me that Courtney might have just weeks. He was doing his job and I will forever be grateful to him for what he did for us, but the Lord knows more.

Psalm 91:9 *Because thou hast made the LORD, which is my refuge, even the most High, thy habitation;*

Psalm 91:10 *There shall no evil befall thee, neither shall any plague come nigh thy dwelling.*

If your dwelling place is the Lord (verse 9), no plague can come nigh your dwelling (verse 10), because nothing can touch Him. Things might touch us, our family, our earthly dwelling, but they can never, ever touch the eternal dwelling place that we have in Him. The most anything of this world can do (whether enemies, illness, accidents, whatever) is let us go to our eternal dwelling place earlier, and they can't even do that unless He allows it.

In Him
Justin

My cousin wrote a nice note about the frustrations of not being able to be with Courtney. It *was* frustrating, but I wrote back—*Every time I think about not being with her, I remind myself, "You didn't think this operation would happen." It's easier not to fret when I remember to be grateful!*

From California, USA
Please keep us updated as you can. We are First Reformed Church in Yuba City continue with our prayers.

11 December 2020 (Friday a.m.)

"I Feel Alive!"

I just received a text from Courtney saying that. I told her the evidence suggests that it is more than a feeling.

I finally got to speak to one of the doctors this morning, not the surgeon who did the operation but one of his colleagues. So, here's what I've learned.

Yesterday's MRI suggests they were able to remove about 90% of the tumour.

In about a month's time, depending on the pathology report, they will likely want to start radiotherapy and chemotherapy to keep the tumour from growing.

They are also optimistic that after 30 days or maybe a little more Courtney may be able to travel, which would allow us to return to the States and see family.

He confirmed what the nurse told me about possibly coming home within days.

Since, Courtney tells me that:

The physio came, had her on her feet, and has cleared her for home, from his perspective.

They have removed the "helmet" that she was wearing that, she said, was to help prevent brain swelling.

She says she has a black eye and looks awful, and then told me to look up "I Feel Pretty" from *West Side Story* on the Internet. I had no clue such a thing existed, and don't feel particularly that my life has been enhanced by learning it but am glad she is having fun!

She is still in the high dependency unit, so I don't think getting cleared by the physio means she's waltzing out of the hospital today singing. But how things have changed in two weeks! In human terms, the prognosis is still pretty tough with some hard days ahead. Will keep you posted as I learn more. Thank you for your prayers, messages, and offers of help.

In Him
Justin

11 December 2020 (Friday p.m.)

"Courtney Update, First Setback"

Dear All

Courtney is running a temperature this evening.

It's not a high fever, she's not delirious or feeling particularly ill from it, but it probably means infection somewhere. Please pray that this will not take hold.

She feels much better today than she has for a while. She just told me, "It's such a joyful blessing to lie flat on your back and be able to lift your knees and roll your ankle from side to side and feel like there's life in your legs!"

There are so many things for which we should be thankful, and we never are until we lose them for a while (or permanently).

1 Thessalonians 5:18 *In every thing give thanks: for this is the will of God in Christ Jesus concerning you.*

In Him
Justin

The fever turned out to be nothing, and Courtney's recovery continued. She might "look awful" in her mirror, but she was beautiful and I couldn't wait to see her again.

Chapter 7

Home!: "The Lord Is All That Matters"

♪

12 December 2020 (Saturday a.m.)

"Incredible News! Courtney Is Probably Coming Home Today!"

Fever is gone.

Walking ok with assistance.

They are optimistic of her chances of getting home today.

Praise the Lord! He has given these people wonderful skills. Three days ago they removed a tumour the size of a small orange from her head, today she may get home. Obviously, still much to pray about.

Fun story. Yesterday, Courtney told the nurse that we've seen friends with cancer stop eating, which makes it harder for the body to fight the cancer, since the cancer consumes so many calories. She told the nurse, "I'm going to live at least five years. Cake and custard will get me there." The nurse said, "I've got this," and went and brought her a SECOND dessert of cake and custard! :)

They've been very, very kind to her.

Thank you for all your prayers, I will keep you informed.

In Him
Justin

12 December 2020 (Saturday p.m.)

"Not Today After All"

Dear All

The hospital is short-staffed of physios on the weekend and the physio did not get to Courtney today to assess her ability to handle stairs. So, we wait another day.

Having talked to Courtney a few minutes ago, I think this may be for the best anyway. Her vital signs are all fine, everything is fine, but she just sounded very tired to me, and the hospital is just over an hour away, so the whole trip is likely to be very tiring. Lord willing, another day's rest will help and we can get it all sorted tomorrow earlier in the day, and the trip home won't be as difficult.

Thank you again for your prayers!

In Him
Justin

13 December 2020 (Sunday p.m.)

"Home!"

Dear All

Home and straight to bed. Very weak and tired, but very thankful!

Thank you for your prayers.

In Him
Justin

From Justin's mom in Louisiana, USA
No better rest than in her own bed, with her own pillows, her own blanket. And hopefully quiet!! Praying Courtney that you will get a good night's rest. God has done an amazing thing for you and your family. Our hearts are singing tonight!

From Oregon, USA
Yay! Rest is a GOOD and perfect gift! Following your journey and praying for complete healing. Grateful you had access to amazing surgeons and God has given you more time together.

From Colorado, USA
That is fantastic news! I praise the Lord that He has given you all the gift of more time together on this side of eternity. God has provided your daily bread and that is all any of us can ask for.

From our daughter Rosa
Hi. Glad you're home. Keep doing your physio exercises.

I'll see you Saturday!

Courtney had decided the National Health Service was the most wonderful thing ever. The nurses (most of them) had been so kind even though they were so busy. The first half of our drive home from hospital had been singing paeans of praise to the NHS. But then she began to talk about another nurse, and some bad experiences, and, suddenly, the NHS was evil incarnate.

The tumour was in the frontal lobe and had impacted Courtney's emotion-control centre. Her highs were going to be high, and her lows low. This would prove hard because she'd always tried to keep an even keel emotionally. She'd be fine and then suddenly feel like she had turned into a blithering, hysterical ninny.

This did have one really nice benefit. Courtney had come home viewing me as the most perfect person in the world, and she never seemed to get over that. It wasn't true, of course, but it made her happy to think it, so I didn't argue much. Fortunately, she never discussed it with the thousands and millions of people who would have corrected her!

14 December 2020 (Monday p.m.)

"Back to Hospital"

Dear All

Unfortunately, we are having symptoms tonight, so they are sending an ambulance to take Courtney to the hospital. This may be nothing, but it needs to be checked.

We would appreciate your prayers.

In Him
Justin

From southern Asia

Praying.

From Colorado, USA
May God give the doctors wisdom to help Courtney. May He also give you guys energy, patience, and comfort in addition to the strength He is obviously supplying and the witness you are bearing. I will also keep praying for all those helping. God bless you guys, you will remain in my (and my family's) thoughts and prayers.

15 December 2020 (just after midnight, Tuesday a.m.)

"All OK"

Medication adjusted, have to watch to make sure symptoms are resolved, but back home.

Thank you for praying!

In Him
Justin

From Dundee, Scotland
Praise the Lord

From Wyoming, USA
Very grateful! Spreading the good news! :)

15 December 2020 (Tuesday p.m.)

Dear All

We're very tired after a very late night last night, but all ok. Courtney was able to come downstairs several times today and got to read a story to our granddaughter. She's very tired and still dealing with after-effects of the operation, but we're very grateful for the Lord's goodness to us. She kept saying today,

"The Lord is all that matters." When you go through things like this, you see that clearly.

In Him
Justin

This day was painful to Courtney in an unexpected way: the top of her head was heavily bandaged, one side of her face was swollen, and the blood draining from the wound had given her a very bad black eye. When our (very young) grandchildren, the local contingent of The Cuteness Roarers, came by, they were afraid of her, because she didn't look like "Nana."

Within half an hour, Daffodil was on her lap for a story, the others figured out it was still Nana, and all was fine. But it really hurt, and to her it seemed much longer. She was still talking to me about it months later. She'd so wanted to see them in the hospital, and then when she finally did see them, they were afraid.

God-given peace and joy through trials doesn't mean the trials don't hurt sometimes. It gives an answer for the pain but it doesn't cancel it, and sometimes the pain really, really hurts.

From Yorkshire, England
Please keep our Bible Study group in Wakefield, West Yorkshire informed so that we too can continue to pray for all of the Martin family.

Justin to our church—
"Bible Study"

I apologise but this isn't going to be possible tonight. Almost no sleep last night, please pray for better rest tonight.

16 December 2020 (Wednesday p.m.)

Dear All

Psalm 4:8 *I will both lay me down in peace, and sleep: for thou, LORD, only makest me dwell in safety.*

Thankful for this verse tonight, we need it. Courtney had a very difficult night last night and we had less than 2 hours sleep. It just seemed like all the minor symptoms from the cancer, the operation, and medication side effects, all piled up at the same time to create a very difficult night.

Praise the Lord, we seem to have most of those things handled this evening, and Courtney is resting quietly right now. It will be very early to bed for me, too.

We have two grandchildren arriving with their parents tomorrow. :) Edward and Marguerite haven't been back since before they were engaged. Rosa arrives on Saturday and the nest will be full.

Please pray for rest tonight.

In Him
Justin

From a childhood friend in Alaska, USA

I purposely haven't sent you any emails with your plate full. I just thought to let you know we are praying, my mom and Sharon are praying, and our church is praying. We update the church each Sunday morning during our prayer time, so just wanted to let you know we are still here and very much appreciate your updates.

From a pastor in southeast Scotland
Praying for rest tonight.

From a cousin in Alaska, USA
"You can't pour from an empty cup." Just read this and thought it appropriate. Praying for good rest and a sweet time with your entire family!

Chapter 8

"The Comforting Presence Is Real"

18 December 2020 (Friday p.m.)

Dear All

Sleep has been better the last two nights. Thank you for your prayers! We are still asking the Lord to help with this, there have been too many nights with too little sleep, and we are still very tired.

Today has been our best day since Courtney went into hospital. She's been able to be downstairs much of the day, been able to eat better today than she had been and has had more energy. ("More" is relative, she's still quite weak, but going the right direction!)

Marguerite and Edward arrived yesterday, with their two little ones, so all our grandchildren are in Scotland! Rosa arrives tomorrow, and everyone will be here. We are very thankful.

Courtney has been writing letters again. :) I won't give you all of this one but thought the following paragraph might be profitable to many readers of these emails, and she said it was fine to pass along.

"Over the past week, I feel like the Lord has been, through His refining fire, bit by bit remaking me. He is stripping away all the silly things that I struggled with, making me more what I've always wanted to be and what He wants me to be. It's actually rather joyous, even if I seem teary about things. I've felt myself growing closer to Him."

That's what James 1 is talking about, and why we count it as joy when we face trials. If we combine James 1:2-4 with Romans 5:3-5 (I'm too lazy to copy them in, you'll have to look them up), we see that the perfect work of patience described in James 1 involves the love of God flooding our hearts (Romans 5:5). We're going through those trials but God is using it to enhance our understanding of just how much He loves us.

Thank you again for your prayers.

In Him
Justin

Here are those verses. You could take out "perfect work" in James 1:4 and insert "experience" and the following words from Romans 5:4-5 to see what I was getting at:

James 1:2 *My brethren, count it all joy when ye fall into divers temptations;*

James 1:3 *Knowing this, that the trying of your faith worketh patience.*

James 1:4 *But let patience have her perfect work, that ye may be perfect and entire, wanting nothing.*

Romans 5:3 *And not only so, but we glory in tribulations also: knowing that tribulation worketh patience;*

Romans 5:4 *And patience, experience; and experience, hope:*

Romans 5:5 *And hope maketh not ashamed; because the love of God is shed abroad in our hearts by the Holy Ghost which is given unto us.*

From a work colleague in Florida, USA

I sent a note to Robert a few days ago, to tell him that I have been in prayer for Courtney and your family since the first note regarding her health was sent. I will continue to ask Him to wrap His arms around you all at this time. Courtney's witness and your witness to your faith in the Lord's working has had a great impact on my faith walk. Your love for each other and for the Lord is very, very evident in each of your emailings. Thank you for allowing us to walk with you at this time.

19 December 2020 (Saturday p.m.)

Dear All

We're on an up-trend with Courtney's health, she's regaining strength daily. There are definitely some symptoms remaining, and some of them may stay with us long-term, but we can now safely let her walk around the house without help (except for the stairs). The possibility of travel to the US next month seems a lot more real now than it did earlier in the week.

Rosa arrived today, so all are now safely here.

The Scottish government is still banning singing in churches, so we record the songs at home and then play the recordings during the service. Nice to have a few more family members join in, for much of the year it was just Courtney, Alyssa, and I. We've always sung a lot together as a family—tonight, we were missing Robert and Manda, hopefully we can sing with them, too.

I'm attaching a recording of one of the songs. Lyrics below.

Also, with all the missed sleep I also missed putting up new posts for blog messages for Courtney and family. That's fixed now.

1 Who is this so weak and helpless,
Child of lowly Hebrew maid,
Rudely in a stable sheltered,
Coldly in a manger laid?
'Tis the Lord of all creation,
Who this wondrous path hath trod;
Christ our God from everlasting,
And to everlasting God.

2 Who is this, a man of sorrows,
Walking sadly life's hard way,
Homeless, weary, sighing,
Weeping over sin and Satan's sway?
'Tis our God, our glorious Saviour,
Who above the starry sky
Now for us a place prepareth,
Where no tear can dim the eye.

3 Who is this that hangeth dying
While the rude world scoffs and scorns,
Numbered with the malefactors,
Torn with nails, and crowned with thorns?
'Tis the God who ever liveth
'Mid the shining ones on high,
God in the glorious golden city,
Reigning everlastingly.

["Who Is This, So Weak and Helpless"
Words: William W. How, 1823–1897
Music: John A. Lloyd, Sr, 1815–1874]

In Him
Justin

20 December 2020 (Sunday p.m.)

Dear All

So nice to have everyone here today. Of course those who just arrived couldn't go to church with us today because of quarantine, but someone needed to stay with Courtney anyway.

Courtney is still trying to regain strength; we're feeding her a lot! She's also been up on her feet quite a bit today, enough to be quite tired tonight.

We have been watching with some concern about the new COVID strain in the UK, and the fact that several European countries are no longer accepting flights from the UK. Our family can't stay forever, and some have connections through Amsterdam and Dublin, neither of which would be possible if they were flying tomorrow. Fortunately, they aren't flying tomorrow!

I don't know whether to hope they can get back on schedule or hope they can't and get to stay longer! Please pray for the Lord's will to be done! :) (Rosa says some of her patients are probably hoping for her to stay longer. Apparently, she's a tough physio!)

I had a talk with someone today who doesn't know the Lord. He simply doesn't understand how we can be joyful with what is happening. It gave me an opportunity to tell him why. Please pray that the hope that is in us will continue to be clearly seen and that the Lord will continue to move people to ask why we are joyful and peaceful (1 Peter 3:15).

In Him
Justin

22 December 2020 (Tuesday p.m.)

Dear All

Courtney is gradually gaining strength, and her balance is improving. Today her husband and her physio daughter have given her permission to go upstairs without being escorted. :) Going down the stairs is another matter, she's not very steady for that yet, but still, another step of progress.

We're feeling more optimistic about being able to move, perhaps mid-January. Much has to come together for the house to be ready to sell and for us to get this international move together—these things don't usually happen in a month, and with Courtney's condition and the things I need to do to help her, the task is difficult. Fortunately, someone somewhere managed to get something right in training these kids and they are doing a tremendous amount of work to help us get there. Please pray for wisdom in many decisions that must be made.

We do want to move as soon as we get medical clearance. We don't know whether the Lord is going to heal Courtney or take her Home, and if the latter, how long this period of improvement will last. But we do hope to be back to the US in time to spend time with family there either way.

Please pray also for wisdom for provision for the church as we leave this ministry after 21 years.

We learned yesterday that a dear friend and brother is critically ill. He's been in a care home since a stroke some years ago, and there's been a major COVID outbreak in the home. Our hearts ache for his family, but he told me many times after his stroke he just wanted to go home to Heaven. As we prepare to leave Scotland, after coming here more than 25 years ago, it is a reminder of why we came. The change in this man when the Lord began to draw him, and then when he came to Christ, was unmistakable, and I am sure we will see him again in Glory.

Please also continue to pray about the travel situation for our kids. The new COVID strain in the UK is wreaking havoc with international travel. For now, we're just enjoying having them here!

Thank you for your prayers for us.

In Him
Justin

For now, Courtney was only writing to me, but she dictated this to me for the family of the man who was dying:

Courtney's letter—
Dear ___ family,

I am so sorry to hear about ____ health struggles. I don't know if this will be of help, but having just been near death myself, I can assure you that the Comforting Presence is real. The peace is real. There was a sense of joy. I believe you can be certain that ____ is feeling enveloped in loving arms now.

I don't know if the Lord will choose to cure my cancer, as He did your other family member's, or take me Home, but I can say with confidence that Jesus doeth all things well.

Thank you for the kind messages you sent me and for your prayers. We are praying that I will be able to be flown back to America to see family, but also to take part in a clinical trial to help find better ways of treating this disease. Even if it doesn't help me, if it helps others that would be a real blessing.

Whatever happens, God is there and He is good and kind!

Much love,
Courtney

The family's response—

Thank you Courtney for your kind encouraging words through this very hard time. Even though my flesh is heart-broken, my spirit is rejoicing for I know with full confidence where he is going. He will soon be in paradise in his new body in God's presence. But this waiting is the hardest part, so I very much appreciate all your prayers for us during this time.

You are still very much in our thoughts and prayers. Praying God will bring such beauty and power from your whole situation. He has you and all under his control. I pray your move will go smoothly and your trials will be a huge success.

I just wanted to say a personal thank you to you and Justin for your ministry here in Scotland. Especially with my family. I love and miss you both and will never forget all that you have done for myself and my family throughout the years. Justin, your sermons always spoke to me and encouraged me greatly in my walk with God. You were very instrumental in my growth and Love for Christ and for that I will always be thankful. I feel so blessed to have known such a true God fearing family and I wish you all the best in whatever may come next.

> *Isaiah 52.7*
> *How beautiful upon the mountains are the feet of him that bringeth good tidings, that publisheth peace; that bringeth good tidings of good, that publisheth salvation; that saith unto Zion, Thy God reigneth!*

Merry Christmas to you all.
All my love

From Oregon, USA
Glad about the progress. That's a big move after all these years. Your labor is not in vain in Him.

From Justin's aunt in Colorado, USA
You and your family are in my prayers, Justin. What a trial and how hard it is to rush a move like that. I am glad you have such great kids to help with everything. I rejoice though, to hear that Courtney is a bit better. I pray that the Lord will give you the clear thinking and energy that you need for all of this. I know you are relying on the Lord and His perfect plan. God bless you.

Email from Courtney to Justin, 24 December at 2:15 a.m.
I don't want you to ruin yourself financially trying to get me back for treatment.

Courtney would get thoughts in the night that really bothered her, and she just couldn't sleep. She would turn on the light (which would, of course, wake me up) and write me an email so she didn't have to wake me up to tell me.

This illogic was one of those "blockages" from the tumour. Throughout our married life, Courtney always worked so hard to protect my sleep, because I was working two jobs. She went to great lengths to keep the babies from waking me up. All that changed when she came home from the hospital. Lights would go on in the night, music would play, audio books, audio Bible, etc.

I didn't know what to do. It was so out of character that I was sure Courtney was simply not processing the fact that some things would wake me up. I knew she would want to know—if she could process it. If not, it would upset her that she was unable to process it. She was highly intelligent, and these strange mental blocks made her feel guilty, like she should be able to overcome them.

I decided to say nothing, but just to ask her to turn the music or audio book down if she kept it on too long. Usually, if I did, she would turn it off, and I could go back to sleep.

Through most of our married life, I knew the most loving way to handle things. When dealing with a frontal lobe brain injury—in Courtney's case, due to a tumour—it's not always so clear. She might surprise me with how well she'd handle something one day and then struggle immensely with the same thing the next day.

We muddled through as best we could. The Comforting Presence continued to be real.

Chapter 9

"How Could We Be Anything but Thankful?"

♪

24 December 2020 (Thursday p.m.)

Dear All

Several encouragements to report today.

Both yesterday and today, Courtney walked down to the end of our street, then back up the hill, maybe 100 yards each way.

As of tomorrow, we're letting her go down the stairs as well as up, without help, as long as she feels ok.

We have an appointment on the 30th to get the pathology report and hopefully an assessment of Courtney's fitness to travel.

Flight restrictions are improving, and it looks like Rosa will be able to return in time to be at work on Monday. We are thankful for this.

Thank you for praying!

In Him
Justin

29 December 2020 (Tuesday p.m.)

We are still encouraged by Courtney's progress. Today, we took three short walks outside, despite the snow and ice, and her balance was fine. She is still a long way from where she was before, but stamina is slowly returning, and today she is bragging to her physio daughter that her Fitbit showed over 6,000 steps today, and 24 flights of stairs!

Please pray for wisdom and clarity at our appointment with the surgeon tomorrow. Please also pray that we will have a good and clear testimony before him as believers in the Lord.

Rosa was able to make it safely back to Virginia in time to see her patients on Monday. The next complication is for Katherine, and Edward, Marguerite, and kids. Katherine had to change her flight, which originally took her to Germany and then back to the US, because of new COVID restrictions. So she changed to be on the same flight as Edward and Marguerite to London, and then from London back. But then the flight from Edinburgh to London that they were all on was cancelled! Now, they are still on the same flight to London, but an earlier one. Not sure what happens if that is also cancelled, but we know the Lord has a plan.

Please ask the Lord for wisdom as to future plans for our church. We're having an online meeting tomorrow night to discuss that.

We know that all these things are in the Lord's hands. We are currently working very hard (with LOTS of help from our kids) to get ready to move, so that if the Lord makes that possible we'll be as ready as we can be. If that turns out not to be possible, well, we'll have sorted through a lot of stuff, and got rid of lots of stuff we don't need! Whatever the Lord has for us, we know it will be good—He never makes mistakes.

A word about the messages to Courtney: please do not send her suggestions about treatment for cancer. You may send them to me, but if you put suggestions in a message to her I will just delete it before she sees it. The after-effects of the operation make it hard for her to process things like that and so it is just stressful for her. We realise people want to help, and I read and consider what I am sent, but it does not help to send messages about treatment to Courtney.

In Him
Justin

We were getting a lot of "try this treatment" messages. We appreciated the love and care, but it distressed Courtney. Someone with a brain tumour doesn't need that, and I decided it must stop.

From a pastor in Pennsylvania, USA

Thus, adding to my theory: Everybody in the local church is a doctor. Just list an ailment that you are going through, and everybody has an opinion and cure!

We have been faithfully praying for your wife.

From a former member of our church in Scotland's Central Belt

God bless you all, Justin. Praying about the things you mentioned and praising God for His great help.

30 December 2020 (Wednesday p.m.)

Dear All

Today we met with one of the team of surgeons in Edinburgh. She co-authored the protocol used throughout Europe for the treatment of glioblastoma.

For those familiar with some of the technical jargon, this is an unmethylated tumour. For those less familiar, that means it is not as responsive to chemotherapy. As a result, they strongly recommend that radiation therapy start as soon as practical—six weeks after the surgery. The prognosis is not as good as with MGMT methylation.

Also, the tumour has PNET features. This means there is a chance the cancer has migrated to the spinal cord. If so, they would use radiation treatment on the spine as well. It would probably also mean the prognosis is worse. They did a scan today to check for that.

The doctor is convinced Courtney will be able to travel. However, the earliest she could travel is 30 days after the operation, it is not certain she could travel that soon, and to do so would make it very difficult to get radiation started by the 6-week target. There is also a risk of COVID-related disruption to travel plans which could make it impossible to hit the target. As a result, they recommended that we remain here in Scotland for the initial 6-week course of radiation, to be sure it can be started on time, and then travel after that. However, they are willing to work with whatever we decide.

We believe that their recommendation makes sense unless the scan shows that the cancer has moved to the spine. If that is the case, I believe we should travel back to the States as soon as Courtney is well enough to fly, so that she can still see family before things progress much further. If the spine is clear, we will stay here for the six-week treatment and then travel back to the States.

For many reasons, related to church, the sale of our home, and winding up various other matters here in Scotland, the extra six weeks will significantly simplify the process. It will, however, mean daily round-trip journeys to the hospital in Edinburgh, over an hour each way. But with what we know at this point we believe this is the best use of the time and abilities that the Lord has given us.

Obviously, not all of this was what we wanted to hear, but we are still very thankful. We have already been given time we did not think we were going to have. Even if not immediately, it appears very likely we will be able to return to the States before very long. And even if that hadn’t been the case, our eternal destiny has been made sure to us—how could we be anything but thankful?

Please pray that the Lord will guide our decisions for His glory in our lives.

Travel from Britain has become very complicated for our kids, please pray for wisdom in rescheduling flights.

31 December 2020 (Thursday p.m.)

Dear All

Well, it’s been a fast-moving day, I’ve been on the phone many times already.

We received a call that Courtney’s scan has already been checked. The good news is that there is no cancer in the spine. Not so good is that the tumour in her brain has grown since the scan after the operation.

That's not really surprising but it does reinforce the decision to proceed with treatment here rather than have potential delays in trying to move first.

Also, they phoned to make an appointment for Courtney to get her mask made for the radiation therapy (that is Wednesday), and also phoned to arrange the release of medical records. They are obviously working fast to help us out on all fronts, and we are appreciative.

Also, we went ahead and listed our house for sale, it went up on the Internet around 10:30, and by noon there were three potential buyers wanting appointments to view it, one on Saturday. Obviously, it would be a blessing if it would sell quickly.

We thank the Lord for the year He has given us and look forward to what He has for us this next year.

Though we didn't know the exact details yet, we later learned the tumour was already 2 cm in diameter. It had grown that much in just three weeks after the operation. It wasn't causing any real problems yet because there was space for it to grow after removal of the 5 cm mass earlier. Courtney's tumour was extremely aggressive. That is usually true with a glioblastoma, but hers was growing very quickly even by those standards.

From South Carolina, USA

We are praying faithfully for you. Trusting in our faithful God—even though there are many unknowns. Give Courtney our love!

From Texas, USA

Everything is moving fast. Thank you so much for your knowledge, thoughtfulness and care of Courtney. You have done well shepherding your kids around.

May the Lord continue to strengthen you.

From Aberdeenshire, Scotland

Brother Justin, all at our church are praying for Courtney as well as you and the whole family. God bless you and if we can help in any way, let us know.

Chapter 10

"We'll Take It"—Twice!

♪

We hadn't been sure Courtney would even see the new year, and she was doing well!

7 January 2021 (Thursday p.m.)

Dear All

Very busy days, I apologise for not updating you sooner.

We went into Edinburgh yesterday for Courtney to be fitted for her mask for radiation therapy.

The treatment starts on 25 January, 5 days a week, for 6 weeks.

We had originally been advised to plan to travel about 10 days after this first course of treatment. That will be about 15 March. Yesterday, the doctor we spoke to suggested 4 weeks later might be better, but we've had further discussions, and we still are tentatively looking at mid-March. We plan to travel to Colorado Springs at that point.

Any travel plans are going to be indefinite because we don't know exactly how Courtney will respond to the treatment.

Courtney appears to have had a couple of minor

symptoms return, which may indicate swelling again becoming a problem, so she is now back on the steroids at a low level.

Despite that, she is still growing stronger. We have been walking more and more each day, and today we took our first walk over a mile. For the day, she's had more than 8,000 steps and 37 flights of stairs!

Our house has been listed for sale since last Thursday, and we have had many potential buyers through to see it. We received an offer today for more than the asking price, but it would be contingent on the sale of the buyer's home, and their house isn't even listed yet. Please pray for wisdom in decisions around the sale of the house.

We are having to be very careful with the new strain of COVID. To reduce contacts, the estate agents do not show the house, that falls on the homeowner, but we are having Courtney leave the house when people are coming through, and I am showing them around when possible; if not, Alyssa is. This, added to the need to get the house cleaned up and ready to show, makes the whole process rather burdensome.

On the other hand, it is also an opportunity. The potential buyers are all warned to be very careful because there is illness in the house. The result has been many opportunities to express our faith in the Lord in this situation.

Travel news for our kids. All of our kids have had trouble with flight cancellations and difficulty with new travel restrictions. Other than Rosa, who was able to return home on time, all are still here. Katherine, Lord willing, returns to Wisconsin tomorrow. Eric is scheduled to return to Eastern Europe on the 12th, Edward and Marguerite (and their two little ones) to

Utah on the 15th. Please pray for them as they return to their responsibilities, and that the Lord would grant them opportunities to serve Him as they travel.

Robert and Manda (and their children) are still here, but also planning to move, and their house will be on the market soon.

Alyssa is also still here with us, but (depending on circumstances) may leave for Colorado before us to help get a place set up there for us before we arrive.

Finally, please pray for the Lord's direction and provision for the church here. There is a godly man who is willing to consider coming as pastor. Please pray that the Lord's direction in this matter would be very clear. Also, churches have again been closed entirely by the Scottish government—online services only are permitted.

12 January 2021 (Tuesday p.m.)

Dear All

Courtney and I walked two miles this morning! We've been gradually building up; we also walked a little over half a mile this evening.

Courtney has been back on the steroid since Thursday and the symptoms she was having have improved. She's on a light dose which isn't giving her any problems, and she is generally feeling quite well. This will likely continue throughout the radiation and chemo treatment, which starts on 25 January and runs for six weeks.

Our flight from London to Denver is booked for the 15th of March. We intend to fly from Edinburgh to London but unsure whether we'll do it all in one day (very tiring for Courtney) or do the first leg on a separate day. The flight is changeable so that we can do differently depending on how Courtney responds to treatment.

Our house has sold! We had two more offers as of yesterday morning, so all buyers were told to give their best and final offer by 11 today. The best cash offer also happened to be the people I'd hoped would buy the house—of all the people who came through to see the house, they were the ones that I thought would most enjoy the house and be the best fit with our neighbours, which matters to us. As they expressed sympathy for Courtney's illness, I told them how we were trusting the Lord, and how grateful we were for all that God has given us. That led to a conversation about some griefs in their life, and I ended up praying with them before they left. They've asked for each member of our family to plant a tree as something to remember us by.

There are many things to do and many decisions to be made! Please pray for wisdom.

From a pastor near Edinburgh, Scotland

Praise God for the good update, Justin.

I haven't messaged often, but we are daily praying. We also are praying for you with our church family. Praise the Lord about the house. I was praying it would be a cash offer. God is good.

On 21 January, we had long discussions with Melissa, a real estate agent in Colorado. I wanted a ground-floor bedroom and bathroom in case Courtney had mobility difficulties later. For several reasons, we were looking at newly built houses. Finally, we settled on one and told Melissa—but late in the evening (early afternoon in Colorado), word came back that it was sold, as was our second choice.

Justin to Courtney and Melissa (9:20 p.m.)—
The Lord's in control; obviously we weren't supposed to get either house.

Melissa to Justin and Courtney (9:29 p.m.)—
Amen to that!

Courtney to Melissa and Justin (9:35 p.m.), asking about yet another house and then—
I think we need to call it a night here and think about it a little more. We'll get back to you in the morning on this one if it is still there.

Echoing Melissa, I thought, *Amen to that!* I turned off the light and tried to sleep, but Courtney had her light on! She corresponded with Melissa for hours while I tried to sleep and wondered what she was doing. Melissa didn't know I had checked out and worked late to help us. She found three houses that fit our criteria.

At 2:00 a.m. our time, Courtney wrote—
Then we will take this one.

I was still trying to sleep, wondering what in the world Courtney was typing to me and wishing the light would burn out. She had just gone rogue on me and agreed to buy a house!

At 3:00 a.m., she was still negotiating—
We would want to do the fence and landscaping on this one,

too. Also, how much would it cost to do just the bathroom in the basement?

At 3:30 a.m., after further emails, Courtney said, "Justin? We've got a house." I said, "Mmmkay," and she said, "I told her to say *we'll take it!*" For wives who want to make sure their husband is wide awake, "I bought a house" works wonders. She was very pleased with herself and showed me the emails. What could I say? "The usual process when spending more than your entire retirement savings on a house is to talk about it together . . ."

Courtney said, "It's the one we wanted!" Actually, it wasn't. Of the three houses Melissa had sent, the one Courtney had agreed to buy wasn't the best. However, once all was said and done, we did get the best of the three.

Courtney never wanted to spend *anything* without discussion to make sure we could afford it—but the tumour had taken out some restraints. *"We'll take it!"* She never did anything horrible financially, but she did a lot to remind me of her silly threat back in the hospital to bankrupt me! We had many jokes about her bankruptcy campaign—until something ruined the joke, but that's later.

In this case, an extra motivation prompted her to disregard the normal restraints. Courtney was laser-focused on making a home for me in Colorado. She wanted a home set up, once she was gone, that would have good memories for me of her. Thus, she was determined to "get a house!" She worked half the night to do it.

23 January 2021 (Saturday p.m.)

Dear All

I've not been in touch because there's not really been any change in Courtney's condition. But stuff has been happening! And we have prayer requests!

Courtney is still on a low dose of the steroids to keep swelling down, and any symptoms at this point are minimal.

Starting Monday, we go to Edinburgh 5 days a week for 6 weeks for radiation treatment. There will also be concurrent chemotherapy.

Please pray for safety in driving, it will be 2 to 2.5 hours on the road every day.

Courtney's tumour is the kind that can (rarely) "leak" into the spinal fluid. Please pray that this will not happen (it had not as of the last scan).

The tumour is also the kind that does not always respond well to the chemo. As a result, they have said they will try the chemo in hopes that it will respond, but if she has difficulty with handling the chemo, they will stop it. Please pray that the side effects will not be bad and that it will be effective.

Pray that Courtney will be able to keep up her exercise. We've found the long walks are hard, but we've been walking 3 and even 4 times a day and her Fitbit is very pleased with her. :)

Moving News:

All is a go for selling our house. We had planned to close mid-March, but the buyers would like to move in earlier and we may do so, because:

We have today signed contracts to buy a newly built house in Colorado Springs. It is due to be finished 15 February and we're supposed to close 8 March, which will allow the house to be set up before our arrival, so if Courtney is feeling poorly after her course of treatment it will be an easy move-in. So:

Alyssa is likely to leave before we do to get the house ready. She's likely to have help with that (family and friends).

We will likely move into a temporary place in Edinburgh near the hospital once our house sale is completed.

Robert and Manda have also put their house on the market and have had one offer. Please pray for a rapid sale for them. They plan to move to Colorado Springs the end of February (house sold or not).

Please pray that we'll be able to get a moving company quickly (COVID seems to be making that difficult).

Other News:
All our state-side family had flights cancelled but eventually made it home.

Eric was supposed to be back to Eastern Europe long ago, but it's been closed. He's still here but has a flight on 2 February which is not cancelled yet! Please pray that he'll be able to get back.

Courtney's niece has COVID, her brother-in-law apparently does, and her sister has a pre-existing condition. Please pray for physical protection and strengthened faith!

Please continue to pray about the Lord's will and leading for our church!

Finally, I just wanted to say that this whole thing

has opened up more opportunities to speak about our faith than we've ever had since we came to Scotland. It's not a topic that people here usually speak easily about, but that door has been thrown wide open many times.

Thank you for all your prayers for us!

Justin

24 January 2021 (Sunday p.m.)

This isn't really a Courtney update but I'm passing it on because it relates to how the Lord has worked through Courtney's illness. The people buying our house have a very real need not related to the house. I have told them about all the people praying for us, and they would like me to ask you to pray about it. I told them that I wouldn't give any details but that the Lord would know what it is about if you pray. Thank you!

Justin

From a pastor in Wales

God Bless you, Justin. Our church are aware of your needs and have been praying for you. It is amazing how He meets our needs and opens doors for ministry during extremely difficult trials.

I will pray for the buyers of your house.

From a pastor of a church near us

Greetings to you in the Name of the Lord Jesus Christ.

You, your wife, and family continue to be very much in our prayers and thoughts during these most arduous of times for you. Thank you for the regular updates, including your plans to return to the US.

I also want to thank you for your friendship over these many years. I have enjoyed and benefited from the fellowship.

Once again, brother, we are praying for you and we know the Lord is with you, sustaining and directing your every development.

With Christian love

30 January 2021 (Saturday p.m.)

Jeremiah 29:11 *For I know the thoughts that I think toward you, saith the LORD, thoughts of peace, and not of evil, to give you an expected end.*

This week, on one of our walks, Courtney quoted this verse to me, and said, "I know He will do good. I know the expected end that He has for me, that I will be with Him in Heaven. I know that you will be happy, and will be ok, and that if I am to go Home, that is what is best for you, too. I know the kids will be ok, and that if I live, that is what is best for them, and if He is taking me Home, that is what is best for them, too. I know all that—but I would like to see my grandchildren grow up."

That's the Christian life, right there. We have to trust Him. There are things we would like, and it's good to like them, and good to admit we would like them. God desires truth and He doesn't want us to pretend. He's given us a heart for things in this life too, and someone who is so "super-spiritual" that they don't value those good things in this life is probably of no use to the Master. But valuing those things does not mean we don't trust the valuation that He puts on them more.

We're in His hand, always. When you have "terminal" cancer, you remember that fact more, that's all. You are just remembering always how much we all are in His hand. We live as if we have tomorrow but trust as if we don't because we may not.

We've now had five days of radiation and six of chemo—1/6th done on this first course! Courtney feels better now than she did a week ago! I asked the nurse if that's expected and she said, *"We'll take it!"* No, it isn't expected—perhaps someone has been praying for us! The latest blood counts looked good, but it's perhaps too early to tell how the chemo is going to go. Please keep praying!

We'll be here for another week and a half, and then the movers will take everything away to Colorado, and we'll head for temporary quarters near the hospital. It will be nice to not have to get up so early and drive an hour each way every day.

The buyers of our house have had a problem that may mean delays in completing the sale of our house. It's probably not a significant problem for us (and I told our buyer that—he was very distressed about it on our behalf). But it would be a blessing to have it all wrapped up by the end of February anyway, so please pray to that effect.

News on the church. I'm preaching tomorrow, but the church has asked Brother Paul _____ from Dundee to come as pastor. Paul was born in Glasgow and grew up in England. He came up to Scotland some years back to help in the ministry at Bible Baptist Church in Dundee. He's known the Lord for 38 years. He has a real heart for evangelism and has been involved in street preaching and children's ministry for years.

After tomorrow, I'll maybe only preach once more. How strange, after all these years preaching every Sunday, to think I might have only one more sermon here! How strange to be doing it over the Internet! (All Scottish churches are closed.) Truly, we never know what the Lord will do in our lives.

Thank you for your prayers for us!

Justin

Eight days after Courtney ended my sleep attempts by saying she'd bought a house, the nurse used the same words—"We'll take it!"—about the surprising news that Courtney felt better after starting radiation and chemotherapy. I couldn't help but remember . . .

So much had changed—adjustments, new limitations, changes in emotions, changes in Courtney's decision-making processes, etc. We didn't know if Courtney would see her grandchildren grow up; we admitted it was unlikely. Yet, she was herself. Her personality hadn't changed. Her *values* were the same. She was still patient with my flaws, still loved me and the kids. Despite everything, she wasn't self-focused like so many people with major health problems. More than anything, she still loved the Lord!

I'd looked at websites about brain tumours and seen how it affected many people. Courtney still could think clearly, except for sporadic blockages. She hadn't lost the ability to talk or listen; she could still walk and was motivated to do so. All those blessings—and after a week of treatment, she was feeling better than before she started.

All I could think was that the Lord had been so very, very kind to us. Why did we get more time? Why was it easier for us than for so many others?

Our Lord is the Master Planner, weaving the threads of many lives together. In this life, at least, we'll never know all His reasons for what He does or allows, but I'm sure one reason we were so blessed was for Courtney to touch many more lives before she went Home.

Now, looking back, I see the impact Courtney had on so many people through the months to come. God could have taken her to Glory right away, and she'd have been so happy and not had the struggles to come. He could have—but He had a purpose for her to stay and communicate to many lives. He would even use her walking.

I didn't know that then, though. As I thought about the nurse using those words Courtney had used, I was just grateful—and said, "Yes, Lord, we'll take it."

Chapter 11

Grace and Glory

9 February 2021 (Wednesday p.m.)

Dear All

Courtney's Condition:
We are now through 2.5 weeks of this 6-week course of treatment. Courtney is still feeling quite well, better than when she started the treatment. We are told that the last three weeks are tougher. We are praying that Courtney will be able to withstand it well. It is encouraging especially that her blood counts are showing no signs of problems.

We are still walking enough that Courtney gets to 10,000 steps most day. They have reduced Courtney's steroid level again, which is really good news. She will have to take a very heavy dosage for travel to make sure that there is no swelling in her brain during the flights, so it is very good news that they have been able to reduce it for now. We are asking the Lord for another reduction next week. Please pray that Courtney will be able to keep walking, it makes a huge difference to how she feels.

We are thankful for safety on the roads, we've

been having one of the worst storms since we came to Scotland, with nearly a foot of snow. It's made road travel to the hospital very difficult and taken a lot of time, but the Lord has protected us. Yesterday, the roads here were horrible. Today, here wasn't so bad but Edinburgh was horrible. We look forward to tomorrow!

We learned last week that when Courtney went in for her scan three weeks after her operation, the tumour had already regrown to 2 cm in diameter. So it was growing back very aggressively. We are told that is not necessarily a bad thing because the faster growing tumours may respond better to the treatment. Please pray that this will be the case.

Our Move:

Things keep changing, drastically. The Lord keeps throwing my plans out the window and replacing them with better ones. So when I ask you to pray for something, I want to be clear that I am trusting the Lord to reverse those prayers if He has a better plan. We want His will, not ours, and these requests are only because they appear to us to be His will. I could elaborate on why I believe that but it's late!

The movers came Monday and Tuesday and packed our belongings, and today put them on a shipping container. (A) We are thankful they were able to get a container, there is currently a shortage. I was praying for a container, and the Lord provided. (B) It is scheduled to go on a ship in Grangemouth, Scotland, on Monday, and to arrive in Denver on 11 March. (C) We are praying for no delay on this schedule, a quick pass through customs, and delivery before our arrival in Colorado Springs on 17 March. None of this is guaranteed. Please pray. I believe God wants me to do all I can to have the house set up as much as possible for Courtney when we arrive.

Alyssa leaves here Friday, Lord willing, and flies to Green Bay to have a visit with Katherine, then on to Colorado. We intend that she will be coordinating the setup of the house. Family and friends will help her. We are praying for safety in travel, the Lord's provision of a car, wisdom in decisions, and all the other needs we don't have time to think about right now! :)

Eric is still here; his flight home was cancelled yet again due to them extending their travel ban from the UK. He is scheduled to fly again on the 20th of this month. We are praying for no travel ban extension on the 17th and that he can get back to serving the Lord there.

Our original flight from Heathrow to Denver was cancelled. Our rescheduled flight was cancelled also, with no direct flights available. The result is that we fly from Edinburgh to London on the 15th, London to Dallas on the 16th, and Dallas direct into Colorado Springs on the 17th. We are praying for no further delays or changes.

We are praying that, despite our bed having gone, the sleeping arrangements we have will work well and be restful for at least another week. We are ready to move to temporary accommodations in Edinburgh if we need to, to save the travel time and stress, but there are things that still need to be done here and it would be nice to get them done first, rather than have to travel back, especially since Eric is still here.

House, Selling and Buying:

The buyer of our house was supposed to close on their house a week and a half ago, but their buyer backed out. They have a new buyer, and they hope to close by the end of this month. That may mean ours won't close before we leave, but it should be virtually done by then.

We close on the purchase of our house in Colorado Springs on 8 March, Lord willing. This should give Alyssa and her Merry Band (whoever she recruits to help her, it seems to be growing) sufficient time to accomplish some order in our living arrangements, even if the container doesn't arrive.

Robert and Manda agreed a sale this week, but the buyer's mortgage has fallen through so it is back to square one. The Lord has provided a place to rent in the interim in Colorado Springs, so it isn't urgent that their house sell immediately, but the rental is only an interim, so we are still praying for a quick sale.

Please pray for all these matters to go through quickly.

Church:

Please pray for a God-honouring transition for the church. Lots of things like bank account, etc., to take care of. Everything is harder with COVID restrictions, which are particularly onerous in Scotland. Please pray for Pastor Paul as he transitions into this new ministry, and for the people of the church. I'm still sharing the preaching until we leave, but we're working on transitioning more into his hands. He's going to be a very different pastor from me in a lot of ways, but that's probably a very good thing.

General:

We are exhausted. The movers coming was very wearing. Additionally, I seem to have done a mischief to my shoulder, and it has disturbed my sleep three nights running. That's not ideal when driving an hour each way to the hospital and then snow makes the hour into two hours. Please pray that we will sleep well tonight.

We are encouraged. Courtney is feeling well, and things are coming together. The last three days have been very hard but they have not made Courtney ill and we are so thankful that it appears to be moving on schedule.

We are thankful. We have had so many opportunities to see our neighbours recently and had some really good and profitable conversations. One of our neighbours, who we hadn't seen since I told them about Courtney's cancer, stopped today and talked. It happened because we couldn't drive our car up our street due to snow—sometimes those "bad" things are just setting up the good things God has planned! She was very emotional about us going and Courtney's illness.

Another neighbour told me to walk home and leave him the key and he'd take care of the car. He dug it out and parked it out of the way of the movers and returned the key, so now it is in our driveway ready for the hospital tomorrow. We spoke to yet another neighbour for quite a while today, and Courtney said as we walked away, "I really hoped we'd see her before we went." We pray that when people here remember us they also remember Christ.

Thank you for praying for us, and for the notes reminding us that you are!

In Him
Justin

I could have gone back and dug out our car myself. We could have left it and walked down in the morning. But our neighbour earnestly wanted to help, and it really did help.

God made people in His image, and even though that image is marred by sin, it was so encouraging to see it, many times, shining through in neighbours, medical staff, people in churches, and people we encountered in daily life. So often I said, "So many people have been so kind to us."

I wrote a relative going through a really difficult time—
I just prayed for you and your wife. Keep anchored in a few things.

1. This world and its trials are temporary. In Heaven, we'll look back and say, "Why was I worried?"

2. You know God is powerful enough to change your situation and loving enough to do it. Therefore, if He doesn't change it, He's decided that this, hard as it is, is for your best.

3. Remember the "no excuses" verse, 1 Corinthians 10:13. (A) Others have gone through this, it is common to man (B) God is faithful (C) He knows what we can handle and never allows anything beyond that (so we know, because of His faithfulness, that we really can handle it) (D) He always makes a way for us.

Love
Justin

Courtney's sister Myra in Colorado was writing me—
I am so thankful that Courtney has you for a husband. An international move isn't easy under any circumstances, let alone with Courtney's health. I am thankful you take such good care of her. God's plans aren't always our own, but He

seems to keep pushing the two of you in a positive direction. I am so thankful for all God has done for Courtney. Be safe. Have some hot chocolate. We will see you soon.

11 February 2021 (Friday p.m.)

"It Will Be a Miracle"

Dear All

The shipping agent just described her view of the possibility of our shipping container arriving before we do. So many things could go wrong and some probably will. The container might get superseded by an industrial shipment and not get on the ship. The ship might have part of its cargo delayed and leave late. It might get an extra inspection here. There could be weather delays. It could be stopped for inspection in America. They might do an X-ray inspection and see something they want to investigate. It could be chosen for a random visual inspection. Customs just might be busy when it arrives. And so on . . .

The Bible tells us that God wants husbands to care for and provide for their wives. Given the stresses of the next five weeks for Courtney, I am sure God wants me to try to get a home set up for her arrival, so I have no hesitation in asking you to pray for that miracle!

Psalm 127:2 *For so he giveth his beloved sleep.*

I slept better last night. :) My shoulder is still really sore, but I slept! Thank you to those who prayed about this.

Alyssa leaves tomorrow, early in the morning, for the US.

Thank you for your prayers for us!

Justin

Courtney's sister Myra again—
Having a wife with a brain tumor and moving internationally should put you in the nut house. But God is good.

My reply—
Me being in the nut house, and God being good, are not mutually exclusive. It is possible for both to occur. :)

Her answer—
Amen, Brother!

The man buying our house was very stressed about his sale completing in time. I had a long conversation with him. They were not concerned about getting our house sooner; they wanted us to stay as long as it made sense for us. He was just very worried about damaging our plans or adding stress to our life, and it was really upsetting him.

It was more of that kindness I mentioned earlier. So many people wanted to help.

I tried to reassure him—
Thank you. This is "miracle-territory" if it actually closes before the 8th. I'm very relaxed about it, either way. I really appreciate your pushing on things but I hope it isn't too stressful, because it certainly isn't for us. So much has changed so fast and I'm just rolling with it—I'm so relaxed about everything I'm wondering if I'm still alive. :)

18 February 2021 (Friday p.m.)

Dear All

Courtney told the doctor on Monday she felt the best she has since this all started. She's not had any negative effects on how she is feeling except maybe today. Today, she was quite tired, but that may just be because it was such a dreich (Scottish, *dreary* or *bleak*) day here today—that can sap your energy!

Courtney is sleeping well here at home, even with our bed gone. If it's not broken, don't fix it. We're staying here unless the travel gets too much—there's no guarantee she'd sleep well somewhere in Edinburgh.

The radiation does cause a rash and hair loss, and she's having both of those this week, but nothing serious. We're still walking at least twice a day and usually three times.

I still don't have clear confirmation of this but it appears our container is still sitting on the dock in Grangemouth. So unless we end up seriously delayed, it won't be there before us. The Lord has a different plan from ours (again!).

Eric is still here—the ban on travel from the UK was extended again, this time for four weeks. That means Eric will be here after we leave.

Robert and Manda agreed an offer on their house last week but it fell through. They agreed another offer today. The movers come and pack them up Monday through Wednesday, and they fly to London Friday, then on to Colorado next Saturday.

Alyssa arrived safely in Wisconsin last week and is with Katherine. She heads for Colorado the end of the month.

So many people have been so kind to us, we're very grateful.

It's strange but good to "pass the torch" of the ministry. I'm preaching on Sunday.

One of the big "busy things" right now is getting all set up with a doctor in Colorado. I'm also very busy with insurance, things related to buying the house, church financial and legal matters, etc. And, my printer died! That makes everything more complicated, but it also had replacement cover, so I think that means I'm going to have a new printer to give to Pastor Paul. There's always a blessing hiding somewhere in the bumps in the road, whether we can see it or not.

My shoulder is improved and not affecting my sleep anymore. The long list of things that need doing IS affecting my sleep, so I'd appreciate your prayers that either the list will grow shorter or my ability to sleep through it will increase! :)

We're doing well and are thankful. We're only on this earth to serve the Lord, after all, and He keeps giving us opportunities to serve we haven't had before.

We have a family joke about "minor inconveniences." We were going on our first real holiday in years, to France. The locking system on our minibus failed and I couldn't open the back hatch, so to put our luggage in, or take it out, I had to fold down the back seat. But it didn't stop us from going, so it was a "minor inconvenience."

This made it into a sermon illustration about how the struggles of this life are "minor inconveniences." They aren't going to stop us from getting to Heaven, nor from enjoying it when we get there. They really don't matter in the grand scheme of things at all.

Everything here is temporary; if it's a little harder than we'd like, it's still only a "minor inconvenience." For several years, every time anything went "wrong," one of our kids would inform me it was a "minor inconvenience." In fact, hearing that became a "minor inconvenience." :)

That came to mind today, driving back from the hospital. All of it, the cancer, the travel, the tiredness, the paperwork, the hair falling out, is all just a "minor inconvenience." God is still on His throne. We are still loved. Our future is His, and it is glorious. One hymn writer wrote that difficult things in this life will just make us smile in Heaven. So, "Until then my heart will go on singing, until then with joy I'll carry on."

Blessings to you, thank you for your prayers for us.

In Him
Justin

That last paragraph paralleled Psalm 84:11, neither the first nor the last time that verse would come to mind.

> Psalm 84:11 *For the Lord God is a sun and shield: the Lord will give grace and glory: no good thing will he withhold from them that walk uprightly.*

God would give Grace for "minor inconveniences." He would give Glory one day, for our future really is His and it really is glorious. And if that was true, the rest was too—nothing really for our good would be withheld if we would live our lives rightly before Him.

That last paragraph brought many responses.

From a pastor in southeast Scotland
Praying for you. I was going to ask your permission to use your last line of your letter in my sermon tomorrow online.

From a work colleague
What a beautiful uplifting email! Thank you, Justin!! Glad all is going well with Courtney, you, and the family—and that your heart is still singing! Praise the Lord!!

When you know, and God makes you *feel*, that He is giving Grace and Glory, your heart does keep on singing—even if the singing is, sometimes, through the tears.

Chapter 12

Sometimes, Spectacles Need Adjustment

I was becoming concerned about "stuff." Some possessions were too valuable to throw away. We believed that if Jesus gave His life for us, then everything really belonged to Him. I needed to try to find a way for this "stuff" to be used for Him, even if it wasn't "mine" anymore. So, I sent the following email to some ministry contacts in Scotland.

22 February 2021 (Tuesday a.m.)

"Two Cars, a Piano, and a Roof Box"

First come, first served. I have:

One piano, dated from the late 1800s, still works fine, probably doesn't have a real long life but working fine now, and we've had it for something like 15 years. Free to anyone who wants to pick it up, and as a bonus, Eric and I will help load it on this end. If you are desperate for help on the other end and the other end isn't too far away, we will pray real hard (and maybe Eric will come). Would prefer to not give it up for a couple weeks but can be flexible.

One Ford Fiesta, 2003, <100K miles, MOT until

December. Speedometer has gone to zero while driving and then started working again so assuming a loose connection, no other known problems. Free to anyone in ministry, preferable that you pick it up but if that's difficult we can work something. Prefer not to part with it until 5 March but would be very happy to see it vacate the premises as soon thereafter as practical. If it is desperately needed before then, I can work with it.

One Ford CMax, 2009, just over 80K miles, MOT due 27 March (but no known issues). For anyone in ministry, make me an offer that's a good price for you, and I'm willing to eat some of the cost if the MOT is painful as well. I don't have time to try to figure out what's a fair price so offer something that will be a blessing for you. I also have roof bars to go with this.

One large Thule Roof Box. The top of it is beautifully scratched up from getting stuck against the roof in a car park (yes, I had to let air out of the tires to get out, yes, there were warning signs, yes, my kids love this story!). It is, however, perfectly watertight and we've used it multiple times since. Great for taking a family on holiday when the car really isn't big enough for all the kids and their luggage—your option whether to put the kids or the luggage in the roof box. Free to anyone in ministry, would be happy to see it gone.

(For American readers, a "cargo carrier" is a "roof box" in the UK. "MOT" is the annual vehicle roadworthiness inspection. A "car park" is British for "parking garage." I really did drive into a parking garage with the thing on our car and got stuck. A "minor inconvenience," I guess, though the worst of it was our kids delighting in it, over and over again!)

The Fiesta went to one of our church members; our piano tuner found a home for our beloved piano; and a pastor took the CMax and the roof box. It seems strange, now, to care about finding places for "stuff" with what was going on, but I'm still glad it all found good homes.

Our house buyers kept asking about Courtney, and I responded—

Courtney is having three minor side effects from the radiation: hair loss, a slight rash, a weak feeling in arms and legs. Still walking and generally feeling good, it's not really affecting stamina, and blood counts are good, so it appears she'll be able to take the chemo all the way through. Perhaps it will get worse but so far, so good. Last treatment is a week Friday.

This letter from a lady in Vermont meant so much to Courtney—

You have been in my prayers for quite a while. This morning as I read your latest letter I felt led by our Lord to reach out to you.

Our pastor and his wife keep us updated by sharing your letters.

As my Grandmother on my Mother's side was born in Scotland (in fact, Edinburgh) and came to America with her Mother and twin brother as infants, I have long loved Scotland. Therefore, your ministry is very special to me.

It is a blessing to me to think that, [with] all Courtney has been through, she can now get out and take long walks. That is a true blessing from our Lord!

You both will continue in my prayers for continued health and healing, your belongings to arrive safely in Colorado, and all your family to be able to travel as necessary. May you be continually blessed.

My reply—

Thank you so much for your kind and encouraging note, and your prayers. Courtney really felt encouraged!

Courtney's walks are shorter, only half a mile now, but still managing 3 a day. The walks help, because the fresh air is good, and exercise helps her sleep at night. Sleep is the most important thing right now; when she sleeps well, she feels really quite well, when not, she feels really tired. But so far, no other real problems, praise the Lord!

We have so much for which to be thankful. It seems strange to say that with what we are experiencing but the Lord just keeps reminding us.

We are still locked down so we can't meet with our church. Yesterday, we had the best turnout for an online service since all this started! What a blessing!

A work colleague got up in the middle of the night to join our online service.

I wrote him—

Your joining was an encouragement. Our little church has been rather shell-shocked. They thought I was here for life, and to also lose my family, and think the church might close. Every door for a new pastor seemed to close, and then the Lord worked.

So, another believer from far away joining was a reminder, even if we are small, even if we're getting smaller, we're not alone. I've been telling them that but it's different when someone appears (even if as just a box on the screen).

I thought I'd let you know it was appreciated!

Courtney asked me to shave her head. So much hair had fallen out that a wig was necessary, and it was uncomfortable with her remaining long hair tucked under it. She always tolerated my preference for her beautiful long hair, even though it required more care, but I cut it off without any regrets. Anything that made her more comfortable was better. When dealing with cancer, many things that used to matter just don't matter anymore.

1 March 2021 (Tuesday p.m.)

Dear All

We're on the last stretch. This is the sixth and final week of this course of treatment, we finish on Friday. We are still at home, we've decided to stay here rather than move to Edinburgh. The travel is tiring but we don't know if Courtney would sleep well in a different place, and this is working.

Treatment Effects:

Hair loss started in earnest about a week and a half ago.

Fatigue really kicked in last weekend but hasn't been as bad the last few days.

The last week Courtney has had minor headaches in the morning which pass before long. This is probably due to swelling in the brain caused by the radiation treatment, so today they've doubled Courtney's steroid dose (they previously halved it twice).

We are still walking three times a day, and Courtney is usually close to 10,000 steps, if she doesn't get there.

Courtney is still mostly feeling pretty well.

It seems pretty clear from talking to the doctors and nurses that they expected more fatigue by now, continually worsening, and other problems as well. We're thankful for your prayers.

Something About Cancer:

Some people reading already know this, but sometimes when you are fighting cancer, you might be feeling pretty good, but your body is struggling with so much that it doesn't take much to tip you over into difficulty. That happened a week and a half ago with Courtney.

As noted above, the radiation treatment causes brain swelling, so Courtney is on dexamethasone to counteract that. That causes changes to the shape of the face—so Courtney's specs were too tight and pressing into the sides of her face. That caused a headache, and a headache caused disturbed sleep, and disturbed sleep when you are already tired and fighting cancer is not a good thing. Suddenly, instead of a little tired, you become very, very tired—and that can make the headache worse as well as other problems.

Who would have thought cancer treatment might mean it is very, very important to get your specs adjusted? But when one thing leads to another . . .

The Christian life is like that, too. If you are spiritually weak because you've let your pride or other sin take hold, or because you've allowed other things to take priority over your time with the Lord, then it won't take all that much to tip you over the edge, where one thing leads to another, to another, to another, and you can be in a spiritual tailspin before you know it. If you aren't spiritually healthy, all it takes is a wee thing and you're in trouble.

Family News:

Robert and Manda and family arrived safely in Colorado on Saturday. So did Alyssa. Eric is still here with us, hoping to return home on 20 March, now.

Robert and Manda have an agreed sale of their

house, but their buyers need to sell their house.

Katherine plans to travel to Colorado about a week and a half after we arrive.

Houses and Flights:

The purchase of the house in Colorado is scheduled to go through on the 8th. The sale of this house is expected on the 10th. Thankfully the one is not dependent on the other.

There is one complication with the purchase of the house. My sister is acting for us, but we need a signed Power of Attorney that has to be notarized by a US Notary Public, which is almost impossible here. We've got a possible way forward but that ran into complications today. We'd appreciate your prayers for the Lord's help with this one.

We fly from Edinburgh 15 March, arriving in Colorado 17 March.

Church:

We have to get a COVID test at the airport on the 14th, which might make us late for church, so this Sunday will be my last Sunday preaching here. Please pray for the Lord's blessing on the service.

We had joyous news Sunday as a young boy in one of our families has trusted Christ! Also, a man from our neighbourhood was saved some time ago through online interaction, and recently contacted us, and is looking for a church. Praise the Lord for the encouragement He has given His people here. Pray for wisdom for Pastor Paul as he leads the church.

Thank you for your prayers for us!

In Him
Justin

We got the Power of Attorney thing sorted out, so Kate (my sister) could buy our house for us. The Lord smoothed away so many problems.

This specs thing was our first "cancer makes you very vulnerable" experience. In cancer, and in our spiritual lives, just one wee thing can cause problems, but God gives tremendous victories and encouragements too. Yes, Courtney had cancer and was losing her hair. And yes, her specs needed adjusting, but neither "inconvenience" could remotely reduce the joy of seeing another soul saved for all eternity. When "minor inconveniences" meet eternal blessings, the latter always wins. When we remember Glory, Grace is always near!

Chapter 13

Farewell, Scotland; Hello, Colorado

6 March 2021 (Saturday p.m.)

Briefly Tonight:
Courtney's first course of treatment is done! We are very thankful that it went much easier on her than we were told to expect.

Tomorrow is my final sermon before we leave. My title is "I'm not Shaking the Dust Off My Feet!" We're still confined to online services only by the Scottish government.

Just when it looked like everything was finally arranged and finalised, we've hit a complication in buying our house in Colorado. It appears we have a solution, but please pray for wisdom for us.

Will try to write in more detail tomorrow or the next day. Thank you for your prayers for us!

In Him
Justin

Jesus said, "And whosoever shall not receive you, nor hear your words, when ye depart out of that house or city, shake off the dust of your feet" (Matthew 10:14).

In titling my sermon as I did, I was saying God was not done with our church and our town yet.

From Lithuania

So happy for God's help for you and continuing to pray for grace and help in the days ahead!

10 March 2021 (Wednesday p.m.)

"Justin and Courtney's Update—Crazy Day!"

Dear All

I received an email a little while ago saying our funds had cleared for closing on the house in Colorado today. Less than 30 seconds later I got a text from our buyer saying the funds for our house here were on the way to our solicitor.

So, one house goes, another comes! :)

Many things happening very quickly but we're getting there! Some very encouraging things happening with the church here, too!

Courtney is still feeling ok. She had to increase steroids a week ago and it makes her feel weak, but she is still able to be active and exercise helps that feeling. The steroids go really high for the flights to prevent brain swelling so please ask the Lord for strength and to limit the side effects.

13 March—hotel in Edinburgh

14 March—COVID test, back to the hotel for church

15–17 March—Edinburgh to London to Dallas to Colorado Springs

Thanking the Lord for all His goodness to us!
Justin

14 March 2021 (Sunday p.m.)

"On Our Way"

Dear All

We're in an airport hotel at Edinburgh, having left home for the last time. How strange it is to say that.

We had our COVID tests this morning which came back clear, so it appears everything is proceeding.

Courtney took her first high dose of the steroids this morning. It's not pleasant but she's ok, and we did get in a couple more walks in the neighbourhood before leaving. Please pray that they do their job and the air travel doesn't give her trouble.

We had a wonderful send-off from our neighbours—when we drove away at about 6:30 this evening, every single neighbour on both sides of the street, entire families, were out to wave goodbye and wish us well! We had no idea that was coming.

We had a good service with the church today. We are thankful that the Lord has brought Pastor Paul to take the ministry, and thankful for those who have committed to support him in carrying out the work here. I told Courtney this week that the church may be better off with me going! It is, after all, the Lord's church, not mine.

There was one couple in the church we hadn't got to see yet, so we stopped by their house briefly on our way out of town. He was actually the first person I met from our town.

Thank you for your prayers for us!
Justin

This was our last email from Scotland.

From a pastor's wife in northeast Scotland

Dear Bro Justin and Courtney,

Thanks for the update. Must have been a bit emotional for you with all the neighbours coming out to wave goodbye!

We're praying with you all the way home to Colorado. Also praying for some special touches of kindness along the journey.

Yes, the send-off from our neighbours was more than a bit emotional. We were very fortunate in the neighbours we had. Some things when we first moved in had brought the neighbourhood together, but that togetherness had been somewhat lost. Twenty-two years later, friendships were renewed during COVID as neighbours watched for and helped one another. We were blessed with great neighbours in Colorado too, but that street in Scotland was special.

There were, indeed, some special touches of kindness. In London, the airline staff took Courtney in a wheelchair (and our luggage) to our hotel, waited for check-in, and then took us right to our door.

Courtney's hair loss showed she had cancer, and one flight attendant on the London–Dallas flight prayed with her before we left the flight. Courtney did have a bit of a headache on that flight, probably because of the change in air pressure, but otherwise, all went well. We had wonderful assistance at every stop from the airline and airport personnel.

Until we got on the plane in Edinburgh, I didn't

really want to leave—I'd made my life there. I loved the people in our church. I knew it was right to take Courtney back to America, but I was never sure whether or not I'd return to Scotland if Courtney passed away. When I boarded, my desire to be in Scotland disappeared. I still wanted to return to visit the people I loved—but I knew I would never live in Scotland again. A chapter closed; God changed my heart.

20 March 2021 (Saturday p.m.)

Dear All

We arrived safely and without trouble in Colorado Springs. Courtney had a minor headache on the long (and high) flight from London to Dallas, but no further trouble. Unsurprisingly, jetlag is harder for both of us this time than usual, but other than that, all is well.

Our shipping container is currently on a ship somewhere in the Atlantic, but it last registered with vessel tracking 4 days ago, so I don't know when it arrives. It's ok, our house is certainly liveable for the short term.

Courtney's first doctor appointment here is Monday.

Eric was not able to return today as hoped. Since his destination is closed for another month, he is coming here and arrives tonight.

There is much we'll miss in Scotland, but we're grateful for the Lord's provision for us here, and confident in His care and provision. Most of our future in this life is unknown, but our Life Planner is well-known and completely trustworthy. We'll follow the path He marks out for us with joy and peace, not of ourselves, but because we know He gives joy and peace to those who trust Him. It is only if we are so foolish as to forget His love that fear would come in:

1 John 4:18 *There is no fear in love; but perfect love casteth out fear: because fear hath torment. He that feareth is not made perfect in love.*

Thank you for praying for us!
Justin

26 March 2021 (Friday p.m.)

So, sometimes life with the Lord is just fun, just to see what is going to happen next.

The basement on our house isn't finished, and we wanted to get some work done so we would have more room for family, since after all, time with family was part of the reason for our move.

A friend warned me that because of the current building boom, getting work done in Colorado Springs can be difficult and jobs can drag on, with a lot of upheaval to the home. I decided to be very specific with the builders I contacted, that the doctors have said we have 9–15 months, and we wanted this to help with family visits, so if they couldn't do it quickly, I was asking if they could refer me to anyone who could. I sent out several emails to that effect.

One builder called yesterday to say they had a 3-week waiting list for estimates, but they moved us to the top because of our situation—and they had arranged for all their subcontractors to come the next morning at 7:15 to get the estimate done, if we could do it that early. Well, our bodies are still half on UK time, so no problem there. At 7:15, our basement was full—contractor, electrician, plumber, HVAC. They said they would move us up to get it done ASAP. And they won't even need to bring dirt or anything into the house; they'll enter through a basement window to minimize dirt, exposure to illness, and family upheaval!

So, that's pretty neat. But it also made our morning walk later than usual. And I've hurt my leg and can barely walk. So, Courtney took the dog around the block by herself, not at the usual time.

Off she went and came back a short time later really excited. She'd met a neighbor (that she wouldn't have met on our usual schedule)—a lady from the country Eric lives in, a Baptist, who is familiar with Eric's church there. They also have just moved in. And she'd just been praying a few minutes earlier for a female friend here. God provided Courtney, a Christian lady just a few doors away who has actually been to her country and has a son (who is here instead of there for reasons best known to God) who speaks her language fluently, so she'll get to speak to someone in her native language, too!

So, why did Courtney get cancer and why did we leave Scotland and why did I hurt my leg and why can't Eric get back home and why did we end up in this neighborhood and why do we need to get this job done on our basement? I'm sure being an encouragement to this lady is only part of His reason for these things—but isn't it fun to see how God weaves the tapestry of our lives together sometimes? And so, we go on finding out what His plan has next for us!

Courtney's Doctor Appointment:
We had our first appointment here on Monday and didn't learn a lot beyond what we knew before.

Any scan now would be inconclusive because there will be brain swelling from the radiation, preventing a clear picture. So, we won't know until June how effective the treatment has been.

We know it has at least stopped the tumor growth or Courtney would be having severe symptoms.

The next treatment starts 5 April for five days, the first of six four-week cycles, with five days of treatment and then 3+ weeks off. This is expected to keep the tumor generally at bay. Beyond that, we don't know.

Other Stuff:
Courtney still feels pretty good except for fatigue. We're dealing with a treble problem here—after-effects of radiation treatment, jet lag, and high altitude (thin oxygen). So, fatigue is an issue.

She withstood the high levels of steroids quite well, though they give a weak and trembly feeling. Exercise helps with that. We're phasing down, the dose is a lot lower now.

Still walking three times a day except a couple times there was too much snow. The walks are shorter due to the fatigue problems mentioned above but we're keeping at it.

God has given us a lovely place to live. The views of Pikes Peak from our house are beautiful, and the views when walking around the block or when driving anywhere are stunning.

We can't buy a car from a dealer without a US driver's license, and we can't get that yet because there are long delays at the state offices. But a friend knew of a car that is loaned out to missionaries and he's bringing it down to us tomorrow, so we'll have that as long as we need it.

After a long shutdown, our church in Scotland opens Sunday! And the government lost a court case which makes it unlikely they will shut churches entirely again. Praise the Lord!

Our shipping container with all our furniture, etc., sailed past Miami today on its way to Houston. I've now been advised it may take as much as 21 business days after arrival in Houston to clear customs, and as much as two weeks later to get here! We're just trusting the Lord that His timing is better than ours.

Thank you for praying for us! I hope you are enjoying seeing the Lord working in YOUR life as much as we are in ours! Of course, there are things we'd prefer to be otherwise, but wow, it's fun to see Him work things together, and to wonder what's next! How foolish it would be to complain about things in our lives when we can see how He can weave things together!

In Him
Justin

We were going through the strangest experience. It was devastating, heart-wrenching, and horrible—and exhilarating, joyful, and awe-inspiring—as well as just plain fun. We were seeing God do amazing things in the lives of many people, including people we hadn't even known before. We didn't know if Courtney and the neighbor she'd just met were going to be close or not, but we certainly knew it had been encouraging to both.

After two and a half decades of British spellings and

wording, I decided, now that we were in the United States, to return to "American English" in my emails. Britishisms might "leak" in by accident, like "treble" instead of "triple" in that last email. You can't wipe out twenty-six years in a day, but I definitely changed. My American readers may feel more at home from here on. British readers may feel less at home, but you've had it all your way thus far, so it's only fair!

Chapter 14

Joy, and Then Disaster

4 April 2021 (Resurrection Sunday p.m.)

"But now is Christ risen from the dead!" That is the message that changes the world, that changes everything. Because He is risen, the trials and struggles of this life mean little—eternity waits, and it is glorious for those who know Him! The Savior who died for me is alive!

Courtney went to church today, for the first time since she went into the hospital in November. When we walked in, the piano was playing "Because He Lives." God doesn't believe in coincidences! For those who don't remember or who joined this list later, that song was Courtney's song, back when she was in hospital, when we didn't know if she would even see 2021. [The letter she wrote about it is in chapter 3.] It was such a blessing for her to be with God's people again. I have to admit there were times when I didn't think I'd see this day—God has been better to me than I deserve!

We are still walking but the walks are still shorter than they were in Scotland. Courtney is finally starting to feel better and have more energy as the steroid treatment has been reducing. She has two more days of steroids and then that is done. What a relief! We are also getting over jetlag and getting adjusted to the altitude. The church we've been attending puts out doorhangers with church invitations, and Courtney said after church that she wants to get strong enough to help with that. Sounds like a plan to me!

Tomorrow, TMZ chemotherapy starts for five days. This is the first of six cycles of four weeks each, each with five days of chemo and then 3+ weeks without any. At this point we are still on the standard treatment for glioblastoma multiforme. The greatest concern as far as side effects is impact on the bone marrow, which they'll be monitoring. The doctor is quite optimistic, given Courtney's overall condition, that she'll withstand the treatment well.

Family News:
Alyssa and Eric are living with us, Eric temporarily until he can get back to his home.

Robert and Manda are settled in here in Colorado Springs but are in a house they can only rent temporarily. Their house in Scotland has sold so they hope to be able to buy a place before too long—but baby is due in May!

Katherine was able to come from Wisconsin during her spring break for a week and left today. Marguerite and Edward plan to come from Utah on the 17th for two weeks. Rosa plans to fly out from Virginia for the weekend of the 23–25th.

Courtney's sister Myra was able to come down on Friday for a few hours. We got to see my aunt and my cousin, who both live here in Colorado Springs, this week.

Work starts on our basement tomorrow, which when finished should make it a LOT easier for family to come visit.

Our shipping container is not a member of the family, but we would still welcome its arrival. :) As far as I can tell it is in Houston currently.

Specific Prayer Requests:
Wisdom in many decisions to be made as we settle in here.

That we will love the Lord and honor Him in all that we say and do.

That those of our new neighbors who don't know the Lord Jesus might see His love and goodness in us, and that we can tell people of what He has done for us and can do for them.

That we can encourage other believers.

As Courtney has said multiple times, "That this cancer won't be wasted," and that the Lord will use it for His glory.

Thank you for praying for us!
Justin

It was such a joyful day. On the day we celebrated Jesus' Resurrection, Courtney was finally able to be in church! To walk in to the song that captured so much of our thinking topped it off: "Because He lives, I can face tomorrow. Because He lives, all fear is gone!" What a gift our God had given us.

Sunday p.m., I wrote to the church's pastor—
Courtney was crying when we left today. In November we didn't think she'd ever be in church again, she might only

leave the hospital to go home to die, I thought an ambulance would bring her home. Today, she went to church—and when we walked in, "her" song was playing on the piano.

6 April 2021 (Tuesday a.m.)

Dear All

Courtney had a brutal night last night. The nurse thinks it was probably a bug and not the treatment, because symptoms aren't what would be expected. But when something comes along and your reserves are low, it's tough.

It's not surprising. When the Lord gives you a really good day like Sunday, Satan likes to send a really bad one, and the Lord sometimes allows it so we can learn what it is like to love Him in hard times as well as easy ones. There are many examples in Scripture. Please pray that we'll honor the Lord through the good and the bad!

Doing a little better now and managed a short walk a while ago.

From a dear friend in Illinois, USA

Hello Justin and Courtney,

I am praying for Courtney who had a "brutal night last night."

I trust that she is feeling better. Yes, Satan, after a good day and a good report, likes to send a bad day. We will love the Lord and praise Him, causing our words of praise to be weapons against Satan. We love God in good and bad times. I pray for His peace for you two and the family.

I do pray that you will honor the Lord in good and bad times. Me, too. I need to honor God all the time. Say "hi" to Courtney and give her a hug for me.

Things settled for Courtney; she got through the rest of chemo week without much trouble, though it left her very tired. But the following week, we had an apparent disaster.

14 April 2021 (Wednesday 3:46 p.m.)

Courtney had a bad seizure a while ago. We are at the hospital. Will update when I know anything. Thanks for your prayers.

"God is faithful, who will not suffer you to be tempted above that ye are able." Sinning in doubt or fear isn't an option.

Love
Justin

The seizure went on for more than two minutes. Courtney went to the hospital by ambulance with a suspected stroke. Her smile was lopsided (a real danger sign for stroke), and her left side was unresponsive. Her left shoulder was very sore. She injured it when the seizure hit; we didn't yet realize how badly.

14 April 2021 (Wednesday 4:35 p.m.)

Epilepsy triggered by brain trauma. No stroke, no bleeding, no obvious massive tumor growth. May be here overnight due to pronounced left side weakness (which initially made them suspect stroke). But that's starting to improve.

Thanks for praying!

They got her in for a scan very quickly and eliminated all the worst possibilities.

> 14 April 2021 (Wednesday 6:37 p.m.)
>
> Home. Weak and tired and left side still not right, but that is common with these kinds of seizures and expected to be temporary. Courtney is able to walk with help.
>
> Very thankful for the Lord's kindness to us!
>
> Also thankful for the Lord's protection for Alyssa. She was in the left of three lanes of traffic and someone in the far right lane decided to turn left (!!!) and hit the side of her car. She's ok and no serious damage.
>
> Courtney is now on anti-seizure medication, which can make some people irritable. I told the doctor that's a good thing. If I do something Courtney doesn't like, I can just tell her it's the medication making her feel that way! Courtney's had to put up with my bad jokes for 36 years.
>
> Thanks again for your prayers for us.
>
> In Him
> Justin

We didn't know what caused the seizure, but the scan appeared to show growth in the tumor, and Courtney had some other symptoms too. If so, it was very bad news indeed. The tumor was supposed to be quiet for at least another five months if the treatment was effective.

Quality of life is often stressed with glioblastoma patients. There's no real hope of a cure, and often doctors cannot extend life beyond twelve to eighteen months. They try to give the best quality of life possible for that short time.

We did not realize it, but Courtney's quality of life had just taken a major hit. She was now at very high risk for seizures. Because the seizure had been a long one, the doctors feared the next one could be severe. I was always to have emergency medication in case of a very severe seizure.

Courtney couldn't take a bath or shower unattended; she wasn't allowed to walk alone; and she couldn't even go in the back yard without someone watching in case of a seizure. For stairs, I had to be in position to catch her if she had a seizure and fell. The huge loss of freedom made her feel like a horrible burden. I still needed to work, and now she could do nothing without me. This was all extremely unpleasant.

Added to all that was Courtney's shoulder injury. She couldn't dress or undress by herself, and many clothes were difficult even with help, due to shoulder pain. Laundry had to be done more often to wash the clothes she could wear, and she couldn't do the laundry either. She couldn't even roll over in bed without help.

As time went by, the results of the seizure pressed on Courtney. She felt her time passing, and she could do so little because of it.

16 April 2021 (Friday p.m.)

Dear All

The CT scan taken after Courtney's seizure gave indications that the tumor is probably growing, and she's had other symptoms that are consistent with that. So we're going in for an MRI first thing tomorrow to get a better handle of the situation. I am praying that the swelling from the radiation treatment in Edinburgh will not hinder a clear picture of what's going on, so that wise decisions about next treatment can be made.

Also, when Courtney had the seizure, she hurt her upper arm/shoulder, and it is giving her a lot of pain. She is unable to turn over in bed by herself and standing up and other "ordinary" things are requiring assistance right now. This is compounded by the fact that her balance is beginning to be affected, perhaps by the tumor. I'm praying that this shoulder problem will resolve very quickly.

Lastly, our shipping container arrived today (yay!) with a moving crew engaged by the shipping company. Unfortunately, Alyssa's work computer appears to have walked out the door sometime during this process. Since it was in an upstairs bedroom, it's virtually impossible for it to have been anyone but one of the moving crew. I'm praying for the Holy Spirit to convict and for the person who took it to be saved.

In Him
Justin

From a pastor friend
I'm praying for you, my friend. You are weathering the storm well with God's Grace.

My reply—
I believe what I've preached all these years, that's all. Some may find that "commendable" but either the Bible is true or it isn't. I set to my seal that God is true when I was four years old and I won't go back, after 56 years of abundant blessings,

just because the road is suddenly tough. Of course, I could stumble, and I appreciate your prayers that the Lord will protect me from that, but I am determined that by His grace I shall honor Him to the end.

Sunday, despite everything, Courtney was in church. She had often grieved over the weak commitment of some to the Lord. Years ago, a lady told her, "It's easy for you to obey. You have a loving husband, great kids, a happy home. Your life is perfect."

That was nonsense, of course. We had blessings because of obeying; we didn't obey Him because we had them. Courtney's life had never been easy; she'd had her share of heartaches. But she always remembered those words, and her determination kicked in. She may not be able to do much to honor the Lord—she was too shy to say much, she was physically limited, but she *could* and *would* be in church. If she could walk (and even when she couldn't), she would be there, whether anyone thought it was easy or not.

This Sunday was Courtney's first "no matter what" Sunday. "No matter what, I'll do all I can to be in church. I'm going to be there, to smile, to praise God." Cancer effects made it hard to sing, but she was there trying.

19 April 2021 (Monday p.m.)

Dear All

Good report on the MRI today. What appeared on the CT scan to be a growing tumor was swelling in normal healthy brain tissue. That's the cause of the concerning CT scan and also the cause of the other symptoms Courtney has been having.

They had a problem with reading the images from Scotland so we don't know if there has been any growth at all, but if there has been, it is relatively minor.

The swelling is an after-effect from the radiation treatment Courtney had in Scotland. It was supposed to be reduced by now, so she has to go back on a higher dose of the steroids for a while, which is unpleasant. But better that than a growing tumor! It means hopefully within a week or so Courtney should start feeling better again.

In Other News:
Our house is in total chaos after our container arrived on Friday, but we're slowly moving toward sanity.

The remote Cuteness Roarers, Neil and Charlotte, arrived safely from Utah yesterday. We're thankful they brought their parents with them, too!

Yesterday, we became members of Colorado Springs Baptist Church. I was looking for a church with: (A) A doctrinal statement I could affirm (B) The practical doctrine (what they do) of the church to be Biblical (C) a church that matches John 13:35.

Thank you for all who have been in touch in the last few days. It is encouraging to hear of your prayers for us!

In Him
Justin

The higher dose of steroids reduced the seizure risk, but we still needed to be very, very careful. Courtney was beginning to realize how burdensome that would be. Later, she would feel differently, but for now, the seizure felt like a disaster.

We wouldn't complain—how could we, with all we had been given? But being thankful doesn't mean things don't hurt sometimes; this one really did. Even knowing now how the Lord used it later for our good, it still hurts to write about it.

Courtney worried about my eyes. She'd say, "What's the white stuff in the corner of your eyes? You need to get that checked. I keep seeing it." I figured it out—it was salt. She would see it after I'd been fighting back tears. To cry in front of her would have hurt her so I fought it, but I was grieving at how hard it was for her. I wiped my eyes more, to clear any "white stuff" before she saw it, and never explained. It would have pained her, and for no benefit.

It would get easier, but this phase was very hard. Courtney didn't want it in the emails, though. We wrote about the problems, but it was too personal for her to write about how hard she found it. I tell it now to say God's peace and joy can carry you through the really difficult times too. Even with "white stuff" in the eyes, we kept on singing, for Grace and Glory were always coming our way. We never doubted that.

Chapter 15

Small Gifts and Better Days

We now entered a "quiet period." For a time, not a lot was happening. Courtney was feeling pretty well; we were walking a lot; we were settling into our home in Colorado. It was a happy time.

One surprising tumor effect was a change in Courtney's musical tastes. Our music had been mostly hymns and classical music. We didn't want our kids to acquire a taste for the sounds and styles heard in the pubs and clubs (those used to push drugs, alcohol, and immorality), so we kept it very conservative.

Courtney began playing Gospel music (mostly fine) but also some music we had decided to avoid. Her brain didn't recognize the change nor retain conversations about it. Since the kids were grown, I felt it was doing no damage and let it go. Most of her music still fit the standards we'd held, but it was all rather random. I never knew what she might play on any given day.

In April, some randomness went away as one song became a regular. The Gospel group His Own came to sing at our church. Their first song, "I Trust in You," written by His Own member Maegan Stewart, brought us to tears. Her words seemed to perfectly capture our experience—and our commitment. The things happening were not what we'd dreamed, but we were determined to stand for the Lord like never before.

Courtney created a Morning Playlist, at first with just this song, and listened to it every morning for the rest of her life (commonly more than once a day). Ms. Stewart kindly allowed me to include it here.

I Trust in You

Verse 1:
When the end of the day is not what it seemed
And things that are happening are not what I dreamed,
And the hopes that I had for what might have been
Have turned into tears once again;
My cross is heavy and this road unsure,
But, Jesus, You are mine; and I am Yours.

Chorus:
Help me stand for You like I've never stood before;
Help me sing to You until I can't sing anymore.
Lord, increase my faith that I may rest in Your Truth
So whatever comes my way,
My heart can truly say,
I trust in You.

Verse 2:
Though the enemy comes to tear me apart
And finds ways to hurt what's close to my heart;
I have found strength down on my knees,
Trusting by faith what I can't see.
The battle's raging, but the victory's won;
Lord, take this heart of mine, Your will be done.

Repeat Chorus

Bridge:
Lord, You've opened my eyes,
And now I can see
The beauty in this story
You're writing for me!

Final Chorus:
I will stand for You like I've never stood before;
I will sing to You until I can't sing anymore.
Lord, increase my faith that I may rest in Your Truth
So whatever comes my way,
My heart can truly say,
I trust in You.

www.hisownministries.com

30 April 2021 (Friday a.m.)

Dear All

Sorry for not updating you sooner. As it stands now:

Courtney is still on high steroid treatment, which is unpleasant, but is definitely helping. Most of the symptoms that made us think the tumor was growing are now gone.

She is still weak and tired and has some troubles with balance. She does well in the mornings and afternoons, generally, but by evenings she's very tired. We've been able to get in a couple walks of about two miles each, so that's progress!

We are still on seizure watch, but no new seizures, thankfully.

Courtney is still having a lot of trouble with the shoulder she hurt when she had the seizure, but is now having physical therapy, and there's been some improvement.

The next treatment is Monday night, and she will take tablets for five nights. Last time, this was very difficult for Courtney.

BIG prayer request. Tomorrow morning, our church is going around the doors again, and Courtney very much wants to go. Please pray that she will be able to do so.

Other Stuff:
Eric FINALLY appears to have clearance to go home. He has to transit through a third country, but this is explicitly permitted according to the embassy websites. Lord willing, he leaves on Tuesday.

Neil and Charlotte are taking their parents :) back to Utah this weekend. It's been great to have Edward and Marguerite here—and the kids!

Rosa was able to visit from Virginia for a quick weekend.

We hope to have more family coming to visit in the next few weeks, once schedules are finalized.

Thought from Today's Proverb:
Proverbs 30:8 *Remove far from me vanity and lies: give me neither poverty nor riches; feed me with food convenient for me:*

Proverbs 30:9 *Lest I be full, and deny thee, and say, Who is the LORD? or lest I be poor, and steal, and take the name of my God in vain.*

Maybe sometimes the Lord gives us less than we would ask or allows things to come into our lives that we'd rather not have, so that we don't become so complacent that we stop relying on Him. Maybe we should let Him decide what is the "food convenient for me" rather than trying to dictate to God how we think He should take care of us. Perhaps the porridge that He gives us sometimes is a little better for us than the Frosted Flakes that our tastebuds might prefer.

In Him
Justin

Courtney was able to go put out door hangers. Of course, she didn't have the stamina she had before, so we didn't do a lot. Even so, it was such an encouragement to me and many others to see her out there doing what she could to serve the Lord.

It was instructive to me as well. We want to do great things for God, but it's silly. All we do for the All-Powerful One is weak and feeble, like a cancer patient walking from door to door with door hangers. He doesn't love and bless our service because it is awesome, but because we do it out of love. That's what He really wants and blesses.

3 May 2021 (Monday p.m.)

Dear All

Courtney was able to go out on Saturday and help put out door hangers with the Gospel. Praise the Lord! Please pray that the Lord will work through the literature we and others put out.

Today the physical therapist seemed to get

the problem on Courtney's shoulder, and it seems significantly better this evening. She's not really been able to use the arm for almost 3 weeks, so this could be a real blessing!

On Friday, the doctor cut Courtney's steroid dose in half—no adverse effects so far. And there's now a plan to mitigate one of the bad side effects, disturbed sleep. No further reductions in the steroids are planned for at least three weeks, though.

This is treatment week—last time, it was a very tough week. Our son's mother-in-law is coming to help, which is a real blessing. (Are we "co-parents-in-law" or something? :))

Eric returns home tomorrow, which is both an answer to prayer and something we might not really prefer! But we believe this is of the Lord and are thankful he can go.

Please pray for the Lord to work in the Scottish elections on Thursday.

Lots of encouraging news—but we're ready for a difficult week if that's what the Lord deems best for us.

Today is the 123rd day of the year:

Psalm 123:2 *Behold, as the eyes of servants look unto the hand of their masters, and as the eyes of a maiden unto the hand of her mistress; so our eyes wait upon the LORD our God, until that he have mercy upon us.*

I hope you've read somewhere in your Bible today. If you find Bible reading hard, the Psalms are a great place to start.

In Him
Justin

There was some trepidation about this week—chemo week the prior month was rough. This time was much better, though still not easy. Courtney was still on seizure watch, and her shoulder continued to be a huge problem.

6 May 2021 (Thursday p.m.)

Dear All

Briefly:

This week started MUCH better than last time but has been getting progressively tougher for Courtney as the week has gone on. Still better than the last treatment week, able to walk more and function better. One more treatment tonight and another tomorrow, and then she's done for 3+ weeks.

Courtney's shoulder is significantly improved but still hard for her to get dressed and still affecting her sleep.

Having Manda's mother here to help Courtney has been a real blessing for us this week.

Eric made it as far as Chicago, and then Lufthansa decided (despite what the embassy website clearly said) that he wouldn't be allowed to fly on *from* Frankfurt, so they wouldn't let him fly *to* Frankfurt. He was given a flight back to Denver, but they are refusing to refund his fare. He flies tomorrow to London, then on, this time avoiding Lufthansa and Frankfurt. We are praying that he will be able to get back to where he believes the Lord wants him to serve.

That's all for tonight.

In Him
Justin

To keep our medical insurance, I needed to average working thirty hours a week. Because Manda's mother was here, I worked more than thirty hours during a chemo week! That helped make up some time I'd lost during our move.

On Sunday, Courtney was so tired I doubted if she should go to church, but she was determined.

9 May 2021 (Sunday p.m.)

Dear All

Did you make it to church today? Courtney did. She was so tired she had to rest her head on my shoulder while listening to the sermon, but she was there!

This week of treatment was much better than the last one, but still very, very fatiguing. Having Manda's mom here to help has been a wonderful blessing and very much lightened our load this week.

Courtney's parents fly in tomorrow for 2½ weeks. We are very much looking forward to seeing them.

Eric finally made it home! One overnight on a plane from Chicago to London, and the next night spent in an airport, but he arrived safely Sunday morning, and was able to at least make an appearance at church. I'm not sure, after traveling for 2 days and 2 nights, that he was able to add to or benefit from the service! The last message we've had from him was simply "bed." :)

The work on our basement is hopefully going to be finished this week, and then we can finally get the boxes out of the garage and finish this unpacking process.

Psalm 127:2 *"For so he giveth his beloved sleep."*

I think this must be a verse that cancer patients (and their families) come back to frequently. Please pray for restful sleep for us. But we are very thankful that this treatment has gone so much better than last time. Of course, we know sometimes the difficult times are for our good, to teach us to trust Him and be thankful even when it is harder to do so. But that doesn't mean we can't be thankful when it isn't so difficult!

In Him
Justin

17 May 2021 (Monday p.m.)

Dear All

Courtney came through treatment much better this time. The last couple days were quite difficult but she bounced back quickly.

Manda's mother came and stayed with us for over a week during the treatment and recovery. What a blessing, in so many ways!

Courtney is now feeling the best she's felt since we arrived in Colorado! Far from normal, of course, but she's finally over the jetlag and altitude adjustment.

We saw the neurologist, and we're still on 24/7 seizure watch. Having Manda's mother here really helped with that! It meant that even with the seizure risk I was able to make up some work time, which really helped.

Eric is safely home! It's a good thing—his room here has been inhabited by Manda's mother and now by Courtney's parents.

Our basement is "done"—the carpet company

brought the wrong carpet! They just went ahead and installed it anyway, so we'd have the use of the basement until the right carpet comes in, then they'll come and install that. Courtney's sister Myra is the first occupant, she arrived today and stays until Friday. We also saw our nephew this week.

My mom and sister Kim arrive on Saturday as well, though they'll be staying with my aunt for a few days before moving in here.

We're very grateful that the Lord allowed us to come here and have these family times. Of course, we don't know how much time He is giving us, so we want to use it well.

That's always the case, of course, none of us ever knows how much time has been entrusted to us. It's just that we usually tend to forget that. When you live what we're living, you really become aware of what you should have known all along—your time isn't really yours. It's a sacred trust, something that the Lord has placed in your stewardship, to use it in ways that honor Him. It really belongs to Him—if we misuse it, we're stealing from Him. A sobering thought as we look back on our lives, but it's a reality you can't avoid when you see how limited your time might be.

In Him
Justin

"Every day is a gift." So many times we said that. Looking back, I am glad we didn't forget to say it, even in these days when Courtney felt better. Yes, she was tired and her shoulder still caused a lot of trouble, but these were far better days than the first three weeks after her seizure. Too often, we get complacent and forget to be thankful when things are better. Perhaps God left just enough difficulties during this phase to remind us to be thankful for the improvements.

Colorado Springs has a wonderful zoo, and during this time we went with Courtney's parents and the local contingent of The Cuteness Roarers. It was a lot of fun! We didn't stay as long as we might have normally because Courtney got pretty tired—but then, so did the younger kids. It was a good day.

21 May 2021 (Friday p.m.)

Dear All

We went to the physical therapist again today. Courtney is still having trouble with the shoulder she injured in her seizure, and though it is improving, she's still getting treatment for it.

But the other thing she has been there for is to work on her balance. Her first visit, soon after the seizure, she got a balance score of 17 out of 30, which made her a definite risk for a fall. Today, her score was 28 out of 30! The PT told her she didn't even have to do some of the balance exercises anymore!

Courtney has been working really, really hard on her exercises, and today her Fitbit did its "happy dance" when she hit 10,000 steps, for the first time in a long time. No doubt the steroids have done their job in reducing the brain swelling that was part of the problem. But none of this would even happen if the Lord hadn't blessed the treatment and the exercises, and we are very grateful.

We are still on 24/7 seizure watch. Courtney

has an EEG on Monday which could lead to a reassessment, if it shows the risk is lessened. We are praying so.

Courtney's parents are here from Idaho and will be here until Wednesday. Her sister Myra was able to come to stay the last five days. My mom and Kim fly in tomorrow from Louisiana and will be here until the 31st.

Courtney's next treatment starts the 31st. In early June we expect a scan that will hopefully give us a little more insight into what is happening with the tumor with all this treatment.

Of course, we know that it is all in the Lord's hands, and if He decides Courtney's time is to be short, it won't change the fact that we'll praise Him for all eternity for all He's done in our lives, including this. He made us and He bought us with His blood, and we're doubly His, to do with as He lovingly deems best.

In the light of our eternal blessings and destiny, it seems so small to say it, but we're thankful that Courtney is having good days right now, anyway. And I'm persuaded He wants us to thank Him for the small and perhaps temporary gifts, as well as for the great eternal ones.

Thank you for your prayers for us.

The only time Courtney really had trouble with her balance now was in the night. When she would first get up, she was quite unsteady. Her brain's balance mechanism took a minute or three to process that she was standing now, and if tired/sleepy, she could be very unsteady. Long before, I had trained myself to wake the instant she started stirring, so I could help her if she was getting up.

Other than that, she was handling stairs and walks

around the block; even walks over rough terrain were encouraged as a balance exercise. The only restriction? Someone always had to be with her because of the seizure risk. That bothered Courtney more than me; I was glad to walk with her—but it always made her feel a burden. That's a trial of cancer I'd never thought about before, the false guilt of being a burden.

Looking back, it is interesting how quiet my email inbox was during this time. We were still getting encouraging emails, of course, but much less. I think our Lord knew when we needed encouragement the most, and then He laid it on the hearts of His people to write us more. In times where our circumstances were getting easier, it wasn't as important to get as many emails—and we didn't. But we were always surrounded by the love of God's people—it was part of that Grace we kept experiencing.

Chapter 16

Milestones

28 May 2021 (Friday p.m.)

Dear All

Best news of the week! We're a Nana and Papa again! We stopped to see our grandchildren and their little brother must have decided he didn't want to miss our visit, so made a rapid appearance. This is the second time we've arrived after a birth but before the midwives! Perhaps this whole midwife thing is overrated? :) Seems like the babies come whether the midwives are there or not! Anyway, we're very grateful for the Lord's protection for our daughter-in-law and new grandson. And we can't help remembering that we thought Courtney wasn't going to get to see this child!

Hard news of the week: We've had a dual reminder of how vulnerable you are when cancer becomes your companion along life's journey.

On Monday, Courtney had an EEG to check her brain for "seizure activity." (We don't have results yet.) But one requirement was, "no more than 4 hours of sleep the night before." Well, normally that just means you take a nap and get a good night's sleep the next night, but Courtney has really struggled to bounce back from it, and hasn't slept well since, either. She says it gave her jetlag all over again. There's just no reserve for things like that.

Now, Courtney also has a cold, and it's a doozy. Again, when the body is weakened . . .

When your body is vulnerable, the littlest thing can knock you way back. (Here Justin puts on his preacher's hat :) and notes that if you aren't reading your Bible and praying, not meeting with fellow believers, not serving the Lord, but instead you are reading/listening to/watching things you shouldn't, you are spiritually vulnerable and might get knocked back hard.)

My sleep has really suffered this week too, I think this is the most exhausted I've been since Courtney was diagnosed.

The next treatment starts Monday. We may not have another scan until July but we were told today that we should feel pretty optimistic that the treatment is (for now at least) controlling the tumor, or we'd be having symptomatic trouble by now. So that was encouraging.

In Other News:

Courtney's parents were able to be here for 2½ weeks but left Wednesday.

My mom and sister Kim arrived last Saturday and will be here until Monday. Mom has really struggled with this trip; she had an infection and also has had to go on oxygen (perhaps due to the altitude).

Due to some family history, they suspected a genetic link to Courtney's cancer. All tests came back negative, for which we are thankful. We've always assumed there was no obvious human explanation and that we should accept this as something God allowed for His purposes alone, but it's also nice to know it isn't signaling a particular risk for our kids and grandkids.

We're expecting another invasion of our kids—Katherine in late June, Edward and Marguerite in early July, hopefully Rosa will also be able to come. Now, we have some room to accommodate a crowd!

A work colleague came and installed some garage storage for us, which was a real blessing. We're a long way from "organized" but we're moving in that direction!

In Him
Justin

Now there were six Cuteness Roarers, four local and two in Utah! We found out just days after Courtney's diagnosis that Miles was coming, and it didn't seem like she would get to see him. She saw him (and we got a picture of her holding him) before the midwives arrived! He arrived six months after Courtney first went into the hospital. This Miles-stone :) was the first of several "milestones" in a very short time.

My inbox was full of responses about my "preacher's hat," pictures of what it might look like, or simply appreciation—*I enjoy it when you put on your "preacher" hat. Keep it up.*

Courtney was very tired on Sunday, and we had to leave partway through the service. Courtney's phone was left behind, but we were able to get it the next day.

I wrote—

Hi, Pastor, thank you, we got the phone back ok.

I felt bad leaving yesterday. It can be a distraction and perhaps even a discouragement to others. I've assumed that (on balance) people will be encouraged that Courtney tried, rather than discouraged if she has to leave, and so when she's up to trying, we come, even if we aren't sure she will last.

How strange it felt to go from behind the pulpit every week to thinking about partial attendance.

1 June 2021 (Tuesday p.m.)

Dear All

Happy Anniversary to us! At times we did not think Courtney would be here by this date, nor did the doctors, but today we celebrated our wedding anniversary, and we thank the Lord. Every day is a gift, and so is every year!

Thank you for your prayers for us!

In Him
Justin

A second milestone—our anniversary! This meant a lot to Courtney. We didn't go anywhere special, but we were still together. She would have been a lot happier in heaven, of course. But I was so thankful that she was still with me!

5 June 2021 (Saturday p.m.)

Dear All

Another week of treatment done. We're learning more and more how to cope and minimize the side effects. The only real problem has been fatigue and it's been manageable this week. We were able to go for a long walk this morning—and Courtney came back and had a long nap. Walking is still the best way to handle the side effects—when walking, she feels good; when she sits down to rest, things get worse. But obviously she can't walk all day!

We had good news this week—Courtney is no longer considered a severe seizure risk. This means we can relax most of the precautions we were taking. Courtney no longer has to feel like I'm spying on her all the time! :)

Cancer triggers one thing after another, all of which need treatment. Eating right, exercise, and good habits can help but they don't help everything. So you end up with seizure medication, steroids to reduce brain swelling, anti-nausea medication, etc., etc. They all have their side effects, and most of them seem to have "tiredness" or "can disturb sleep" (which ends up the same thing) on the list. This all can affect/slow down mental processes as well, which Courtney finds frustrating. I keep telling her she's just as intelligent as ever, it just takes longer to connect things sometimes.

In asking you to pray about those things, we'd like to be clear, though. While cancer is no picnic, the Lord has made it easier for us, so far, than we'd expected. So much of the treatment has been easier than we thought. So many people have helped us with small and large kindnesses. Instead of going through months finding out the best ways to cope with things, we seem to keep finding good answers quickly (at least, good answers for us).

And of course, over it all is the peace which God gives both for eternal concerns and temporal ones. We know Whose hand is holding our eternal destiny as well as our path in this life. I can see now many ways in which He has been preparing us (and others) for this through the years, so it's not hard to trust that He's even now preparing us and others for what comes next.

Of course, we don't know what the future holds. But it would be silly to complain about that, when instead you can trust the Lord. No problem is improved by worrying about it (with apologies to our church in Scotland who must have heard me preach that about 50 times!).

My mom and Kim made it safely back to Louisiana this week. We're back to "just us"—Alyssa, and Courtney and me. We're still not really close to "settled" after our move, but we keep making progress, even during treatment week. We're looking forward to the week of the Fourth of July—it looks like all of our kids except Eric will be here.

Thank you for your prayers for us!

In Him
Justin

From a pastor in North Carolina, USA, that we'd known for over thirty years

As for walking all day—you could put a treadmill in the main room and just keep her on it—a hamster wheel for humans!

Praying for y'all daily

From a dear friend in Scotland who wrote so faithfully

Thank you for this encouraging update. It's always good to hear how the Lord is faithfully taking care of you, and helping you navigate through this on a steady course.

And thine ears shall hear a word behind thee, saying, This is the way, walk ye in it, when ye turn to the right hand, and when ye turn to the left. Isaiah 30:21

12 June 2021 (Saturday p.m.)

Dear All

We were able to go up to Denver to see Courtney's sister Myra and brother-in-law Miles this week. It's the farthest we've traveled since arriving here. It was good to see them.

Courtney is still having physical therapy, both for the shoulder she hurt in her seizure and for the balance problems. Both are very, very significantly improved over where they were, but both still can use some improvement. The PT identified a tendency yesterday that is very good to know about and work to overcome.

This week has primarily been a "steady as she goes" holding pattern. We're in this weird phase of life, where every little headache, every little balance wobble, the little memory breakdowns that happen to all of us, the extra fatigue one day, all make one wonder, "Is that because the tumor is growing? Or is it the medication? Or is it nothing?" You wonder, but all you can do is just keep on serving as He enables us and trust Him that all of that is in His control and His plan is perfect. Since you can't do anything about all that, the best you can do is just keep on doing what you are supposed to do!

It's been very hot this week, for people who just moved here from cool and rainy Scotland! That's very draining when you are already tired. But there's been no illness, no drastic changes in symptoms, no particular problems. Courtney's found it hard to walk quite as much in the heat, but this morning wasn't too hot and we managed about 2½ miles, with only one short rest.

Last week, I got to speak briefly to a young man

about knowing the Lord—we agreed to meet this week, and I am praying that will happen. We also had a really good conversation with a new neighbor this week about trusting God through times like this. We continue to find that Courtney's condition opens doors to conversations that move beyond the surface discussions of weather, etc.

We are praying for several families in our church struggling with COVID. (Courtney's blood counts have held up very well and we were told at our last appointment that she should have a good immune response.)

Our eldest, Katherine, plans to get here in time to help during the next treatment week, which starts the 28th. Most of the others arrive late that week. We'll have a very full house!

Thank you for your prayers for us!

In Him
Justin

From Lithuania

Praying from Lithuania, and thankful for the testimony of Christ in you as you go through this all for His glory.

Yet another milestone was 20 June—a Father's Day we hadn't expected to see! We mostly saw Mother's Day, Father's Day, and Valentine's Day as clever marketing tricks to separate you from your money. This one, though, meant a lot to Courtney. As these milestones passed, I could tell she had not expected to see them and didn't expect to see them again. I hoped for next year, but it didn't seem likely. Every day was a gift.

I wrote a long letter after Courtney went to bed. Our

pastor had asked how we were doing, and I'd given the brief answer you give in a crowd, but it hadn't really told the story.

Hi, Pastor. You asked how Courtney is doing. The real answer is I don't know. There have been several "Whoa!" moments recently that make me think the tumor is likely growing. On Tuesday, she got ready for church because she thought it was Sunday. I haven't seen that since before her operation.

Incidents keep happening but are few and far between. She's feeling fine. I do not think she is connecting the dots and thinking it is growing and I don't want to ask her because then she will connect it up, which could just be unnecessary turmoil for her.

They are sporadic enough to just be delayed effects, from the tumor, the operation, the radiation, the chemo, the seizure. It's enough that I suspect tumor growth, but little enough to think the chemo is restricting the growth (in a full-scale glioblastoma growth phase new symptoms would appear every day).

I'll be discussing all this with the doctor on Wednesday. We've expected another scan in mid-July and I suspect he'll continue with that but may decide to get it earlier.

If the chemo is losing effectiveness and letting the tumor grow, I'm not sure there's much they can do.

As always, in God's hands. Certainly, if I get complacent, Courtney says or does something that hits me with a sledgehammer and reminds me just how dependent we are on Him.

Anyway, "She's fine" wasn't a very good answer to give you today. :) Of course, we're fine, but perhaps not physically. God knows.

I appreciated the message. God used a sermon on Ephesians 2:1-10 to call me to the ministry. I had career opportunities,

I was studying chemistry and physics. But when my pastor preached on dead people becoming alive, I knew that was something for which God wanted me to give my life, and a whole lot better than chasing money. So, a favorite passage, and you handled it well and faithfully. Courtney liked that you preached on one of my favorite texts on perhaps our last Father's Day together.

In Him
Justin

As I'd just written, I didn't want to "connect the dots" for Courtney and make her suspect the tumor was growing (if she didn't already). By Wednesday, she said she also was suspecting growth, so the conversation with the doctor was much easier.

It can be hard to know when and how to talk freely with a brain tumor patient. I did not want to upset her unnecessarily if she wasn't thinking the way I was—especially if I turned out to be wrong. But neither did I want to hide things, and I didn't always know just how well she was processing facts.

20 June 2021 (Sunday p.m.)

Dear All

We thank the Lord for another week of His blessings. Courtney's stamina is, I think, continuing to slowly improve, and after next week, she'll only be seeing the physical therapist once a week, rather than twice. The problems that called for PT are improving, though she still has trouble with her shoulder, and her balance is still occasionally suspect.

One cannot have a brain tumor, operation, and

radiation treatment on the brain without having some effects, and those are with us in varying degrees. But we are so grateful our Lord has given us this time and given us a quality of life that I never dreamed of before the operation. This week brings another milestone we didn't know Courtney would see. I remember well Courtney being unable, in the hospital, to cope with the simplest decisions, and now she's planning my birthday dinner.

Courtney and I were able to put out some door hangers this week with a Gospel message and a church invitation. We pray that the Lord will use them. Also, I was able to meet with the man I mentioned last week and share the Gospel with him. I told him lots of people are praying for him, even though none of them would know who he is, God knows! Now, you have to pray for him, or I'll be a liar! He seemed very open, though of course Satan is very deceptive.

Stuff:

The carpet is done in our basement, so now we can begin to unpack some 200 boxes that came from Scotland—books upon books (not just mine!), etc., etc.

We have had some very unpleasantly hot weather here—and our air conditioning wasn't working. It was repaired Wednesday. Yay! What a difference!

Katherine arrives next weekend and will be here through treatment week and for most of the next month.

The following weekend, Edward and Marguerite (and OF COURSE, Neil and Charlotte) arrive for a month. Also, Rosa and a friend arrive the same weekend, for a week.

We've learned my mom's cancer has returned

again. The doctor expects to be able to treat it, but I know she would appreciate your prayers.

This week is the American Olympic Trials, which takes me back to my running days (not that I was ever close to THAT good). But it does give a reminder that we are to run with patience the race that is set before us (Hebrews 12:1-2).

I remember one track meet when my coach had me run the mile, even though the two-mile was my best race. It wasn't the race I'd have chosen, but it was the one that was set before me. But I HAD chosen to go out for track and run for him, and so I did the best I could with it. I didn't win the mile, but my coach was working to a plan, and I beat those other two-milers at the end of the season when it mattered.

Revelation 2:26 *And he that overcometh, and keepeth my works unto the end, to him will I give power over the nations:*

Revelation 2:27 *And he shall rule them with a rod of iron; as the vessels of a potter shall they be broken to shivers: even as I received of my Father.*

Revelation 2:28 *And I will give him the morning star.*

In Him
Justin

Milestones—or as Samuel said when he raised a stone as a marker for Israel, "Hitherto hath the LORD helped us" (1 Samuel 7:12).

These passing days (Miles's birth, our anniversary, Father's Day, my birthday) were milestones—but our Stone of Help was the Rock of Ages. Yet these milestones gave occasion to say, "To here, the Lord has helped us." They were markers on His path to Glory, by His Grace.

Chapter 17

Heartaches, and More Heartaches

26 June 2021 (Saturday p.m.)

Dear All

The last few weeks, Courtney has had a series of differing neurological symptoms that come and go. The doctor tells us this is consistent with what he would expect from swelling that presses on one part of the brain, then another part, but not at all what he sees when cancer is growing.

So, good news that the things we've been seeing aren't tumor growth! But it does mean we won't be reducing the steroids at this point. It's not enough to make him think we need to increase the steroids, though, for which we are thankful!

Courtney's had a strong tendency to lean to the left ever since the cancer started, which has been part of her balance problems. Last Sunday, suddenly, she had a very pronounced lean to the right, apparently because of pressure on a different part of the brain. Unfortunately, in working against that, she seems to have strained a muscle in her side. That, combined with the shoulder problem she's had since her seizure, is not always pleasant.

We went out to do church doorhangers again

this week, but we only managed about 10 minutes before Courtney had to quit. Fatigue has been tough this week, perhaps because the soreness in her side has affected her sleep. We're still walking every day but mostly only twice a day. We met one of those neighbors who knows everybody :), and she said everyone knows us. We've spoken at least briefly to many in our neighborhood.

Upcoming Medical Stuff:
Treatment starts again on Monday, for five days.

The doctor (at the physical therapist's recommendation) has ordered an MRI on her shoulder to see if they can get at why it isn't getting well. It's definitely better than it was, but just won't clear up.

They'll try to get another brain scan in before Courtney sees the neurologist on 14 July, and that compared with her scan in April should give us a really good picture of what the tumor is or isn't doing.

Upcoming Family Stuff (if I can keep it all straight):
Katherine is driving from Wisconsin, arrives today, will stay for two weeks, fly to Louisiana to see my mom for a week, then fly back here.

Edward, Marguerite, Neil, and Charlotte arrive next Friday, for four weeks.

Rosa and her friend arrive next Friday for a week.

Alyssa will fly out with Katherine to Louisiana for a week, then on to Virginia to be with Rosa for a week, then back home.

Other Family Stuff:
My mom is moving in with my sister Kim (the girls will help with this while there).

Our brother-in-law in Denver, Miles, is quite ill in the hospital. We are very thankful we were able to get up to see him a couple weeks ago, but I'm even more thankful for the faith he expressed to me while there. He's ready for whatever the Lord brings and expecting to see Him before long.

If you only pray for one thing for us, please pray that we would be able to faithfully honor the Lord and be a witness of His goodness to others. We heard a song a couple months ago that said it all: "I want to stand like I've never stood before." In times like these, the importance of standing for the Lord comes through like it doesn't at other times.

In Him
Justin

(The song mentioned at the end of that email, of course, was Maegan Stewart's "I Trust in You," mentioned in chapter 15.)

I hoped the doctor was right, but I wasn't sure. We knew Courtney's tumor was very aggressive, even for a glioblastoma. Was the chemo really keeping ahead of it? Was it really just swelling? There was no way to know and nothing to do about it. If it was growing, it was growing. God was in control, whatever the cancer was doing.

3 July 2021 (Saturday p.m.)

Dear All

Short update today.

This was a rough week but we're through with the treatment for another month.

Scans are scheduled for this Friday for both

Courtney's shoulder and the tumor. Unless the news is bad, we won't get word on the tumor until the 21st.

We've got a full house—Edward and Marguerite arrived Friday afternoon, Rosa and her friend arrived late that night.

This week was "coming," next week is "going." Katherine and Alyssa fly to Louisiana to see my mom on Wednesday, Rosa and her friend return to Virginia on Friday.

Edward and Marguerite will be here for a month, Katherine returns after a week, Alyssa after two weeks.

I saw a doctor this week who told me they have several believers there and asked if they could pray for us in their weekly prayer meeting.

My brother-in-law Miles is very ill and now on home hospice care.

I told someone this week that we know where we're going, and we know where we deserved to go, and that makes all the difference. And we know that in this life also, the Lord knows what is best and we're here to serve Him. But I told him, you can have all the faith in the world, and it isn't necessarily going to make you less tired!

But faith does affirm that the fatigue has its purpose in refining us, in teaching us to trust Him rather than our own strength, to teach us to set our affection on things above and not on things on the earth—and a host of other good purposes in making us more Christ-like.

In Him
Justin

From a former church member in Scotland's Central Belt

Precious gift of faith! It doesn't take away tiredness HERE, simply because it's not focused on HERE, but on THERE and in the One enthroned there!

Rosa's "friend" in this email was a young man. It was really too early in their relationship for her to bring Ward home. But no one knew how much opportunity he would have to meet Courtney, and they decided it was better not to wait. We were very glad to meet him.

I was glad our kids were "front-loading" visits, rather than waiting until we were settled. We had no guarantee Courtney would feel well enough later to enjoy the visits. All except Eric were present (plus all six grandchildren) for the Fourth of July. The Cuteness Roarers got along very well together, with lots of cuteness and lots of uproariously rowdy fun. It was a very good weekend.

4 July 2021 (Sunday p.m.)

For those who prayed for rest after last night's email talked about fatigue—Courtney had her best night's sleep in the last 2½ months (since her seizure). Praise the Lord!

In Him
Justin

10 July 2021 (Saturday early afternoon, written from the airport)

Dear All

This will have to be brief.

Courtney has had a pretty good week this week physically.

Scan was yesterday, we may not have results before we see the oncologist on the 21st but hope to get some information when we see the neurologist this Wednesday. We are praying that the scan will show the tumor has not grown, and that the shoulder scan will show clearly if there is anything that needs further treatment.

My mom had a fall in the middle of the night and is in intensive care in Louisiana. I am flying in about an hour and will be gone until Tuesday. This will be difficult for Courtney to have me gone but Edward and Marguerite are still here.

Fortunately, Alyssa and Katherine were already in Louisiana to help my sister and brother-in-law.

From the Martin travel agency: Rosa left yesterday, Katherine returns here from Louisiana Wednesday, Alyssa goes from Louisiana to Rosa's in Virginia. Edward and Marguerite are here until the end of the month. Much of this could change.

The biggest prayer request is for Courtney to be able to sleep.

Mom has known the Lord for many, many years.

In Him
Justin

Mom had a platelet problem, and there was bleeding in her brain. It would take a miracle for her to survive.

10 July 2021 (Saturday, an hour later)

"Further Update"

Dear All

I wasn't free to tell you in my last update, but I can, now. Our brother-in-law, Miles, passed into Glory early this morning.

When we went up to see them in Denver a few weeks ago, we went out for lunch. The ladies left the table to go get our beverages, and as soon as they left, Miles started talking about the Lord. He'd never done that with me before, and clearly, he really wanted to talk to me. He told me he knew he was dying, and that he was totally at peace with the Lord. He knew he was in God's hands, that God loved him and had forgiven him, and that he was ready. He said this wasn't what he wanted to be happening, but he knew it was happening and that God's time for him was near.

Miles was able to see his daughter graduate, and he felt at peace about his family. He was able to work until just a very short time before passing, and that was consistent with what he always wanted, too.

I believe Miles was ready both in terms of his spiritual condition and in terms of having accomplished the things in this life that were important to him.

I'll always be thankful that we drove up to see them that day. I can't tell you how I knew but I just knew I needed to get Courtney up there. We certainly didn't know Miles would be leaving so soon. I believe the

Lord laid that on my heart, and we're thankful to Him for it.

The last 24 hours have been an awful lot for us. When I asked you, a little while ago, to pray for the Lord to help Courtney sleep, I meant it! Please pray also for Courtney's sister Myra, and for all of the family, for comfort and peace.

Thank you for all your prayers for us.

In Him
Justin

Once I knew we were moving to Colorado, I was really looking forward to getting to know Miles better. In fact, I only saw him once—but it was the best conversation we'd ever had. I would always be grateful. Nevertheless, this hurt—with more hurt to come.

On 11 July (Sunday), I wrote to Courtney and our pastor—

Mom just asked, "Is there any hope?" So I sang "My Hope Is in the Lord.":) Which made her laugh. I told her, if God stops the bleeding, she'll come through, and if not it's because He's taking her Home to see Dad again but even more, the Lord. Either way, it's ok.

All is peaceful here. I've seen the other kind of hospital watch. It's such a difference when you really know the Lord and have lived for Him for years. Mom really wanted to see me again and say she loves me, and she really wants to see my brother again, but it really doesn't matter to her whether the Lord takes her now or later.

My brother made it later that day, so all four of Mom's children were with her through her last two days. We were thankful for that, but Courtney loved Mom and was heartbroken that she didn't get to see her again.

16 July 2021 (Friday p.m.)

Dear All

Mom went Home to be with her Lord and Savior on Tuesday morning. We don't know how everything works there, but I like to think she has also seen Dad again, even though we know there is no human marriage anymore in Heaven. We do know that God has better ideas than us, so everything there is going to be better than we can think up. Mom knew the Lord for 70 years and it showed in her life.

We really appreciated her church planning a service for Tuesday evening so my brother and I could be there. Because of Courtney's condition it would not have been right for me to stay longer or to return later for a service, so their pastor just put together a service for Tuesday evening. He based his sermon on two passages from 1 Corinthians 15 that my brother and I told him were real favorites of Mom's. We believe the service pleased the Lord and would have pleased Mom.

Courtney did sleep reasonably well most nights while I was gone—thank you for your prayers!

We got some preliminary results from Courtney's scan from the neurologist (we'll learn more from the oncologist next week). It shows "minor progression" of the tumor. The main part of the tumor doesn't appear to have grown but it has spread to 2 new areas in her brain.

The growth is so small, however, that the neurologist was ready to reduce the seizure medicine.

We don't have to take as many seizure precautions, at least for now, as we did before! This is a real blessing.

This is kind of fun to tell you about. Courtney needed new glasses, so had a thorough eye exam. She's had macular degeneration for some years. The exam showed that it's really quite advanced in both eyes—but when it comes to the center part of the eye, which is what matters the most for vision, there's none in one eye and it is just starting in the center of the other eye. Her optometrist in Scotland was amazed at how well she could see given how advanced it was, but now we understand better. It's maybe not quite a miracle that her eyesight is so good but it's a gift from God, and the cancer would be a lot harder if she were struggling to see.

We would have preferred to not have any cancer growth, obviously, but then, we'd prefer there be no tumor at all! God's thoughts and ways are not ours and are higher than ours (Isaiah 55:8-9, and if you are too lazy to look it up, His ways are higher than yours, too! :)). If we could really learn to set our affections above (Colossians 3:2), and not on things on the earth, our thoughts would begin to be a little closer to His, and we'd begin to see that our preferences are so temporary and irrelevant, compared to eternity, as to be silly.

As the hymn writer wrote, "When we've been there ten thousand years," there will be no fewer days to sing God's praise than when we started—and no fewer days to look back and shake our heads and say, "Wow, the things that bothered us on earth were so ridiculous!" I didn't want Miles to die yet, I didn't want Mom to die yet, I don't want Courtney to have cancer—but after a few million years in Heaven (and I'm pretty sure we won't even be counting years there), who will care about all that? Ok, done preaching, for now.

As far as we can see, Courtney is not yet having any symptoms from these new areas of cancer, or if she is, they are so minor that she hasn't noticed them. We're still walking, and Courtney is keeping up with her exercises, and has done well enough with her balance that the physical therapist will be releasing her at the end of this month for several weeks to see how she does without so many appointments.

One of our neighbors (from Vietnam) told me Courtney is "an inspiration" and brought freshly cooked spring rolls while I was gone. Another neighbor, who is a nurse, told Courtney she would come and stay with her while I was gone if Courtney needed someone. People in our church are ready to help in whatever way we need. Edward and Marguerite were here so it wasn't necessary, but we appreciated the kindness.

Katherine stayed a couple days longer in Louisiana to help my sisters and returns tomorrow. Alyssa has gone on to Virginia now to visit Rosa and returns next week. Eric told me today that more borders are open so it won't be so complicated for him when he returns—currently he's planning on November but he has more flexibility now.

Thank you for your prayers for us!

In Him
Justin

In five short days, our brother-in-law and my mom went to be with the Lord, and we learned that Courtney's tumor was again growing. I believed everything I wrote in that email about how these things fit in an eternal viewpoint—but it was still a very hard time.

23 July 2021 (Friday p.m.)

Dear All

This week we celebrated Courtney's birthday, another "It's a gift" milestone. When Courtney was diagnosed, I couldn't even get a promise she'd see Christmas and the New Year, and here we are!

We saw the oncologist this week and got a little more info on Courtney's scan. He said the new growth is so small he personally can't see it on the scan, but it's enough to suggest that "something is starting to stir up." Obviously, the chemo is still having some effect because the growth is so small, but that means it is time to look at other treatments.

We always knew this type of chemo was likely to be temporary. It works really well for a short time but is usually only given for six months because it loses effectiveness. Next week, Courtney takes it for the fifth month.

We're thankful to those who have studied and tested different treatments. I've read that before TMZ (this kind of chemo) was found to be effective, the average life span of glioblastoma patients was 7 months, and TMZ took it to 12–18 months. It appears to have kept Courtney's tumor pretty much in check, without major side effects, up to 7 months after her operation, about the time most GBM patients used to die. We always knew it would be temporary and that we would then be looking at alternatives. We've reached this point perhaps one or two months earlier than we had hoped, but we know the Lord's timing is perfect.

One option being considered is further radiation treatment. We have an appointment to discuss that on Monday. This also would likely only be a temporary measure. The only permanent cure to this kind of cancer is a miracle.

We also learned something else. The MRI on Courtney's shoulder shows that she dislocated her shoulder when she had the seizure and suffered what's known as a Hill-Sachs fracture. That at least partially explains why she's had so much pain and weakness. This also means I need to write a letter to the hospital where she was taken, because they never examined her shoulder. (This means I need you to pray that I'll honor the Lord in how I write that letter because I'm more than a little displeased with them.) Of course, we know that the Lord allowed all that to happen for His purposes. But His sovereignty doesn't mean they should not be held accountable for providing poor care.

But we want to say this!!!

The seizure was extremely difficult, and resulted in a lot of pain, and a lot of inconvenience, over the last three months. But it meant that instead of scans being done in early June and then early September, they were done in mid-April and mid-July. The result of that seizure which we found so difficult was that the timing of the scan was perfect for catching the new tumor growth very, very early. It probably wouldn't have been there in early June. It probably would have been more advanced in September.

Instead, because of the seizure, we caught it now. That means there's a much better chance for whatever treatment is used going forward to be effective for longer. We don't know what God is going to do, but we do "know that all things work together for good to them that love God, to them who are the called according to his purpose." "All things" includes seizures. Perhaps He sent the seizure just so the tumor growth would be found sooner. It wouldn't be the most mysterious way in which He has worked, His wonders to perform!

In Him
Justin

That awful seizure. We never complained (we knew God must have a purpose), but we did grieve over it. It injured Courtney's shoulder and marred her quality of life more than anything else. It meant I had to watch her constantly, she needed help with everything, and she couldn't walk up or down stairs alone.

All that—*and* it saved her life. The growth was caught early—and when it grew (as we later learned), it was exploding. The seizure was God's Grace; now we could see it. We were still on His Grace and Glory path, and He let us see it now—when the heartaches were mounting, and we might have lost our way otherwise. His Grace goes beyond mere circumstances and is always there even if we aren't seeing it. But when we most need to see, He graciously shows us.

Chapter 18

"This Is the Worst Possible Scenario"

28 July 2021 (Wednesday p.m.)

Dear All

Monday, we met with the oncology radiologist. She is very unhappy with Courtney's scan, she says the level of blood flow indicates the main tumor is active and likely taking off, that we're not in a good scenario.

We've said all along this would take a miracle, but we feel like we've already had miracles, and every day is a gift. Certainly, the medical prognosis is not very promising right now. But the two best words in the Bible are "But God . . ." He, not the doctors, decides our future, and Courtney's time on earth could be much shorter, or much, much longer, than the doctors are saying. If her Father wants her to come Home, He wins, and so does she. If He wants her to stay longer, then their prognosis is pointless and powerless. "For me to live is Christ, and to die is gain" (Philippians 1:21).

This week, Courtney is taking the chemo, perhaps for the last time. It's obviously still having an effect but diminishing. Soon, probably next week, she will have radiation. The plan is to hit the tumor (both the main tumor and the growth areas) with a high and targeted dose of radiation for five days, in the hopes to knock it back temporarily to give time for other things to work. This may, of course, have side effects. A second operation is almost certainly not going to happen. We are still not sure what the next treatment will be.

For those who have written about different treatments: many treatments can't cross the blood brain barrier to reach the tumor. The Bible says, "I am fearfully and wonderfully made" (Psalm 139:14). One of the amazing things in the way God made us is to protect the brain with a barrier that prevents many things from passing into the brain through the blood. It's a wonderful thing God has done which protects us from many serious problems attacking our brains. But it also means that many things that might work well on other kinds of cancer don't work on this kind.

When sin came into the world, illness and death came in, too (Romans 5:12). One of the things that "got broken" is that some of the things God made for our good get twisted, in some ways, to our harm. That's what happens with auto-immune diseases when the immune system attacks the body. The blood brain barrier is similar in treating problems in the brain—that which was a good gift from God becomes a hindrance to dealing with a cancer that attacks behind it.

That's why this particular form of cancer is considered incurable. If we understand Scripture, we understand that these things will happen in a sin-marred world. We also know that God has all the answers and can heal beyond anything that human attempts can ever achieve. And ultimately, we know that the time will come when He will wipe away all tears from our eyes.

There are a lot of things being tried with this cancer. Part of God's plan for man was to "subdue and replenish the earth," so He has put within mankind both the desire and the ability to pursue solutions for these problems. A quick online search shows a wide variety of things being tried. Nothing (in either formal or informal medicine) has been found (except a miracle) to cure this kind of cancer, but some things are having some limited success. We believe that God has made us stewards of the life we live, and that we should do our reasonable best to protect it. So, we're focused on treatments that (1) have a chance to reach the tumor despite the blood brain barrier and (2) can have an effect on Courtney's particular kind of glioblastoma.

Ultimately, it's in God's hands, and that's always the best place to be, anyway.

Courtney is mostly feeling ok but is very, very tired. She is having some headaches which could be consistent with tumor growth, or with increased swelling in the brain, or may be simply as a result of the fatigue. She's not having any other significant symptoms at this point.

Family News:

Edward, Marguerite, and the kids leave Saturday for Utah. It's been really nice to have them here for the last month. Katherine leaves on Monday or Tuesday, back to Wisconsin via Idaho to see her grandparents. Courtney's sisters arrive on Saturday for maybe a week. We're so thankful that the Lord enabled us to move so we could have these family visits.

Miles' funeral was on Sunday. Please pray for his family, and that they would know the Lord and the peace He gives, as Miles did.

Courtney's dad is having some health problems and

would appreciate your prayers. We are so thankful that Courtney's parents were able to visit earlier before this became such a problem.

Thank you for praying for us!

In Him
Justin

From a childhood friend in Alaska, USA

We've been praying, and let Courtney know that Alaska is praying for her!! And I keep our church updated on your reports, and we pray for Courtney on our prayer chain, so I just wanted you to know that. I also celebrated with your family as your mom passed this past month. She was such a testimony to all of us, and I remember our time as kids hanging out at your old house, and riding bikes to school. Those are good memories for me. :) Your mom and dad were such a testimony. And all those nights going to Bible club with your family. You know, as I've gotten older, I think back about how I didn't have a dad growing up and it was people like your dad who made such positive impressions on me that helped me later when I became a dad.

Anyway, I just wanted to drop a note to you. God bless you all. Thanks for sharing Philippians 1:21. One of my favorite verses! Maybe we can visit you one of these days.

To a dear friend in Scotland—

Been a tough week—the oncology radiologist walked into the room, looking and sounding upset, and said, "This is terrible. ***This is the worst possible scenario****." First, not entirely true. Second, with frontal lobe issues, you don't need melodrama, you need calm. Left Courtney, who is completely ready to die in the Lord's time, so upset that she was sick all night. It's* *simply physically impossible for her to bring her emotions under control, as a result of the tumor/operation.*

I was very upset with that doctor—her initial comment was both unprofessional and unkind. She did, however, really seem to care; she seemed knowledgeable and competent; and she helped us with what was to come. We had been half wondering if things weren't worse than the reassurances we'd heard. We wanted someone to give it to us straight. Now, though, I wondered if someone was magnifying rather than minimizing the problem.

After some initial discussion, the doctor left the room briefly, and Courtney (through tears) said, "Tell her we're trusting God. I'm ready to die if it's His time, that I don't want to die but I'm ready. I can't tell her; I'll just cry." When the doctor returned and I told her these things, she shook it off with, "We need to keep you from dying." Indeed, it was her job to try to do that, but it didn't raise my opinion of her bedside manner.

After a sleepless night, I took some time off work. One of Courtney's goals was a settled home. I spent three weeks arranging furnishings, putting up curtains, and hanging pictures—reminders of all the blessings we'd had. Seeing the pictures brought Courtney peaceful memories and turned her thoughts from the doctor's words. She needed these things done; they had lagged, but it was time to do them. I got further behind on work, but work would just have to wait.

Courtney and I talked one evening about the tumor's effect of making her cry so easily, even if she wasn't particularly emotional. Sadness made her cry, as did happiness. The tears just flipped on and came. She said, "I want to tell people I'm okay, that I'm trusting the Lord. I'm going to heaven and I'm so happy, but the stupid tears start, and that ruins it because it looks like I'm sad." We agreed we'd just have to trust the Lord to take care of it.

The very next day, as we were walking around the block, some neighbors popped out to talk, and this dear lady told Courtney, "You know what's special? You are dealing with some really heavy stuff, and the light of Jesus just shines out of you."

When we got home, Courtney told me, "That was really nice." We both remembered the conversation the night before. As with so many problems, the Lord had it in hand before we even talked about it. It is always good and right to speak of the Lord to others when we can, but it was silly of us to think He needed our words. For having been Christians for so long, we still had a lot to learn.

31 July 2021 (Saturday p.m.)

Dear All

Briefly this evening. Starting Monday for five days, Courtney has Cyber Knife treatment. This is not some weird video game, it is very narrowly targeted high dose radiation on three areas of the brain, the original tumor and each of the new growth areas. Potential side effects include additional brain swelling (so her steroid dose has been increased at least temporarily), headaches, and possibly seizures. Almost certainly it will also cause fatigue.

We are doing well and trusting the Lord. At times this week has been hard, but there have also been some unexpected encouragements, for which we thank the Lord. We don't know what the future holds, but we know the One who holds it, so we know it is good.

Courtney's parents are going through some difficult times and have decided to go into "independent living." Because of this, her two sisters that were coming this week are needing to delay their visit. We would appreciate your prayers for wisdom in all the decisions that have to be made, and for all the new needs arising because of this.

In Him
Justin

Meanwhile, the doctor was working to get Courtney into a clinical trial as a volunteer to help find better treatments for glioblastoma. This was something she had wanted from the first day she learned of her diagnosis. So many times, she said, "Even if it doesn't help me, if it helps others, it will be worth it." Now, it looked promising. Perhaps we could forgive a poor bedside manner after all!

6 August 2021 (Friday p.m.)

Dear All

Courtney has completed the Cyber Knife radiation treatment. She had some headaches consistent with swelling and is now taking 3 times the previous steroid dose, which is not pleasant, but the headaches are under control.

Of much more concern, an MRI yesterday evening showed the tumor is progressing.

The main tumor again appears "stable to minimally larger" but has higher than normal blood flow at the margins which suggests the cancer is alive and ready to grow.

The smaller new growth has gone from 2 mm to 3 mm in the last four weeks. This is still very small and the doctor is not certain it is even cancer, though it's highly likely it is.

The biggest concern is the larger new growth. It has grown very, very rapidly in the last 4 weeks and is now 3.1 cm x 1.6 cm x 4.1 cm.

This larger new growth has been hit by the Cyber Knife which may have slowed it or temporarily stopped it—we have no way of knowing yet. But the doctor couldn't say with any confidence that it would—she said it has grown much larger than the scan on which she was operating and so she is not sure whether we hit all of it with the radiation or not. If not, then some of it, at least, will be alive and still growing.

Courtney has been given preliminary acceptance into a clinical trial of a new anti-cancer treatment for glioblastoma in Denver. We hope to get more answers on this at an appointment on Monday, but if I understand it, among other beneficial effects, the medication reduces blood flow to cancerous cells and so prevents them from multiplying. Earlier trials were more limited but found no serious side effects yet and found that there was a real improvement in tumor control and life expectancy. This is definitely not a cure, however.

It's worth mentioning that news has just come out that doctors in Houston have found a non-invasive, non-chemical use of magnetic fields to stimulate the production of a chemical within the cancer cells that kills them. It has been used in animals effectively and has been used with a single human patient, who had a 30% reduction in his tumor over 36 days, before he tragically had a fall and died. This is only one patient, of course, and no one knows whether there will be significant side effects or whether it will work as well in reducing the tumor in other patients or for how long it will work. But we thank the Lord for giving doctors the ability to research these things, and it would be truly a blessing if better treatments could be found.

Courtney was just telling me she is pleased that she can stand on one leg while getting dressed. It's actually incredible how few symptoms she is having when you discover she has yet another tumor that is more than an inch wide and an inch and a half long. And today, on the fifth and final day of an intense radiotherapy course, her Fitbit says 11,500 steps. God has allowed her not only to have a glioblastoma, but probably just, about the most aggressive type of glioblastoma, but He's also been incredibly gracious in protecting her from so many symptoms that others suffer.

We have two songs for you today. Courtney's grandma loved the Oak Ridge Boys and Courtney ended up with an album with this song when a teenager, and it came to her mind a couple weeks ago. The song, "Why Me, Lord?," asks what we've done to deserve God's blessings and love. We wouldn't endorse everything in it (as sung by the Oak Ridge Boys or Johnny Cash, it *is* better than the original lyrics), but the first verse and chorus reflect an awful lot of Courtney's thinking when she thinks about the life God has given her.

When we were talking about it, Courtney says the Lord used it to remind her of the right way to think about the current situation when she was in danger of a pity party. And she referred to this verse:

Luke 17:10 *So likewise ye, when ye shall have done all those things which are commanded you, say, We are unprofitable servants: we have done that which was our duty to do.*

Next, we are still working on recording hymns from our hymnbook for the church back in Scotland. Alyssa and I were recording the other night and came to "Now I Belong to Jesus." It struck me as we sang it that anyone who can REALLY sing that, who really believes it, can smile in the face of cancer or whatever. "From Him no power of evil can sever"—and no power of cancer, or anything else, either. I realize that not everyone receiving this may be able to say, "Now I belong to Jesus, Jesus belongs to me"—but if you can truly say it, if your sins are forgiven and washed away by the blood of Jesus, nothing this world can throw AT you should ever throw YOU.

Family News:
Everyone has now left except Alyssa. Katherine left Monday and went to Idaho to see her grandparents, but unfortunately her car decided to give up the ghost near Billings, MT, on her way back to Wisconsin. We're still figuring out the best way for her to get home!

Courtney's parents move into independent living tomorrow. Dad is still having a lot of health problems, and we are praying for the Lord to help him.

We're still hoping Courtney's sisters, and mine, will be able to visit soon.

Also, Lord willing, I'll be preaching this Sunday evening.

Thank you for praying for us!

Justin

The secondary tumor had almost tripled in size in 4 short weeks. If not for the Cyber Knife treatment, Courtney would have been in a terrible condition within a couple more weeks. If not for the seizure having changed the scan schedule, we'd have never known the tumor was growing until it was beyond what the Cyber Knife could help. It was only now, with this second MRI showing the explosive growth, that we really understood what a gracious gift of God that seizure had been.

"Why Me, Lord?" made it onto Courtney's Morning Playlist, and she put it first on the list. "I Trust in You" was still her favorite, but she wanted to start the day with a reminder that every blessing from God is an undeserved gift.

So many people ask "Why me?" as a complaint. How much better it is to ask it in amazement at the Grace that leads to Glory. We deserve none of this life's blessings; far less do we deserve those of eternity with our God and Savior. It was good to be reminded of that every morning.

Another song was added, too. The chorus of the song "God Wants to Hear You Sing" includes the words "When the wisest man has spoken and says your circumstance is as hopeless as can be, that's when God wants to hear you sing!" Well, the doctor said it was "the worst possible scenario," so that's pretty much where we were, and Courtney wanted an every-morning reminder to keep praising God.

"Now I belong to Jesus, Jesus belongs to me! Not for the years of time alone, but for eternity!" When you can sing that knowing it is true, you are never in "the worst possible scenario"—even if your glioblastoma just tripled in size in four weeks.

Chapter 19

Courtney's Clinical Trial

Now began a new phase in our life-with-cancer, the clinical trial. Courtney was delighted to do what she'd wanted all along, to help with the research for better treatment. She was determined to do all she could to be the perfect patient.

9 August 2021 (Monday p.m.)

Dear All

We spent hours today with the researchers and doctors in Denver. We have agreed to enter into this trial and they have agreed that Courtney is a good candidate. It now requires some lab work and submission to the final approval, but it seems very likely that Courtney will be entered into this trial.

This study is only 56 patients because it is so experimental. It involves two medications which have demonstrated synergies in animal trials, but they have not been given together to humans prior to this study. There are no guarantees that it will work for Courtney, or that the side effects of the two when used together will not be bad enough that she will be unable to continue with it. But both medications have been used separately without severe side effect problems, and both medications have been found separately to help control this kind of cancer.

One other interesting fact that came out of the discussions today. The apparent tumor growth on the latest scan may be overstated—some of the apparent growth may have actually been cells killed by the radiation treatment Courtney was having, rather than live tumor cells. So perhaps the tumor hasn't been growing quite as quickly as we thought, but there's no way to know at this point.

However, because it obviously has been growing, they are going to try to get Courtney started on the new treatment as quickly as possible—hopefully by the 23rd, if not, by the 30th. That means we have at most two weeks before we have to be in Denver 3 times a week.

That has pushed me into a quick decision on something I'd been considering. Courtney's parents are simply not going to be able to travel here again. So (unless something changes in the next 12 hours or so) I am intending to take her to them. My current plan is to go to Denver again tomorrow to get the necessary lab work done and then go on from there. I don't know how far Courtney will be able to travel in a day, and we aren't going to be able to be in Idaho long, because the researchers will need us back around the middle of next week. But I don't know when or if we would be able to go see them if we do not go now.

Finally, the lead doctor today told us he is hopeful that this new treatment might give us a year, and that he is very hopeful that another new treatment (which has already gone through trials and is awaiting FDA approval) would be approved by that time. None of this is a cure, and none of it is remotely close to certain. The only certainty is that which God decides,

> and He is the only One who knows what He has decided at this point.
>
> We are still in that weird situation of Courtney mostly feeling well, and yet knowing that she has a growing brain tumor, that the doctors don't have any assurance that anything they do is even likely to stop it (or even slow it down), that really significant symptoms could start at any moment, and that she could be leaving this earth soon. As Courtney says, "It's totally beyond our control. We're in the Lord's hands. Underneath are the everlasting arms."
>
> Thank you for your prayers for us!
> Justin

Our main researcher, Joy, was very kind and thorough in her explanations. She walked us back down to our car, told us where best to park, and promised to meet us the next day at the lab. Our life was going to be much easier in some ways.

We had to drive to Denver three times a week, but never again would I have appointment hassles. The researchers made all appointments and always reminded me. The research sponsor (a pharmaceutical company) paid for the researchers to be with us every step of the way and helped with our travel costs, too. I hope the medicine works out and pays off for them; they were wonderful to us.

One difficulty of life-with-cancer is remembering everything (paying bills, making and keeping appointments, taking pills at the right time, etc.). You are so tired, and so much is unfamiliar at first. Now, if fatigue turned me into a gibbering idiot, Joy would set me straight and not even make fun of me! Even while we were at Yellowstone and in Idaho, Joy called three times to update me on appointments.

We did not yet know what a blessing they were going to be to us. The home visit nurses in Scotland after Courtney's operation had been very nice and helpful, but the researchers took it to another level.

We learned about ethical oversight. Volunteers take risks when vulnerable, and safeguards ensure the researchers, doctors, and drug companies never pressure anyone to join or stay in a trial. If it is no longer in the volunteer's best interests, it ends. Often during our time in the trial, I was asked, "Is this too hard on Courtney?" If I had ever said it was, that would have been it.

Joy met us for the lab work too, and then we were on to Yellowstone! Because of fatigue, we walked less than in the past, but we really enjoyed the trip. We dodged elk outside our cabin at Mammoth; we saw deer, antelope, buffalo, wolves, a fox, and human wildlife! We missed the bears until the last day, when we saw a grizzly right next to the road! It was a wonderful trip to perhaps Courtney's favorite place on earth.

Then, it was on to Idaho, where we saw Courtney's parents and all three of her sisters—Myra, Lynn, and Fiona—as well as a nephew and several nieces. We really appreciated the effort they made to come. We knew, even if the trial succeeded, that Courtney might never see them again. And since Courtney's tumor was so aggressive, we knew the trial would have to be extremely successful to stop it.

I didn't send emails while traveling, but my inbox was full of questions about the clinical trial. As all along, there were also many short messages like this:

From Japan

I just wanted you to know that we are praying for you all.

17 August 2021 (Tuesday p.m.)

Dear All

We are safely back from Idaho. We were so thankful to see Courtney's parents settled in a good and safe place, and to have some really good time with them, and with other family members.

We drove through Yellowstone on the way. Yellowstone was a huge part of Courtney's childhood (her grandpa worked on building projects on the Old Faithful Inn during the Great Depression, and later they often met relatives there), and she really wanted to see Yellowstone again—another gift God gave that we didn't think we'd see. He also put a grizzly bear right next to the road for us!

Courtney has another MRI tomorrow to assess whether the radiation has slowed the tumor growth. We'll see the lead doctor either later tomorrow or Friday to get the results.

Courtney is still not formally accepted into the clinical trial (the MRI is needed first) but she is scheduled for the first treatment Monday. They've done in 2 weeks what normally takes 4 weeks because her last scan showed the tumor was growing so fast. They don't want it to kill her or do irreparable harm because they've delayed unnecessarily, and it was growing fast enough to justify moving quickly. The lead researcher told me everyone (doctors, researchers, sponsor) really wants her in this trial.

So, please pray that nothing on the MRI will

preclude Courtney from the trial! This is what she has wanted all along, ever since her diagnosis.

If this experimental treatment works, it will be yet another gift from God, extending Courtney's life longer yet again than we had been told.

If it doesn't work, Courtney will probably die sooner than if we had used a standard treatment that might have gained her a couple months more. But even so, if her participation gives them information that will help treat other people, then we're reflecting Christ. He gave His life for our eternal benefit, that our sins could be cleansed and forgiven for all eternity. It's not a bad thing for Christians to reflect Him (if feebly) by putting our lives on the line for others, even if only for earthly gain. Jesus said in John 15:13, "Greater love hath no man than this, that a man lay down his life for his friends."

Thank you for praying for us!
Justin

We lived with constant uncertainty: would the trial shorten or lengthen Courtney's life? We also had a constant certainty: to honor God was good, even by volunteering for experimental treatment. Grace and Glory were ours; we would stay true. Even if the treatment didn't bring bad effects, trips to Denver would bring extra fatigue and take time Courtney could have been using to read stories to The Cuteness Roarers. But we believed it would please God, and we were determined.

Coming home from seeing her sisters, Courtney saw a Target truck with a red circle target and a dog with a black nose. It brought back a childhood memory of singing "Snoopy vs. the Red Baron" with her sisters. This song was outside our normal standards, but she said, "I keep getting knocked down and having to try again, just like Snoopy." It wasn't the most spiritual song on the importance of perseverance, but Courtney didn't know whether she would ever see her sisters again, and it went on the Morning Playlist.

Joy needed to know every preexisting symptom, so new symptoms could be investigated as potential side effects. Courtney hated this part of it. She didn't want to complain. It took several conversations and emails with Joy to get them all.

Appendix B contains the best list I can reconstruct now. I include it for cancer patients who may read this to say, "Yes, us too." We knew we were more fortunate than many, but there's still a "fellowship of cancer patients," and "Yes, us too" is worth saying sometimes.

From a friend in Florida, USA, after a family tragedy
You know this better than me, but at times like these there are so many questions but no answers. The truth is that if we had answers, it would not help. The only answer is Him and He is our comfort.

There was so much truth in that statement that it still "grabs" me. If we knew all the "whys" that Courtney had cancer, all the answers, it wouldn't have taken away the pain. But we knew the One who is our comfort.

19 August 2021 (Thursday p.m.)

Good news and good news!

We don't yet have a radiologist's report from yesterday's MRI, but the neurologist looked at it and says there is little change. So, it appears the Cyber Knife treatment has at the very least significantly slowed the growth of the secondary tumor!

Courtney has been formally accepted into the trial and receives her first treatment on Monday!

Because this is using a very untested experimental medicine, there will be a lot of medical screening/evaluations going on. They want to be right on top of anything that is going on with side effects or anything else.

Monday's appointment is for 9 hours. Wednesday is for 3, Friday probably 4.5 hours. After that, it will be 3 hours for most appointments, 3 times a week. All of these will be in Denver, an hour away by car (when traffic isn't bad, and it often is bad on Interstate 25). So, busy times ahead, but we're thankful and excited.

Thank you for praying for us!
Justin

We were in, definitively! It was a Phase 2 trial, and Phase 1B results had looked promising, so there was hope that it would really work well for Courtney. But whether it did or not, we were in! It was a happy weekend. Courtney really liked and trusted Dr. Diamond, the lead doctor for the clinical trial in Denver. But the biggest thing was that we were in the trial. Now, it wasn't "the trial"—now, it was "our trial."

A song called "Lord, I'm Thankful" was added to the Morning Playlist, as was "Ballad of the Green Berets." They were daily reminders that the trial might cost us something, but that self-sacrifice for others is honorable and worthwhile.

23 August 2021 (Monday p.m.)

Dear All

We're home after a very, very long day. Fatigue is a huge issue with cancer anyway (sometimes for the spouse, too!). But Courtney just told me she's so tired that even if I brought her some Peanut M&Ms, she wouldn't be interested. That's REALLY tired! :)

As of now, there are no noticeable side effects from the treatment. It's strange to walk out of a hospital having just received a treatment that might be a tremendous blessing to many thousands of people. Or it might end up being a huge disappointment and not do any good at all. Or it might have serious or at least significantly unpleasant side effects. And we don't know which of those scenarios, if any, will play out. But we're coming back Wednesday, and Friday, and next week, and the week after, over and over again—without knowing which of those scenarios it will be.

There's an element of excitement in it. As one of the researchers said, "You're doing science here." Not just reading about it or playing around in a lab, but real life-impacting science. But I can only imagine how scary it could be, too, if you didn't know the Lord. It's one thing to try a treatment that might mean you will die sooner than you would have otherwise. It's quite another to try a treatment that might mean you will be in Heaven sooner than you would otherwise, and to be confident that the Lord is pleased with you for doing it.

We've learned this week how much muscle weakness the higher dose of steroids brings. It means a lot of hard work to try to regain muscle strength. Courtney's had to do this before, but this time is harder because the high dose she had during her Cyber Knife radiation treatment was kept up for longer, and while it has now been marginally reduced, it's still pretty high. Courtney has kept up her walking, still getting over 10K steps most days, but it's going to take harder exercise (stairs, etc.)—harder exercise when the cancer and the treatments are making her tired anyway.

Some really good sleep would be a blessing, too.

Thank you for praying for us!
Justin

Joy had spent virtually the whole day with us, making sure we were where we were supposed to be and generally supporting us. Even with her support, it was just a long, tiring day. But no one was complaining; it was what Courtney had wanted all along, and I was thrilled for her.

Chapter 20

Platelets and Low Blood Pressure

27 August 2021 (Friday p.m.)

Dear All

Not such good news today. When we arrived in Denver today, blood tests showed that Courtney's platelet count was low enough that the doctor decided she should not have treatment today.

This was not particularly expected, as it is not a known side effect of the experimental drug, and the other medications Courtney is taking hadn't previously had this effect. We'll return on Monday to check again.

One of the goals of participating in this trial was to help them learn more about this new medicine and its side effects. If we're learning more in this way, that's not a bad thing—but obviously, we're hoping the treatment will also work. So, we're praying that this is just a blip and that Courtney can get treatment on Monday and be back on the regular treatment schedule.

This week, we went to a hymn-sing service at Robert and Manda's church. Courtney chose the following hymn, one of her all-time favorites, and we asked them, more than anything, to pray for this for us. As Courtney told me on the way home afterward, little is gained if she lives longer but the words of this hymn aren't true of her.

If we aren't living life as described here, we aren't accomplishing much of anything of value for eternity. So, by all means, pray for the platelet count to come up, for Courtney to be able to have treatment, and for the treatment to work. But more than anything else, please pray for us for this.

1 May the mind of Christ, my Savior,
Live in me from day to day,
By His love and pow'r controlling
All I do and say.

2 May the Word of God dwell richly
In my heart from hour to hour,
So that all may see I triumph
Only thru His pow'r.

3 May the peace of God, my Father,
Rule my life in ev'rything,
That I may be calm to comfort
Sick and sorrowing.

4 May the love of Jesus fill me,
As the waters fill the sea;
Him exalting, self abasing,
This is victory.

5 May I run the race before me,
Strong and brave to face the foe,
Looking only unto Jesus
As I onward go.

6 May His beauty rest upon me
As I seek the lost to win,
And may they forget the channel,
Seeing only Him.

["May the Mind of Christ My Savior," Kate Wilkinson, 1859–1928]

My inbox flooded with people saying they loved that hymn. It captures so much of the Christian life—what we should be, what our thoughts should be, how we should be toward others, our motivations, and our dependence on God.

Something else in the inbox really touched our hearts.

From someone we didn't even know, in Florida, USA
Could anyone help donate to platelets? If so how could I go about getting quickly tested to try to help?

We couldn't have that kind of medical intervention—a platelet infusion could skew the results in a scientific trial. A new friend couldn't give Courtney platelets—but he certainly gave a beautiful example of Christian love. It was love *from* God but *through* His people.

31 August 2021 (Tuesday p.m.)

Dear All

Courtney's platelet count yesterday was still low but stable, and so they decided to proceed with the three treatments this week. It's not in the danger zone, so stable is ok, but last week it was both low and dropping which caused the concern.

There's a mystery here. Courtney's platelet count dropped by half in the 13 days before she received the first experimental treatment. It dropped further from Monday to Friday but has now stabilized. But why did it drop before the treatment? We have no idea. There's no obvious medical reason. It's one more thing in which we need to trust the Lord.

What is obvious is that the Lord knows, and He allowed it, so it has a good purpose, even if we don't know what that purpose might be. But it's certainly not discouraging. Courtney wanted to go into a clinical trial to help find better treatments, and anything (whether it seems bad or not) that helps them learn more is a positive thing, not a negative one.

One of the difficulties with a new medicine is "how much, how often?" What's the right dosage and how frequently should it be given? No one really knows. If Courtney's next MRI shows that it is working well despite her missing a day of the treatment, that may tell them that they can get good results with lower dosage or less frequent treatment. A later study might look at reducing the treatment—maybe the next people would only have to go to Denver twice a week, not three times. Or maybe they can lower the dose for each treatment and so have lower risk of side effects.

So maybe God had a good purpose for the platelet count that actually had nothing to do with us. Maybe He allowed it to help the researchers learn more, and so allow them to help more people. We tend to think that the good and bad things that come into our lives are all about us. Maybe He brings things into our lives because of the needs of other people, instead. Despite our tendency to have an inflated opinion of our own importance, the world really doesn't revolve around us, and things that happen to us may not be primarily about us.

But certainly, He doesn't waste these things in our lives, either. We learn more about patience, more about trusting Him, more about how absolutely dependent we are on Him. If we need to know what caused the platelet drop, I'm sure He'll work it out for us to find out. If we don't need to, well, then we'll trust Him.

Back to Denver on Wednesday and Friday for treatment!

Thank you for praying for us!
Justin

I didn't think there was anything special about that update, but person after person wrote that it was exactly what they needed to read. Their stories are not mine to tell, but God kept reassuring us that, however difficult things might be, He was working.

On the way to Denver one day, Courtney said, "These mountains make me think of 'Highland Cathedral.'" We decided if the Highlands can be considered a cathedral to the glory of God, so also could Colorado's Front Range, even if the bagpipes aren't usually associated with Pikes Peak. "Highland Cathedral" was added to our Morning Playlist.

7 September 2021 (Tuesday p.m.)

Dear All

Brief tonight. Courtney had all three treatments last week. The first treatment this week was deferred until today because of the Labor Day holiday yesterday. Courtney's lab tests came back good today, with her platelet count still below normal but significantly better than last week.

It was a long day in Denver today, and we return in the morning for this week's second treatment.

Status on the Treatment:
Fatigue is worse, but we don't know if that is due to the treatment or the earlier mornings and the travel. Other than that, there's no real evidence of any negative side effects at this point. Courtney's not having any new symptoms that would make us think the tumor is growing, either.

We've had multiple reminders in the last week of the way God can work in the midst of trials. We are thankful for all He is doing!

Thank you for praying for us!
Justin

The next morning, headed for Denver, we stopped to get Courtney a snack from the back. She got out to walk around, and when I finished in the back seat, she was sitting on the ground fifty yards up the road. I ran up and said, "What happened? What are you doing?" She said she fell, and then, "Well, I didn't fall. My legs just went wobbly, so I sat down."

Her blood pressure had been really low the day before, and she'd had a history of low blood pressure. Dr. Diamond suggested more salt in her diet, but we'd not had anything like this for decades, and I was pretty sure there was something else going on.

11 September 2021 (Saturday p.m.)

Dear All

Courtney had some trouble this week with unsteadiness after standing up, and in one case on Wednesday, she fell. Fortunately, no injuries. The doctor says it is likely due to low blood pressure. Courtney's had a tendency to low blood pressure in the past, and on Tuesday when she went for treatment, it was quite low.

We don't know why this low blood pressure got worse. It could be an effect of the anti-seizure medicine Courtney has been on, or just fatigue. It could be a side effect of the experimental medicine, though it's not one that has been observed or is expected. Or it could be something else.

What it certainly does provide is a reminder: we are totally in God's hands, totally dependent on Him. There are so many things that could go wrong and, if they do go wrong, could be serious. A fall could mean a broken arm or leg, a scrape that gets infected, or severe bruising due to Courtney's platelet count being low. And while I can try to be sure to be there when Courtney first stands up to help her keep her balance until she adjusts to being on her feet, what are the other things that I should be guarding against, and the other things I simply can't guard against? Only God knows, and we just have to trust Him.

We have another EXTREMELY TROUBLING problem! Since Courtney's platelet count was so low, she researched and found that production of red blood cells generally also means more production of platelets as well. So eating red meat is recommended, and that meant that our last trip to the grocery store ended with the acquisition of some small steaks that she is eating once a day. The problem? My doctor recently told me to watch my cholesterol, so I'm NOT eating steaks and she is.

We used to tell our kids that "nothing's fair" and intentionally dish out unequal servings of dessert, to resist a selfish entitlement mindset. I still believe that, but somehow this steak thing seems to be taking it too far! :)

Thank you for praying for us!
Justin

From our daughter Rosa
I feel like this is a case of reaping what you sow. No symphony.

"No symphony" was a Martin family joke for "no sympathy."

My response—
Rosa, you sound bitter! :p

From Lithuania
It isn't fair that Jesus took our sins on Himself, yet we can't complain about it!

Thank you for your encouragement in these updates, especially at the beginning. We should have been the ones encouraging, but it definitely seemed the other way around! That's not exactly fair, either!

From a pastor in North Carolina, USA
Don't you just love it when the lessons you tried to teach others come back to bite you?

You made me laugh this morning, and I truly appreciate that. You are both in my prayers.

From a pastor in central Scotland

I guess you could always be thankful that she isn't on a kimchi diet. If you have never smelled it, count your blessings!

15 September 2001 (Wednesday p.m.)

Dear All

Courtney had another fall today. It wasn't really a fall, more like her legs just slowly gave out from under her and she sank to the floor. No dizziness or loss of consciousness, just extreme leg weakness. Again, it was after getting out of the car. We're not so sure it is low blood pressure, we'll be talking to the doctor about it. It doesn't hinder Courtney at all once she's been on her feet for a few minutes.

Today we met a man (and his wife) who has just joined the same trial Courtney is on. His initial diagnosis was a year ago in June. He has 7 secondary tumors (8 total). This is much of the difficulty with this kind of cancer; it spreads in the brain. We are praying for them.

Courtney's platelet count is still a little below normal but more than 50% higher than it was 2 weeks ago! Those steaks must have helped! :) But really, we know Who is in control of this, a few small steaks could never have that much impact. We don't know why the Lord allowed the platelets to drop so low, but we are thankful that He's brought them back up.

Today, Courtney had her first MRI since she started on the clinical trial. We'll probably not have the results until Monday, which might give us our first hint as to how well this new medication is or isn't working.

Thank you for praying for us!
Justin

We were now stopping twice on the way to Denver so Courtney could walk to counteract the low blood pressure. I wasn't convinced it was just low blood pressure; something must have changed for low blood pressure to suddenly be such a problem. I was to regret that I didn't push harder.

In addition to the low blood pressure and other stuff, we had some "Oops, it's a brain tumor" moments. Often Courtney's memory was fine—we'd forget the memory blips—and then boom, something happened.

On Friday, after treatment, we stopped at Costco. Courtney went to the ladies' room while I bought some stuff. We were to meet at checkout. I finished the shopping, checked out, and waited. And waited. And waited some more.

My phone rang. Courtney was in tears, in the car, looking for me. She had forgotten the meeting plan, so she went to the car—but forgot where it was. She walked through the parking lot, pushing her key fob until she heard the car honking. Only when back in the car did she think to call me.

Courtney could still form a coherent plan—just not always the best one. She knew I would not leave without her; she could have called me, waited at checkout, waited near the door, or even gone to customer service for help. Any would have been better than wandering the parking lot—but she did wander with a workable plan, after all.

By now, I knew not to ask, "Why didn't you . . . ?" The answer? Her brain was damaged, and it wouldn't be kind to force her to say that. She knew her solution was flawed. It was just a mental block, one not helped by suggesting alternatives after the fact. Either she would have a mental block next time or she wouldn't. I gave her a hug, then held her hand and drove one-handed. I couldn't take the hurt away, but I could at least hold her hand.

Rarely did Courtney struggle with faith through these trials, but this one was very hard. A super-spiritual person might say, "Trust the Lord. Heaven is still there." I guess we weren't super-spiritual enough. God gave grace and peace, and we really believed Glory was still there and where we were headed. Even so, Courtney really struggled this time. She just didn't see why God could let her forget where we were supposed to meet.

When I think of this event now and how much it hurt her, it hurts me badly. At the time, I was okay. That was a special grace from the Lord. Courtney's only real fear was that I would not cope without her. If she had seen me hurting badly, it would have made that fear worse. God gave me a peace through these events that protected her. My pain would come later, but it would not grieve Courtney. That's one of the kindest gifts my Father ever gave me.

This, like some other painful things, didn't go in an email update. People didn't have to understand everything to pray for us.

I did email our pastor about it, and closed with this—
Not complaining. Every day is a gift. :) *See you Sunday, Lord willing.*

When things hurt, it helps to remember: every day is a gift.

Chapter 21

Infection!

As the weather cooled, Courtney often (even in the house) wore her yellow hat. A sweet neighbor had asked her favorite color and then knitted it for her. Courtney often felt cool, so the hat was a double blessing—it brought warmth, and the warmth of being loved.

We had a new researcher. Joy was still very much a part of our life, but now Felicia came into the picture. Both were such good friends to us and so helpful throughout.

Just before Felicia joined, I had a talk with Joy about her work. I thought it must be very satisfying to help find new treatments. She said it is, but many experimental medications don't work out. They spend so much time with volunteers, forming real friendships, and then the results are disappointing, or worse. Sometimes, her job is painful.

It is even harder with children. Courtney knew the research might not help her but might help others, and that was okay. Child volunteers often come when parents are desperate—and it's heartbreaking for researchers and parents when it doesn't work out. We were seeing firsthand how much we owe to those who work in the medical research and pharmaceutical fields.

We were growing quite fond of Pete, the other

patient with us in the trial, and his wife, Eve. It was sad that Pete and Courtney had glioblastomas, but if it had to be, it was good to go through it together. Pete's glioblastoma wasn't the same strain as Courtney's, so while we hoped the treatment would help her, we hoped he'd have an even better result.

In mid-September, I was spamming Felicia and Joy with emails, but I'll let the one to our distribution list tell the story.

20 September 2021 (Monday p.m.)

Dear All

Some eventful days but finishing with good news!

Friday and Saturday:

The weather has started to turn cooler, and attention turned to warmer clothes (especially since Courtney feels cold all the time now). Unfortunately, Courtney's healthy wardrobe of warmer clothes from Scotland doesn't fit anymore! Months of steroids and seizure medication will do that to you. So, we started buying a few of what Courtney calls SAD clothes. SAD for Steroid-Adjusted Dimensions, but also SAD because she likes her other clothes.

We also bought a few "compression" things because the doctor seemed quite sure that Courtney's problem with collapsing was due to circulation issues and/or low blood pressure.

Saturday Night:

Courtney slipped and dislocated her shoulder again. It popped back in quickly, but it was very sore, which meant a very badly disturbed night with little sleep.

Sunday Morning:

Courtney felt quite unwell and unsteady, partly from fatigue, partly from pain—and then, she collapsed again, and this time lost consciousness briefly. We're pretty sure this was fainting due to a combination of low blood pressure, fatigue, and pain.

Sunday Evening:

The shoulder pain began to improve, but it was still not a very good night's sleep for various reasons.

Monday Morning:

Courtney woke up with her shoulder feeling much, much better.

We got our scan results this morning and the tumor is stable with no measurable growth since the last scan a month ago! This tumor more than doubled in size in 4 weeks this summer.

Courtney's platelet count is up again, now well within the normal range!

Courtney got the treatment again today.

The doctor is pleased enough with the scan that he's reducing her steroids for a week, and all going well will reduce them again next week. All going well, the following week he'll stop them entirely! It's just possible Courtney can get by with just a few SAD clothes until some of her other stuff starts to fit again!

The doctor has prescribed more salt in Courtney's diet to try to get her blood pressure up some. I'm quite enjoying this, feeding her more and more salty stuff after years of her telling me I need to keep my salt intake moderated. Doctor's orders! :)

Monday Evening:
It was a long, long day in Denver, we were gone over 8 hours. So, early to bed tonight, but we're very thankful. An entire month without any tumor growth or any serious side effects from the new medication, when just a few weeks ago the tumor was exploding in size.

I know that some of you knew yesterday was a rough day, and you were praying for us. Others didn't know it was a rough day and were praying for us anyway. Isn't it great to know that God knows what someone needs when we pray for them, even if we don't know?

And have you ever noticed that sometimes God allows us to have a tough day just before we are getting good news? Perhaps we need to learn to love Him more for who He is, rather than just for what we get from Him!

Thank you for praying for us! Remember, every day is a gift. Today, we learned we've been given not a day but a whole month without tumor growth!

Justin

We had been getting ready for church when Courtney fainted. Thankfully, she was right next to the bed and just lay back on the bed so there was no injury. But it did mean she missed church for the first time since April. That was hard, but Monday was wonderful!

Our kids were all planning to come for Thanksgiving. I had never been sure Courtney would have Thanksgiving. Now that it appeared the treatment was at least helping some, Thanksgiving looked promising—but there were difficult days ahead.

25 September 2021 (Saturday p.m.)

Dear All

It's not been an easy week.

Courtney's shoulder pain eased pretty quickly, but she popped it out again on Wednesday. It popped right back in and wasn't sore for too long.

Fatigue has been a real problem.

The last couple days Courtney has been really struggling with nausea.

The low blood pressure is still giving Courtney a lot of difficulty.

Obviously we're extremely grateful for God's gift on Monday of a report of no growth in the tumor over the prior 4 weeks. We're even more grateful for His gift of eternal life to those who trust in Him. We're not complaining, we're grateful—but it's still been a hard week.

Blessings:

Courtney's sister Myra came down to see us today (she goes back tomorrow).

We've been able to get to know another couple in the same trial. Pete and his wife said I could give you his name and ask you to pray for them.

We met a really nice Christian lady getting treatment for another kind of cancer.

Despite having a really difficult week, Courtney has still been able to keep walking.

Some Specific Requests:

Please pray that we can be an encouragement and help to others who are receiving cancer treatment, and to those who are trying to help them.

Please pray that, as Jesus said, our light will so shine before men that they may glorify our Father in Heaven.

Please pray that harder circumstances will help the light to shine brighter.

Please pray that people will see clearly that it is not us, but Christ in us, that is shining.

In Him
Justin

From a former work colleague, Florida, USA
I have been praying for Courtney, you, and your family through all of your very trying times. Of course, the first part of my prayers has to do with Courtney's healing. The second part, which I now think perhaps has been placed in the wrong order, has had to do with your faithful witness to the Lord's working in your lives.

This friend was right, the second part was more important. It all mattered! We wanted Courtney to see her grandchildren grow up. Neither of us wanted me to be alone. But the second part was of eternal importance.

If that week was tough, the next was worse.

Late Thursday, I wrote to Felicia and Joy—
As I told you yesterday, I'm convinced something other than low BP is going on. I'm more convinced today. The weakness and unsteadiness is significantly more pronounced.

Her walking is the worst and the hardest since the days after her seizure in April.

I was really starting to suspect infection. We went in for treatment Friday as usual, but things were just getting worse.

2 October 2021 (Saturday p.m.)

Dear All

I'm sorry I haven't responded to many of your messages in the last week.

This week has been perhaps the most difficult since Courtney's first week home after her operation. Courtney has been dealing since Tuesday with extreme weakness, with her legs giving out at times. Instead of 10–12,000 steps, today she had less than 2,000, and this evening when we tried to walk around the block, she had to sit and wait while I got the car. Our neighbors have all been so supportive. One of them was out to check on Courtney almost immediately and was keeping an eye on her until I got back.

This is clearly not low blood pressure as we originally thought, though that might be contributing to the problems at times. It could be an infection, or a side effect of the anti-seizure medication, or something else. It could be a side effect of the experimental medication—one of the difficulties in a trial is not all of the side effects are necessarily known, nor is the optimal dose to maximize good effects and minimize negative side effects. No matter what they do to try to figure those things out, ultimately human volunteers will have to try it. Courtney has always wanted to help them learn how to better treat this cancer, so if we're helping them learn important things about this medicine, we're glad of that, even if it isn't very easy to go through.

Pray that in all things we will honor Christ—in the treatment, in our interactions with other patients, with our neighbors, with our church family. It's good for us to remember when suffering that Jesus didn't have to suffer, didn't deserve to suffer, and chose to suffer for us. No doubt, this week has been very hard—but we deserved far worse, eternal suffering. We have nothing of which to complain, and everything for which to be thankful.

We'd appreciate your continued prayers for Pete (the other patient we've met in this trial) and his wife.

Courtney's anti-seizure medication was reduced on Thursday, and the experimental medicine will likely be reduced Monday if there's not an improvement before then. Whether these will solve the problem or not, we have no way of knowing. We don't think it's tumor growth—this weakness was starting to show up before Courtney had her last scan, which showed no growth. But of course, we don't really know for sure.

The only One who really knows what's going on is also the One who can change it. We're content to be in His hands.

Thank you for loving us and praying for us.
Justin

My inbox filled again with encouraging and loving messages. Just one example:

From Scotland's Central Belt
"Underneath are the everlasting arms".

That night, I wrote to our pastor—
Hi, Pastor. You'll see from my update, Courtney's really

struggling. I don't know if she'll make it tomorrow. If she does, it will be with a cane or possibly even in a wheelchair.

I hate not being reliable. It's probably because my horrible pride kicks in, to be proud of being dependable. So, I'm guessing the Lord is taking that away from me, at least for a time.

It's funny how we never get completely cured of pride until we're in Heaven, when all the qualities of which we might be proud will be far better than they are here—and we won't be proud of them.

Instead of church, we ended up in the ER. They didn't think it was an infection, because her white blood cell count, though elevated, wasn't that high. Only the next morning did I think, *Her cancer meds affect white blood cells! It shouldn't be elevated at all!* One would expect the doctors to think of that.

5 October 2001 (Tuesday p.m.)

Dear All

Jesus said, "Let your light so shine before men, that they may see your good works, and glorify your Father which is in heaven." I think sometimes our Father does let our circumstances grow dark just so the light can shine more clearly, but His love is always there. And we certainly learn a lot more about loving and being loved in those darker circumstances.

But our circumstances look brighter today than they did over the weekend. Sunday morning, in a phone call with a cancer nurse, I was told to take Courtney to the Emergency Room to be checked for an infection. So off we went to the hospital, where we were told there was no clear evidence of an infection, and back home we came, for Courtney to spend the day in bed, since she was too weak to do anything else.

Monday, we went to Denver and saw our doctor there, and he diagnosed Courtney as indeed having an infection. He wasn't entirely complimentary about the ER doctor . . . :) Nevertheless, I'm sure the Lord has His reasons for the ER doctor not picking up on it. It's one of those things where you might ask, "Why, Lord?" Maybe someday you'll find out, but maybe not, and we don't have to. Would we do anything differently if we knew why? Or should we just do right anyway, whether we know why or not? The answer is obvious—we should do right anyway.

There are some very strict ethical standards around clinical trials, and though Courtney would have chosen to proceed with the cancer treatment, the doctor can't do that until she is stronger. So, she's on antibiotics since yesterday, and this afternoon started to improve. This evening, we walked around the block again. But there won't be treatment tomorrow either, and Friday is unlikely—it depends on how quickly Courtney regains strength.

We'd obviously love for her to be able to get back to the cancer treatment. It seems to be working! So, it's disappointing to miss it. But Courtney isn't the first to have an infection while using this medicine, so it appears to be a side effect that will appear on warning leaflets in the future. Maybe one day one of you will use this drug and will read about infections and remember this! One of our prayers is that Courtney would help them learn more about this medicine, and that seems to have happened. We don't want her to experience every possible side effect, however! :)

Courtney's next MRI is Monday, so it won't be

that long before we get a further update on how the tumor is responding to the treatment. We have to be there at 7:30 a.m., which would mean leaving home at 6, so I was thinking about getting a hotel up there for the night.

A Christian brother in our church phoned me today. He told me to book the hotel, and also do it for any other nights where it makes things easier for us. Effectively, he said to spend money on anything that makes things easier for us, and he'll pay. Such a blessing—though I'm not even surprised by this kind of thing anymore. God uses dark circumstances to let others shine their light, too, and puts within the hearts of His people a desire to love and to shine.

This kind of thing, in big and small ways, has happened over and over again in the past year. I'm now convinced that part of the reason for Courtney's cancer is to give a lot of people a chance to exercise their Christian love. There's no way I could even think to list them all.

Blessings to you all and thank you for praying for us!
Justin

Dr. Diamond's view of the ER doctor was not an elevated one. Courtney should have been on antibiotics a day and a half earlier. Did the delay make a difference? There is no way to know. Did the infection contribute to the blood pressure problems? Again, I don't know.

I do know the blood pressure problems kicked up shortly before the infection became obvious and went away not long after it cleared. Maybe there was no connection. Looking back, I could have insisted earlier that something was wrong—but real life doesn't give look-backs. We do our best at the time and trust the Lord despite our imperfect knowledge and actions.

Maybe our Lord allowed the infection to motivate people to love us more, as I said in that email. Infection is a temporary-in-this-life problem, but love is eternal. Maybe in giving us love, people developed habits of love-giving that would touch many more lives. Maybe someone (who loved us) went on, through love, to win someone to the Lord, and we'll meet them in heaven! We can only speculate how God works, but I am pretty sure that heaven has lots of wonderful surprises! We know of God's Grace now—but not like we will know it when we get to Glory.

Chapter 22

The Mountains Were Still There

♪

Mom's burial and memorial service was 9 October in South Carolina. Several of our kids went, so we were well represented, but Courtney and I clearly could not go. It was harder than I expected, and we cried afterward. It was the first time I'd let her see me cry since December, and the last time I let it happen. She was hurting and knew I was, but God gave me grace to be strong for her.

It was also a tough phase in other ways. Courtney was still very weak and had collapsed again on Thursday. We were using a wheelchair to go anywhere, though she could still walk around the house (with help). She'd had no treatment all week, so it was likely the tumor had grown. That evening, she had another collapse.

> 9 October 2021 (Saturday p.m.)
>
> Dear All
>
> Brief tonight. Courtney had much trouble with this infection, but it seems to have cleared. She is very, very weak, and collapsed Thursday, and again this evening, with a sore elbow as a result.
>
> If possible, we'll go to church tomorrow, but will probably be using a wheelchair if so. Tomorrow later

we'll drive to Denver. Courtney's next MRI is early Monday.

Please pray for a recovery of strength and stamina. It is a little better, Courtney has consistently been able to get out of bed, and into bed, on her own the last couple days, which is an improvement, but the strength doesn't last long. Please pray for sleep for both of us, the last two weeks have been rough.

Courtney asked me how God's strength is being made perfect in her weakness. I told her it's motivating others to love us and giving them opportunities to do so.

Thank you for praying!
Justin

Courtney was so tired of being confined to the house, so we walked one hundred yards up the street, then she sat and I wheeled her back. Struggling up the street, she asked that question about God's strength and her weakness. My answer struck a chord with many people. Perhaps God's strength was using our weakness in other ways in other lives, too.

We did make it to church. The "parking lot guys" helped Courtney out of the car, and I wheeled her in while one of them parked our car. The ushers cleared room for the wheelchair and kept a seat next to it for me. After the service, our car met us at the door, and off we went. They always took such good care of us.

Courtney had always been impressed by our pastor's wife. Confined to a wheelchair for years after a car accident, she was always competent, cheerful, and committed. Now Courtney, needing a wheelchair, said, "She makes it look so easy!" She felt inadequate by comparison, but it helped so much to see someone else honoring the Lord through years of difficulty. This lady was another gift of God's grace to us.

12 October 2021 (Tuesday a.m.)

Dear All

Mostly good news today. Courtney is still very weak, and we mostly use a wheelchair when we go anywhere. But each day she's done something more that she wasn't doing a week ago, so we're moving in the right direction. Other than the weakness, all signs of the infection are gone, for which we are very thankful.

Courtney was able to have the cancer treatment yesterday and is scheduled to go ahead tomorrow and on Friday as well. She had her MRI yesterday morning, and we get the results of that next Monday.

Yesterday was an extremely long and tiring day. We didn't get home until after 6 p.m. Fortunately, there was about a 2½ hour gap in the day, and the researcher had told me to get a late checkout from our hotel, so that Courtney could go back and rest during that time. They really do try to take care of us. I can't imagine what the day would have been like if we'd had to leave Colorado Springs at 6 a.m. and hadn't had that available to us.

It's funny, in a "God is so good" kind of way, that I'd previously never considered getting a hotel for one of our days up there, and this day was so much more important than any of the others for that to happen. We have an early start next Monday as well, so will be spending Sunday night up there again. We're very thankful for God's provision.

Pete (the other patient in the trial) got his first MRI results back—no significant growth in the first month. His wife called it "the best possible news." For patients with recurrent glioblastoma, even slow growth is almost a miracle. Some of Pete's symptoms have improved as well. They are very thankful, and they do appreciate your prayers.

Our daughter Rosa is in for a quick visit this weekend from Virginia, and Courtney's sister Myra is coming down from the Denver area as well.

And this is kind of fun. My company had a user event scheduled at the Broadmoor, a local luxury resort. Due to COVID it was canceled, but they wouldn't refund the rooms, so they had to be used. We have two nights at the Broadmoor this week. I hope no one discovers that we aren't really quite posh enough for such a place. I suppose I should be on my best behavior—but will my best be good enough? :)

Heaven's better than the Broadmoor, by the way. And my best will never be good enough for Heaven. And it doesn't have to be, because Someone paid the price to get me there, and my best doesn't matter. Since Jesus paid the price, I can't get kicked out of Heaven for not being good enough. And anyway, He'll make me good enough to be fit for Heaven.

Courtney will probably make me behave well enough for the Broadmoor, too, but that will just be external. Inside, I'll still be the same troublemaker I've always been. But the Lord cleans us up from the inside out!

If I don't see you at the Broadmoor, or even if I do, I hope to see you in Heaven! No excuses, it's been paid for!

Thank you for praying for us!
Justin

Joy's late checkout suggestion was brilliant! She seemed to think of everything. She was tough on me, though, if I forgot the Peanut M&Ms! They *had* to be in Courtney's lunch when we went for treatment. If I forgot them, Courtney, Joy, and Felicia ganged up on me and made me go for my emergency stash in the car. If I wasn't quick, I'd catch it when I got back, too. Pre-tumor, Courtney didn't like chocolate (and still mostly avoided it), but now Peanut M&Ms just had to be.

We didn't always see Joy. Felicia was our usual babysitter now, ensuring we were well cared for and behaving ourselves, but Joy popped by Wednesday. She said, in very general terms, that sometimes an MRI would show minor growth that might not mean much. It might just be the way a different technician read the MRI or maybe even "false progression."

I already suspected the tumor was growing again, if slowly, but Joy set my radar pinging. If she knew what the MRI showed, she wouldn't have admitted it, but I suspected she was preparing us so we wouldn't despair.

Of course, despair wasn't in our picture. If Courtney went to heaven earlier than we hoped, it would be better for her, and the Lord would make sure I was okay. There would be no despair. Sadness, yes, but despair? "This world is not our home, we're just a-passing through."

After Wednesday's treatment, we headed for the Broadmoor. We did have fun. We were told there was one free suite upgrade, and we'd "won the lottery." I was suspicious that some kind person had upgraded us or someone had skewed that lottery on our behalf. So many people were doing things for us.

It didn't matter. Whether it was because God directed a "lottery" our way or touched a kind heart to give us something, ultimately it came from Him. If someone should be rewarded, He would take care of it. Our Father wanted us to enjoy it, and we did.

Before going, I was asked if Courtney needed anything or if there was anything she would like waiting when we arrived. I mentioned fresh fruit, and also as an afterthought her craving for Peanut M&Ms. The Broadmoor does really nice fruit salads. And a huge jar of M&Ms was just waiting for someone to gorge herself!

We had a tower suite with a lovely view. We enjoyed walking through the hotel, over the bridge, around the lake, and through the buildings. It was cold, but you could always find a fire and rest. Mostly we used the wheelchair, but Courtney did walk a little. She really enjoyed the paintings and the pictures of famous visitors to the Broadmoor. They never took Courtney's picture to add to the collection, which was their loss—none of those famous celebrities could hold a candle to her.

Even there, the tumor was with us. The first morning at breakfast, a fellow employee of mine, originally from the country where Eric lives, stopped by our table. Courtney had always wanted to meet him—but when the chance came, the tumor had her in a "fixation" moment and she was locked in on something else. I couldn't break through, and then the chance was gone, and she never met him.

18 October 2021 (Monday p.m.)

Dear All

Driving back from Denver today, Courtney said, "It's at times like these that you need to focus on God's love." It was another long and hard day. We got Courtney's MRI results today and they were not as we had hoped. They showed 22% progression of the tumor since August.

That's significantly better than the 150% progression in 4 weeks that we saw in July and August, and it's significantly better than glioblastoma patients usually see once the tumor starts growing again. So, the experimental medicine seems to be working somewhat. But it's not as good as hoped, based on earlier studies.

The doctor did say that it's possible that some or all of this growth is what's known as "false progression" in a delayed reaction to the radiation in August. But he definitely thinks there is some real growth happening.

Other Things:
Courtney may be having a recurrence of her infection.

Her platelet count was pretty low again today. We now know that other patients have had low platelet counts. One of the goals of the study was to identify side effects, so it appears we've helped accomplish that.

We've known all along that Courtney's tumor is just about the worst kind of glioblastoma. So it's not surprising that its growth is faster than the medicines can stop.

The doctor hopes to add another medicine to the mix. It may or may not slow the tumor further, but it should reduce swelling in the brain and help with other symptoms. It's known as primarily a quality-of-life medicine rather than an extending-life medicine, but he hopes that it might also make the other medicines more effective. We don't know if this will be possible, but we should know this week.

We know that many of you have been asking the Lord to extend Courtney's life, and even to heal her. We would never rule out miracles, but it seems we are in miracle-only territory for those things. We do hope to stay in the clinical trial for as long as we can, but that may also have a limited time frame. These things are totally in God's hands, and we're at peace with that. What He gives, we'll accept gratefully.

As we drove back today, I looked at Colorado's awesome mountains, and told Courtney, "It's nice to think that, when we're both dead and buried, those mountains will still be there testifying to the greatness of our God."

Thank you for praying for us.
Justin

For me, 22 percent growth (rather than 100 to 150 percent) meant we'd have Thanksgiving (with all six kids one more time) and almost certainly Christmas. Since the last Christmas had been in doubt, to have another was good news—even if not as good as we'd hoped.

Dr. Diamond had hoped this treatment would give us a year—and perhaps bridge to another treatment. Now, he had to admit that was unlikely. That's hard for a doctor to say. I felt for him and said this news must not be pleasant to give. I thanked him for being straight with us. No one in the room was happy, but we hadn't forgotten all God had given us and tried to make it as easy as we could for the doctor, Joy, and Felicia.

We had a peaceful drive home. Courtney often slept on the drive, but not this time. The mountains really were a comfort. They also shall pass away, but they've outlasted many lives of men and women on this earth. The God who made those mountains has lasted and will last far longer, and He's the Guarantor of our home in Heaven.

Back in Colorado Springs, we suspected Courtney's infection was recurring and went to our local clinic. We were to see his colleague, but our own doctor (always so kind and praying for us) came in. He had been given the wrong room! Courtney started crying and told him the tumor was growing. We only had a moment, but I think she needed to tell someone she knew would care, and I think God arranged an "accidental" mix-up of room numbers for that.

The tests didn't show infection, but the doctor ordered a full culture (which would take five days) to be sure. He didn't think it was anything, but we were pretty sure we were dealing with both a moderately growing glioblastoma and a recurring infection.

That was tough, after hopes the treatment would stop the cancer for a while. It meant time was getting short and would probably be marred by infection. That day, Courtney began seriously planning her funeral, especially the music. The Morning Playlist soon had several additions. Courtney's favorite hymn "Wake, Awake, for Night Is Flying" made the list, her beloved "Ashokan Farewell," and John Rutter's beautiful "For the Beauty of the Earth." She wanted this funeral to honor God with beautiful music.

Courtney was excited about how God might use her funeral. It was so strange to be talking about that and not be devastated by it, but that's the peace God gives. It wasn't easy, of course. But if the heavens declare the Glory of God, so also do the mountains. The mountains and sky were still there—and so was the God of Grace.

Chapter 23

A Bad Fall!

20 October 2021 (Wednesday p.m.)

Dear All

Courtney just had another fall. She's banged her elbow and her head, both are sore. (Likely a low blood pressure faint.)

The research sponsors are doing another MRI to get a better read on what's really happening re: real growth or "false progression." This may be as soon as Friday but within a week at the most.

Today we reported what the researchers call "an adverse event" yesterday and mentioned that we could see how the Lord had used it for good. The person to whom we were speaking commented on our attitude, and it gave us opportunity to speak of the Lord's goodness again. We're so blessed to have a sure hope in a risen Savior! That makes it so much easier to have a "different" attitude from so many others.

In the "this was fun" category. One of the nurses at the hospital is a very kind person, but also extremely energetic. He's always laughing and talking with the patients, etc. On Monday, he was much quieter, and as we were leaving, Courtney said, "He is quiet today. It's like Tigger got unbounced." So, I stuck my head back around the corner and told him what she said and asked if he was ok. All his colleagues loved it! He promised to be more bouncy when we came back. So today, he literally bounced into the room where we were to say hi! :)

Thank you for praying for us!
Justin

We were in the living room. Courtney was on her computer, ordering a stuffed Tigger for our bouncy nurse! I was working, locked in, concentrating, and didn't notice her get up. Suddenly, I heard a loud thump, looked up, and didn't see her. I called, "Are you okay?" and got no answer as I rushed to find her. She had gone for a snack and fainted. Falling on her back, her head missed a bench by inches and it landed on a rug, which helped, but it was a very hard fall. By the time I reached her, she was starting to come around.

I got the wheelchair and helped her into it. She wanted to lie down, so I wheeled her in to bed and moved my work into the bedroom. Other than sore ribs, a sore elbow, and a headache, she seemed okay, so I didn't make much of it when I sent the email above.

I wrote to Felicia and Joy—
I haven't been working in the bedroom but now it is "not out of my sight" mode. If she starts to get up unassisted, I can rebuke her sternly and have her laugh at me for my pains!

Only later did we learn that her left leg wasn't responding normally. She could put it on the floor but couldn't lift it. Her left hand was misbehaving too, with a strong gripping reflex. If she handed something to me, she couldn't seem to let go.

A cognitive effect I had seen developing also worsened after the fall. Courtney wasn't stringing requests together. She might ask for four things, but it wasn't, "Can you get me A, B, C, and D?" Even things that normally come together might be several minutes apart—and at night, too. Sometime after midnight she asked for an extra pillow, and a couple minutes later some water. After I got back to bed, it was the heating pad for her ribs, then Tylenol, and finally a snack. As I was dropping off, she asked me to get rid of the extra pillow.

I was very tired, and realizing I was about to get even more tired. Still, I did not say, "You just asked for that extra pillow." What's the point of telling a brain tumor patient, "Try to remember," or, "Try to think of what else you might want"?

Courtney so hated to be a burden that I was determined not to make her feel like one. My go-to response to "I'm such a burden" was "You're worth it!" To deny it would have been pointless—she knew the truth, and it would have only made her feel worse. "You're worth it" was far better; it made her feel loved. I think many times I didn't say the best thing, but I got this one right!

We were both trying to be patient. I was too slow to respond at times, not strong enough for some needs, and I made mistakes and forgot things. My innate selfishness kicked in at times. Courtney had limitations she'd never had before and didn't always respond well. She tolerated my inadequacies and failures, and I put up with hers.

The next morning, I decided to get Courtney

checked. Her "gripping" reflex on the left side was stronger, her headache bad, her neck and ribs sore, and she could only walk if I half carried her—not a great thing with sore ribs. We went to Denver; they had her scans and would communicate better with Dr. Diamond than the local hospital would.

Reporting to Felicia and Joy, I wrote from the ER—
This left-side thing is weird. When asked to put her hands out, only one of them moves. When asked to move the left one specifically, she'll do it. Same with the foot.

Three times, the resident asked her to hold or squeeze her hand, and Courtney did just fine, but when she asked her to let go, she just didn't let go. I've been pulling stuff out of her hand all day. :) *"Would you please let go of that?"*

The scans showed no brain changes and nothing broken. It was a long day. They were very thorough and talked frequently with Dr. Diamond, who stayed on top of it even on his day off. Maybe clinical trial volunteers get special treatment or maybe they were told she was royalty in disguise, but in any event, we got great care. Finally, after a strong painkiller they let us go.

We had cancer treatment again in the morning, so we got a hotel. The next day, we had treatment, more painkiller, and went home.

Later, I wrote again to Joy and Felicia—
Her walking still isn't good, but it's better. She figured out the left foot problem. She has to "let go of the floor" and then she can move it. Something is triggering a "hold on and don't let go" reflex in both hand and foot, apparently. When she consciously tells her foot to let go of the floor, she is better able to walk.

23 October 2021 (Saturday p.m.)

Dear All

Courtney's faint on Wednesday ended up with us in the Emergency Room all day on Thursday, until 8 p.m. We went to Denver because they have all her records and scans up there.

The problems were pain in various places including her neck, bad headaches, and significant loss of use of her left leg. Everything checked ok on all the scans and x-rays and they gave her pain medication. Since we didn't get away until late and had to return in the morning, we stayed in a hotel. What a blessing to not have to be concerned about the cost!

The chest x-ray did show a little bit of non-infected fluid in her lungs, which is of some concern.

Yesterday, Courtney had her cancer treatment as normal in the morning, and some more painkiller. While there, we met another patient and had a wonderful opportunity to talk to him briefly about God's ultimate love in sending His Son to die for us.

The additional MRI to try to identify false progression was not needed after all. We still don't know what they are going to decide but at least we don't need another MRI.

By yesterday evening, Courtney was losing some function in her right leg as well. However, this improved through the night (though we didn't really get any sleep all night).

The right leg is definitely improved today, and the left leg seems to be regaining a little functionality as well. Courtney still can't walk without significant help.

We're using the wheelchair to go anywhere, and some around the house as well. I told a neighbor this and she is going to try to organize some of the men in the neighborhood to build us a ramp at the front of the house. So many people have been so kind to us.

We are very, very tired but thankful for God's goodness to us. Courtney's fall was a bad one and it's definitely causing some problems, but she was within a couple inches of hitting her head on some metal furniture.

Thank you for praying for us!
Justin

On Friday, Bill (another patient) watched me get Courtney her lunch, help her into her wheelchair, wheel her to the bathroom, back out, help her into a recliner, and adjust her pillow and blankets. After treatment, I got her coat on and knelt to put on her boots before leaving. He called me over and said, "What I just watched was the ultimate in love."

He was mistaken, for our love was mutual. The ultimate love is one-sided, when one loves having received nothing. That's what God gave when Jesus died for me, and if there was anything special in my love for Courtney, I'd learned it from Him. I was thankful for the chance to talk about it with Bill.

My sister Kate arrived. It wasn't the pleasant visit she and Courtney had planned, but what a help! Courtney's pain was debilitating. She wasn't sleeping, and it was such a difficult time. Extra help from someone Courtney loved and trusted meant I was sent to the basement a couple nights to actually sleep. (I didn't sleep well, but much better than if I'd been caring for Courtney.)

Late Saturday night, there was another twist. I

checked my email and learned that the lab culture from earlier in the week had come back with bad news.

> 25 October 2021 (Monday a.m.)
>
> Dear All
>
> Late Saturday night we learned that Courtney is struggling with two nasty antibiotic-resistant infections. Her new antibiotic was tested against the bacteria in the lab and should work. Her cancer treatment can't go ahead until these are cleared, which is obviously far from ideal, since it was at least slowing down the tumor growth.
>
> We are thankful to finally get a good diagnosis, and hopeful that dealing with these infections will make a big difference to how Courtney feels, as well as getting her back into cancer treatment quickly. Courtney does seem to be getting a little more comfortable and slept a little better last night.
>
> I've heard from Pete, the other patient we've met who is on the clinical trial. He's been feeling quite good and some of his symptoms have reduced since starting. It's very encouraging to know that the medication seems to really be helping him! He and his wife are very grateful to all who have prayed for them.
>
> Thank you for your prayers!
> Justin

The tumor was growing; the treatment that seemed to help was stopped again by infections (two this time); Courtney could barely walk; and she had sore ribs, back, neck, shoulder, and legs from a bad fall.

But determined as ever, Courtney did make

church that Sunday! She might have a gripping reflex that wouldn't let go, but she was also clinging to her commitment to honor the Lord. We got up early to get ready, used the wheelchair to get her to the car, and headed for church.

The "parking lot guys" cleared the closest handicapped spot for us and helped get Courtney into her wheelchair. (This was so difficult one man told me later he thought it would be her last time at church.) The ushers took care of us, and God's people loved us. I sat close to the wheelchair, and she rested her head on my shoulder and slept for part of the service, but if anyone noticed, I'm sure they didn't care.

Monday, after a discussion with our local doctor, Courtney went for an IV antibiotic to try to clear the infections quickly so cancer treatment could restart. After the IV she also got another painkiller, which helped her sleep a little better that night.

On Thursday, Courtney started on oxycodone to control pain and help her sleep. It was not a happy choice. It made her sleep but she was still in pain, and it made her so sick she couldn't even keep water down. For two days she was sick to her stomach, unable to stay awake or talk much, and now her right leg stopped working. When helped to her feet, she could stand momentarily, but she couldn't get either leg to move to take a step.

29 October 2021 (Friday p.m.)

Dear All

Courtney's infections seem to have cleared, for which we are very thankful.

She is still in A LOT of pain since her fall last week, bruises, sore joints and muscles, etc.

She had barely slept at night since the fall. Yesterday she had a painkiller which made her sleep—probably 24 of 30 hours since her first dose. Unfortunately, side effects hit her hard so she's had to stop it, but it still seems to have broken the no-sleep cycle. The pain is still very much with her.

She's been unable to walk by herself since the fall, and not at all since she started the new painkiller. We're hopeful this will improve once it is out of her system.

There's been no cancer treatment this week. As far as human knowledge goes (unless God has chosen to directly intervene) the tumor is probably growing.

The wheelchair ramp idea won't work because our house is on too steep of a hill at the front, so I'm having a chairlift installed in the garage early next week.

My sister Kate has been here all week, which has been a huge help and blessing. She leaves Sunday morning.

Pete is still doing well, in fact, his symptoms are improving, which suggests the treatment may work better on his kind of glioblastoma than on Courtney's.

We're very tired, and Courtney's feeling miserable. There's no point in sugar-coating that. As I often used to say in preaching, Christianity isn't for wimps and faith isn't stupid. We don't expect times to always be good, and we don't pretend that they are. Our God gives strength and peace for the tough times, He makes us strong when others would crumble. It's not us, it's Him, which is why it works. If it were us being strong, we'd be in trouble in the times when we're weak and it's too hard for us. Because it is His strength and peace, we're ok even when it's too hard for us.

I'm not sure "early to bed, early to rise" will make this man healthy, wealthy, and wise, but if I don't do it, I'll pay for it, so I'll close. Thank you for all your prayers and encouragements. I've fallen horribly behind on answering which I greatly regret, but we read everything you send us.

God's blessings to you all.
Justin

From a former member of our church in Scotland
My dear big brother and sister! You don't have to feel "horribly behind" with replies. Please don't feel the burden to do so with me/us. I know you; you're my big brother in Christ and you've a lot to deal with just now.

I just want you to know that as I read your updates, I feel and I pray, and our God is more interested in you (and each one of us) than any of us are. He knows the thoughts He has for you.

From Bangladesh
Justin and Courtney, you are in our hearts and prayers. I'm sorry for the painful journey you are on, but the path of Jesus is so full of light and life! May the beauty of Christ be a present reality in the midst of the pain.

From a new work colleague I'd never met personally
Still praying for you diligently. May Christ Himself be your peace.

By Sunday, Courtney could again eat and drink but still couldn't use her legs. Kate asked if she should stay, but I (fool that I am) said I would be okay with Alyssa's help, so she flew home. Within two days things would turn upside down again and she'd be coming to our rescue!

We didn't make church; it just wasn't possible. Someone at church told Alyssa, "If *they* aren't going to make it, it *must* be bad." We hoped to motivate others to be more faithful! Church attendance is only one way to honor the Lord, but it's an important one. It says to others, "We are committed to the Lord and to you; be committed with us!" But we closed October watching online rather than attending in person.

Courtney said maybe we could try to go that evening instead. I knew we wouldn't. I watched while she slept through most of the morning service. I wondered if she'd make church again. I didn't think the cancer would stop her, but I wondered if the infections, the fall, the pain, and the oxycodone reaction had permanently taken her mobility. I also wondered what else could go wrong—a dangerous thing to wonder!

Chapter 24

This Was Good, Too

Courtney was totally wheelchair bound, still reacting to medication, virtually incapacitated. She couldn't even roll over in bed by herself, and if she tried to stand, she would fall. She couldn't possibly go to church.

It was 31 October, Halloween. Some Halloween celebrations treat evil as a joke or a myth, as fun rather than bad, so we always opted out—but this year would be different.

The neighbor kids knew about Courtney's cancer. Always so kind and sweet to us, they loved to see her and would be so disappointed if we didn't answer our door. Sometimes, love has to win, and you do things for love's sake that you might not normally do. We decided to have sweets for our sweet friends. Since we couldn't go to church, that clinched it. We could listen online and still answer the door.

I wheeled Courtney to the door, with extra blankets to help with the cold, to see her little friends as they came. By the time they stopped coming, she was exhausted and went to bed. I started feeling unwell (despite no candy!) and went to bed too.

The nausea was so bad I couldn't hold still. Around 2:00 a.m., Courtney said, "*Please* lie still!" I felt horrible keeping her awake, but I dared not leave the room, lest she get up and fall. I got up so my tossing wouldn't shake the bed and lay on the floor beside it. Then, if she tried to get up, she'd step on me and wake me so I could help her. It was a pointless precaution—I slept not at all.

Later, when the pain started, *it was real*—within minutes, I was in tears. By God's grace, a friend was there when it hit, so he took me to the hospital. Alyssa stayed with Courtney.

Sent by Rosa to our list

1 November 2021 (Monday p.m.)

Dear All

My dad decided that my mom was having too much fun with the medical field or something, and so he joined in for himself today with a trip to the ER for appendicitis. I told him that they've reached the point that kids are taking over and making decisions, and that unless he objected, that included taking over sending an email update. He did not object. So, after many years as the pastor's daughter, this is finally my opportunity to speak on his behalf about him to a very large group of people. I'll be nice. This time. *evil grin*

1. My dad is having surgery this evening to remove his appendix. He's on lifting restrictions for ten days post-op. He told us that he's been instructed to pass on that he's not allowed additional pain meds if he can't form a complete sentence. Based on the texts I was getting, I'd have been cutting him off, but I guess they're nicer than I am in the hospital. Prayers for a smooth, uncomplicated recovery would be appreciated.

2. With my dad on lifting restrictions/recovering from surgery, additional hands are needed to help out. I'm flying out to Colorado tomorrow on a one-way ticket and will be staying as long as needed. My dad's sister is also flying back out to help with getting some longer-term care solutions in place. Multiple other family members are on standby if we end up needing more help.

3. Alyssa and Robert, as the family members already there, are picking up a lot of extra stuff over the next 24 hours with making sure everyone gets to where they're needed. Alyssa is also taking over making sure that my mom is cared for at the moment until reinforcements arrive.

There are a lot of moving parts right now and a lot of things to figure out. We appreciate your prayers for wisdom, and that none of the spinning plates will be dropped as we transition who is responsible for what from my dad to other people.

My dad has often sent out a section of a hymn with his updates. "The Promise of God" by Mary Rose Jensen (https://gardenrosemusic.com) has been a family favorite for many years. The second verse seems especially fitting right now:

> The promise of God is that He will not leave us.
> The promise of God is that He never sleeps.
> As He cares for His own, giving life in abundance,
> Our God will supply all our needs.
>
> [Words and Music: Mary Rose Jensen, b. 1958
> © Garden Rose Music, http://gardenrosemusic.
> com. CCLI#3423291 Used by kind permission.]

Through changes and uncertainties and new types of needs, our Father has promised that He will not leave us, and that He will supply all our needs.

Thank you, as always, for your prayers.
Rosa for the Martins

I sat in the ER for hours. While waiting, I called our pastor—help was needed desperately. Courtney needed help with everything, and Alyssa was not strong enough for all of it. I was sure it was my appendix, and that I would be incapacitated for a while.

I was in too much pain to want to correct errors in texts and thought they would give the kids a laugh. I could have fixed them if I wanted to. That's my story, and I'm sticking with it!

Finally, they did a scan, and things started to happen—fast! Quickly I was on an IV with heavy antibiotics and painkillers, and I felt well enough for dumb jokes with the nurses.

"Who is at home to take care of you?"

"My wife with a glioblastoma who can't get out of bed without falling, and my daughter who isn't strong enough to lift either of us. But she can drug me, so I won't cause trouble if you send home some good stuff."

I did tell them we had help from our church, and that God was in control. When you know God is in control, you can afford to laugh in the face of an appendectomy. It may seem strange to others, but it's a good kind of "strange."

Mainly, I was concerned about Courtney. I kept thinking, *Poor Courtney, when she finds out what this is, she will feel terrible about grumbling in the night, and about me sleeping on the floor.* As it turned out, she never mentioned it to me. I think God graciously gave her forgetfulness—she didn't need that burden.

> From Rosa again
>
> 1 November 2021 (Same day, very late)
>
> My dad is through a successful surgery, down an appendix. He's complaining that a bossy nurse denied him cheeseburgers and is threatening to spend my future inheritance on Skittles as payback for my snarky comments (when he says he's feeling pretty dopey, that means he's back to normal, right?), so I think he's doing OK for now. They're still hoping to get him home late tonight.

My doctor wouldn't like the Skittles plan. I have decided instead to live so long that Rosa will be too old to enjoy any inheritance I leave. They say revenge is best served cold!

I did get home later that night, but the "fun" was not done yet.

> 2 November 2021 (Tuesday p.m.)
>
> Dear All
>
> Yesterday I tried an alternative method to weight loss. It's not recommended. :)
>
> What a series of events! I had an unsettled stomach all night and barely slept, but no pain until yesterday morning. When it came, it really came. By God's grace, someone was here, so Alyssa could stay with Courtney. He took me to the Emergency Room, and we called Robert to come help here. It took them a while to

confirm what I pretty much knew from the beginning, but once they saw my appendix on the scan they began to move pretty quickly. I told the surgeon to take out all the bad bits and leave the good bits. She did that quickly enough that they could send me home late last night, with a whopping dose of painkillers.

By the time I got home, one of the ladies from our church was here to help with Courtney through the night, and I was ordered off to bed in the basement. I awoke sometime around 2:30 a.m. to a thump on the floor above me. A little later, there was the sound of voices, including men, so I dragged myself up the stairs, expecting to find that Courtney had fallen and the ambulance had come to take her to the hospital. I was partly right. It was Martha, the lady from church. Unfortunately, last I heard she is still in the hospital. Please pray for her!

Another lady from church came this morning. As we were working out how to get up to Courtney's doctor appointment today, we learned that the doctor's father was taken to the ER last night so the doctor was leaving early—so Courtney didn't have an appointment with him after all.

As Far as I Know Right Now:
Martha is still in the hospital. The doctor's father is probably still in the hospital.

I am on hefty painkillers which give me an excuse for anything incoherent in this email, if I don't fall asleep before it is done. The painkillers are good, but their effect is currently not lasting to the next dose, so I'm alternating between very dopey and very sore. I am not to do any lifting for six weeks which means I can't really help Courtney with anything.

Courtney is still struggling with a lot of pain from bumps and bruises from her fall, still not able to get to her feet or even to roll over in bed. We still haven't exactly figured out how to control her pain. The medication she was given last week was effective on her pain but had some very bad side effects, such that the nurse said it was probably an allergic reaction.

All that said, we are getting loads of help. My sister Kate, who just left on Sunday after a week, came back and arrived this afternoon. Our daughter Rosa arrives tonight, and thinks because she's got a Doctor of Physical Therapy that she's going to boss us around. Ha! To paraphrase a Scripture, a PT is not without honor except in her own family! :) Courtney's sister Lynn is driving from Eastern Washington and hopefully arrives tomorrow night. She also has some experience as a nursing aid. Eric arrives Thursday from Eastern Europe.

The lady from church spent all day here today. Our pastor brought lunch and someone else in the church brought dinner. People have picked up stuff from the store for us. People from the church are picking up Rosa tonight and Eric on Thursday from Denver airport. There's probably other stuff people have done for us that I'm forgetting but I'll blame the painkillers for that.

Courtney finally restarts cancer treatment tomorrow. I think Rosa and Alyssa will take her. It will be a long, long day for her, she'll be receiving the experimental treatment plus the other medication I've mentioned previously. The result is that she'll be on three medications for cancer. The three together has not been tried before. The doctor is hoping that synergy between the three will peg back even a cancer as fast-growing as Courtney's. We're very much on the front edge of science on this one, with all the risks that come with that as well. We're at peace with it.

I expect there's other stuff I should be mentioning but everything has happened so fast. I'll be getting another painkiller soon and then it will be quickly to bed before my brain turns to mush.

So, I'll close with this. Sunday, Courtney wasn't well enough to go to church, so we listened online. But one of the things about church is being there to encourage others, which we couldn't do. But what I did do afterward is write. Courtney has always liked the tune "Ashokan Farewell" and says that it says, "God sent His only Son to die for our salvation." She's wanted me to write the rest of it for a while.

So, since we couldn't be at church to encourage others, I wrote this. I reserve the right to tweak the wording here or there, but here is its current form. Maybe it will encourage you. I called it "Glory's Path."

Glory's Path

God sent His only Son to die for our salvation,
The heavens were opened, God spoke from above.
His well-beloved Son came to make a new creation,
A people to follow His pathway of love.

Chorus:
I'll follow my Lord, wherever He leadeth,
The road may be rough, or smooth.
Glory's path is the one that I have most needed,
To teach me to live day by day in His truth.

God sent His only Son to die for our salvation,
He cleansed and forgave us, and made us His flock,

God sent His only Son to provide a sure foundation,
Our hope is anchored upon a rock!

God sent His only Son to live as our example,
He calls us to live in His righteousness,
He dwells within our hearts, He says that we're His
temple,
He bought us to show forth His holiness.

God will send His only Son to bring us safely to Him,
The path may be bumpy, its ending is sure.
Glory's lights may be obscured, but they never can
be made dim,
My future is with Him, completely secure.

When I heard the fall above me, I thought it was Courtney. I was too doped for the stairs, and I knew if she was hurt, Alyssa or Martha would come tell me. No one came, and I went back to sleep, only to hear the voices upstairs a little later.

I dared not walk upstairs, so I crawled to the top and opened the door. I could see into our bedroom, and the ambulance people were gathered round not Courtney, but Martha, still lying on the floor! She saw me and said, "Oh, Justin!" She had passed out and fallen, and now felt guilty that she'd let us down! (She wanted to stay despite what the paramedics and I thought, but once her husband arrived, away she went.)

Martha was distressed that no one else had responded to our need, and now she couldn't help. I said, "God knew about this. Maybe someone should have responded and didn't, and because of this they will another time. But He has another solution. It will be okay." Perhaps I was calm only because I was doped! But worrying never made anything better, and later I was glad the medics heard me say that. Christians should still be Christians in a crisis, after all.

The medics helped Courtney settle into bed, and Alyssa spent the rest of the night with an invalid mother, a drugged father, and a house that we thought must be cursed! Another dear friend from church came in the morning. Later that day, Kate and then Rosa arrived, and Courtney's sister Lynn on Wednesday, and we could take on the world again!

Wednesday morning, Rosa and Alyssa took Courtney for treatment. I couldn't lift for six weeks, until mid-December, but for now we had a lot of help. Kate was arranging nursing visits and help from a physical therapist and occupational therapist.

Courtney was a little more mobile but really struggling with pain. She thought if my pain medicine helped me, it would help her—but it included oxycodone. She was confused and upset, and said, "How will our kids feel knowing you let me die in pain?" She wasn't normally manipulative and would never have tried it on me—but the pain was really tough. When I told her, "It was killing you," that finally got through.

Friday, they found pain medicine that worked, and things got much better! It became a joke: "How will our kids feel knowing you are letting me die in pain?" We never stopped laughing together, even (or *especially*) at our own follies and foibles. We were headed to Glory, after all! Everything in this life is temporary, and much of it merits little more than a laugh.

8 November 2021 (Monday a.m.)

Dear All

(An email glitch kept this from sending last night, here it is this morning.)

Martha is ok. Justin is ok. On to Courtney. It may be too early to say this, but Courtney may have finally turned a corner.

A couple months ago, she was walking 10–12k steps a day, when infection hit. The infections were antibiotic-resistant, so they really took hold, and she became so weak she couldn't even walk around the block (about 1,200 steps). Then, she fell, and could no longer walk unaided. A week and a half ago, she was given painkillers for all the pain she was suffering from her fall and reacted badly, and completely lost the use of her legs.

Yesterday, Courtney had her best day in a while. Even though she still wasn't using her legs, she was able to sit up in the living room for much of the day. And today was better. Though completely dependent for getting in and out of the car, and using a wheelchair exclusively, she did make it to church today! And later today, she stood up twice on her own power, and used her legs more than she has in over a week!

Of course, we don't know how much improvement we'll see but it seems hopeful she can get back to a little better capability and some more independence. We're very thankful.

Travel News:

My sister Kate got here on Tuesday afternoon, less than 24 hours after my operation.

Our daughter Rosa got here Tuesday evening.

Courtney's sister Lynn from Washington arrived Wednesday evening.

Eric arrived back from Eastern Europe on Thursday. He's staying at Robert and Manda's right now because our house is so full.

Kate and Rosa both tentatively leave on Saturday.

Katherine, and Edward and Marguerite + kids, all tentatively arrive a week from Saturday.

Treatment News:
Courtney restarted cancer treatment on Wednesday. She now is receiving three different cancer medications. They've varied the trial to allow the medication which has been added. It reduces blood flow to the tumor (as does the experimental medicine) so it's hoped there will be synergy between them, but we're in totally unknown territory.

The newly added medication does have a known side effect of high blood pressure, but Courtney's BP has been so low as to cause problems—we won't mind if it comes up a little bit!

We have home physical therapy and occupational therapy coming this week.

We may have to get some home nursing care.

Courtney will be in Denver for cancer treatment 3 days this week.

The following week, the Denver schedule drops to 2 days a week, Tuesday/Thursday rather than MWF.

Loads of Help:
Two ladies from church spent time here until family arrived.

People from church picked up both Rosa and Eric from Denver airport.

Both church people and work colleagues helped with meals over the last week.

Courtney fainted in the car on Friday after treatment and the nurse next door came and helped, then a couple neighbor men helped carry her wheelchair up the stairs and into the house.

We've now installed a chair lift to get Courtney into the house from the garage, and several family members have helped with the cost.

Neighbors are arranging a meal train for next week after Kate and Rosa leave.

One of the neighbor ladies works at home and says she is available on instant notice whenever needed.

We've needed loads of help. The last few weeks, especially since Courtney's fall, have been pretty rough. It would have been immensely worse this week, with me incapacitated, without all the help. I'm not supposed to lift more than 10 pounds for six weeks, so we will probably continue to need a lot of help. We may have to get a lot of nursing help to come in after this week, though if Courtney continues to improve as she has today, the need may be less.

My pride doesn't like to ask for help, but then, there's lots of things that are good for me that my pride doesn't like, and lots of things that my pride does like that aren't good for me.

We're doing fine. Very tired, I'm still very, very sore, there's been some real difficulties, but we're doing fine. We're thankful for all the help, thankful for the Lord's provision in so many ways, thankful that my appendix (bad as it was) wasn't worse, most of all thankful for His peace that passeth all understanding.

Thank you for praying for us.
Justin

I wrote later that day from the hospital where Courtney was receiving treatment.

8 November 2021 (Monday again, p.m.)

Very brief, I'm writing from the hospital.

Courtney stood unsupported today for the first time in about 2 weeks.

Phenomenal news for Pete and his wife! Their scan shows that one secondary tumor is completely gone and that his main cluster of tumors has decreased in size by 28%!

This is incredible for recurrent glioblastoma. Even though the experimental medicine may not be working as well as hoped for Courtney, it makes us feel like being part of this trial is extremely worthwhile. If the new medication is going to help some patients and we're helping them learn more about which patients will be helped, and about possible side effects, then it's extremely exciting.

We were told last winter that there had been no advance in the treatment of glioblastoma in 40 years. It looks like we're seeing an advance unfolding right in front of our eyes!

Justin

Courtney's tumor had been growing, but the treatment seemed to have helped and seemed to be helping Pete! It was thrilling to be part of something that might be a real advance, even if a small one! How do you value something that might give glioblastoma patients a few more months with their families, a few more months to prepare for eternity?

A week earlier, in the ER, it had looked so dark. Wondering if my appendix would burst before they got around to helping me, I'd also wondered how we would care for Courtney. Yet now, we were rejoicing with Pete and Eve in an apparent answer to one of our biggest prayers—to join a trial that would really help others, whether it helped us or not.

We still had all the problems. I was still sore, still limited, still unable to see how we could manage care. I still didn't know if Courtney would walk again, and her time was still likely short. Lots of things didn't seem very good, but our loving Father handed us another joyous reminder! He was still on His throne, still in control, still loving and blessing us. Nothing would happen that He didn't allow.

Psalm 84:11 says, "No good thing will he withhold from them that walk uprightly." It was our job to walk uprightly and let Him decide which things were good. I didn't know why my appendicitis was a good thing, but my Father had decided it was.

It wasn't until later that the thought hit me—the way I'd been caring for Courtney was unsustainable. I needed more help, and the appendectomy forced me to accept it. This illness and all the struggles that came with it? Yes, this was good, too.

Chapter 25

So Thankful!

12 November 2021 (Friday p.m.)

Dear All

In short, Courtney's much better.

The Physical Therapist worked with her on some standing exercise yesterday.

The Occupational Therapist worked with her on transfer from the wheelchair to another chair by herself.

Pain is under control, and she is sleeping better.

Her left leg and arm, which had mostly quit responding after her fall, are "waking up" again and responding more and more.

She's still not close to being able to walk unaided but that no longer seems like a distant impossibility.

We were able to go to Denver three times for treatment this week. Next week, we move to a new phase of the clinical trial, which only involves two trips to Denver a week, on Mondays and Wednesdays.

We've seen Pete and his wife all three times in Denver this week. She is still so thrilled when she talks about his latest MRI. They are very, very grateful for your prayers. We had a long talk this week about why things happen in a sin-marred world.

Eric arrived safely from Eastern Europe. My sister Kate leaves tonight after coming to our rescue after my operation. Rosa leaves in the morning. It means a lot heavier burden on Alyssa, though Eric will help a lot with that. Courtney's sister Lynn is here and helping with a lot of stuff, though her back hinders her with lifting. Next weekend we have more "reinforcements" with Katherine flying in from Wisconsin and Edward and Marguerite from Utah. The biggest reinforcement is that Courtney is able to do more and more for herself.

I'm still sore enough to keep using painkillers, but not the strong stuff anymore, and I've finished the heavy antibiotics (there was a lot of infection with my appendicitis) that were doing unpleasant things to me. I'm not supposed to lift more than 10 pounds for another 4½ weeks, so can't really help Courtney with a lot of things, but we're getting by. We tried to get some nursing help to come in but there was no one available, they have really bad staff shortages. The Lord provided in other ways.

We have a playlist we listen to every time we go to Denver. Included on that list is "Highland Cathedral." If the Scottish Highlands can be a cathedral, declaring the glory of God, so also can Colorado's Front Range, so it seemed a fitting thing to add to our playlist.

Courtney had said that it would be nice to sing along with it, but the standard words didn't fit what we think the music says, so yes, I wrote another one. I hope it encourages you.

Lord Who Created (Highland Cathedral)

Lord Who created mountains, sea, and sky,
God of eternity, enthroned on High,

Sov'reign before Whom every knee shall bend,
Master and Maker, angels Thee attend.

Chorus:
King of Pow'r, Ruler, Great "I Am,"
We fall before Thy holy face,
Saviour, Lord, Sacrificial Lamb,
We stand lifted up by grace!

Lord Who created mountains, sea, and sky,
Saviour for all upon a cross did die,
Bearing my sin upon that bitter tree,
Bearing my guilt, my shame, my agony.

Chorus

Lord Who created mountains, sky, and sea,
Lord of Salvation, coming soon for me!
Thee I must honour, if by life or death,
Lord, I will praise Thee to my final breath!

Courtney just said a few minutes ago, "I'm ready to go to bed," and Rosa, gloatingly, put on her Physical Therapist hat and said, "You have to do your exercises." I think part of their training is to learn how to like being sadistic. :) Maybe it's good she's leaving tomorrow . . .

Thank you for praying for us!
Justin

Funeral planning proceeded, and we included that song. It seemed even stranger to be planning it now, as Courtney gained strength, but we knew that was temporary. Even as she got stronger and slept better, there was more mental confusion. It was still minor, and I was quite sure we'd have a good Thanksgiving with our family. Our Father was so kind to us.

It took a long time to get Courtney ready in the mornings. On Sunday, I got up at 5:00 a.m. to read my Bible and have breakfast, then got Courtney up at 6:00. I was very limited, but I could get her breakfast and partially help her dress. She napped while I showered and dressed, then Alyssa and I finished getting her ready. It was slow, and by the time we left home, church had already started.

As we drove away, Courtney said, "I didn't get makeup or jewelry!" and started crying. Everything was slow, and if we had gone back, we would have missed most of the service. It just wasn't practical. I told her, "It doesn't matter. Even without them, you'll be the most beautiful woman there, and I won't be the only one who thinks so."

Courtney knew she was well loved and no one else would care, but she still cried. At church, the men helped us wheel her in during the second hymn. The sermon was on Acts 23, where the Lord appears to Paul in prison and says, "Be of good cheer." At the end, she asked me to wheel her forward for the invitation. She said afterward, "I've not been of good cheer." Cancer is tough, but so were ancient prisons. She was right; God wants us to rejoice through the really hard times, too.

About this time, Courtney stopped giving much input on the email updates. Fatigue was catching up to her, and she just didn't care much anymore. She treasured her time with family, but Home was getting nearer and dearer.

16 November 2021 (Tuesday p.m.)

Dear All

Quick update this evening. Two things.

Tomorrow, Courtney has all three treatments on the same day for the first time. We have not been told if anyone in the world has ever had all three before, or if they have had all three on the same day before. It seems likely that if there are bad side effects of the three together, we will find out. It also seems likely, if the three are going to have significant synergy in fighting the cancer, that tomorrow will be maximum impact.

Today, the Physical Therapist told Courtney he's going to try to work with her on walking with a walker on Thursday. He admitted that when he first saw her two weeks ago, he did not think that walking, even with a walker, was a feasible goal for her to look toward.

Walking or not, side effects or not, cancer growing or shrinking, may God be glorified in us. Please pray for that most of all.

Justin

19 November 2021 (Friday p.m.)

Dear All

Courtney's only side effects from treatment this week were some very minor nausea and fatigue.

She was indeed able to walk with the walker when the physical therapist was here yesterday and has been up with the walker repeatedly since. It's still not more than 20–30 steps at a time and then she needs to rest,

> but that's a far cry from 3 weeks ago when she couldn't even shift her position in bed. And her balance and stability are steadily improving.
>
> Right now, Courtney feels like she can do more than it is probably safe for her to do, so we're having to hold her back. That's difficult because she probably really can do most of what she feels she can, but a fall right now could be pretty serious, so we're using an abundance of caution.
>
> We are very thankful. God is so much kinder to us than we deserve.
>
> Katherine, and Edward and Marguerite and the kids arrive tomorrow, so with Eric and Alyssa already here, we'll have quite a full house.
>
> Thank you for praying for us!
> Justin

Sunday night, I re-preached a sermon I had preached in Scotland three days after Courtney's diagnosis, "Scattered Thoughts in a Crisis." I recounted Scriptures the Lord brought to mind over that short period after her diagnosis until the following Sunday.

Courtney listened online. When I got home, I was in trouble! "It was too much about me!" I expected that and was ready. I told of one person after another who said they had really been encouraged or helped by it. Then, I clinched it: "You always said you wanted God to use your cancer. He did!" After thirty-six years of marriage, I finally had an argument-winner!

The next morning, as we headed for Denver, a text arrived. Someone facing a tough struggle had found the sermon so helpful. He was mistakenly (but by God's grace) given Courtney's number, so she was the one who got the super-encouraging text and had to read it to me while I drove. Then, I teased her with "Too bad I preached that" and "God planned it so you would read that to me." Maybe I will grow up someday and won't gloat when proven right, but not yet apparently!

22 November 2021 (Monday p.m.)

Dear All

The last two days were a lot of fun for us.

Yesterday at church, Courtney walked in using a walker. Two weeks ago it took two men to lift her out of the car into her wheelchair. It was pretty exciting for them and others to see her walking, even with a walker.

Today, we took her to the treatment center in the wheelchair but then she got up and walked in using her walker, which amazed all the nurses and other staff. One nursing assistant is a Christian and has been praying for us, and she had tears in her eyes, and all the staff applauded. Pete's wife said, "THAT is an answer to prayer." The manager of the infusion center told me she didn't think she'd ever see that.

Pete is feeling well, he's sleeping better than he had for months, and the headaches are the best they've been since he was first diagnosed.

I preached last night. A lady in our church in Scotland used to tell me if I preached less than 40 minutes, she didn't get her money's worth. I'm afraid they got MORE than their money's worth last night. :)

One year ago today was the first time I began to think something was really wrong. I took Courtney to urgent care at our local hospital in Scotland. They sent her home with pain medication and told us to check in with our General Practitioner in 3 days if she wasn't better. We didn't make it those 3 days. It's strange to think of all that has happened in that year.

Thank you for your messages of kindness, the many kind acts so many of you have done over the last year, and especially for your prayers.

Justin

These really were exciting days. Clouds were on the horizon, but Courtney could do more almost every day. The physical therapist admitted that the patients who do best are usually the ones who do more than he says, and she was very rebellious against his restrictions!

It was also a looking-back phase as the one-year anniversaries came. The urgent care trip, the GP visit/hospital check-in, the first mention of "cancer," the glioblastoma diagnosis, the decision to operate—all these anniversaries passed. We'd been living one day at a time, and it was very strange. Those people from last year, we didn't really know them anymore. We were far different people now. But there is something exciting about passing a one-year anniversary of the day they said you would only have two months!

Thanksgiving Day arrived, something we had long targeted. The whole family had arranged to be here. We'd always been a close family—at times in Scotland, our kids really had no friends outside of our family. We all knew it was the last complete family holiday. Eric had ministry responsibility and wouldn't be "home" for Christmas, and Courtney would likely be *truly Home* before another holiday would come around.

The Cuteness Roarers were all together again—a delight to them, and the death of peaceful quietness! Rowdy when apart, they took it to another level when together. Duncan and Neil, so close in age, were "partners in crime" as only three-year-old boys can be. Courtney found the noise difficult at times, but it was such a joy to spend time with her grandchildren. *Every* day is a gift, but some seem more gift-like than others.

26 November 2021 (Friday p.m.)

"Courtney Martin Update 26 November 2021"

Dear All

Today's email has a different subject line—the year is included, because today we are exactly one year, 365 days on, from the day we were given the diagnosis of glioblastoma multiforme.

Two days before that, Courtney was sent to the hospital by a General Practitioner. The neurosurgeon later told us that was a "really good pickup" by her, that the symptoms Courtney exhibited weren't really enough for her to know. Without that "good pickup," the swelling in Courtney's brain would have done so much damage that an operation wouldn't have been possible. That was the first of many times we've seen God work providentially in ways beyond what we would normally expect.

We never knew we'd have a year. We were told maybe two months when Courtney was first diagnosed, which might have been accurate if they couldn't have operated. With that kind of prognosis, you don't need to give a year, just the day and month is good enough. But here we are, adding the year to the subject line.

Today, Courtney walked more than halfway around the block using her walker, including quite a bit of uphill. Every day, she is able to do more, but this is the first time in more than a month that she's gone out walking in the neighborhood. She's done a few stair steps as well.

We're thankful for this year that God has given us, thankful that Courtney has been able to be involved in the clinical trial she is in, thankful for so many things God has blessed us with, thankful for opportunities He has given us to tell others of His love for us, thankful for the way He has moved in the hearts of others to show us their love.

We had our whole family together for Thanksgiving, and Courtney's sister Myra and her son and daughter were with us. They miss Miles badly, of course, but it was good to be together with them.

The coming week sees a big exodus. A week from now, all of our kids will have left to return to their homes. The last to leave is Eric, on the 3rd—and our good friends Deacon and Christine arrive that day for a week.

We don't know what the next year holds, of course, but then, none of us ever do. We're just trusting the Lord that all He does will be good, whether we understand it or not.

Thank you for praying for us!
Justin

I left it out of that letter (public statements were premature), but Ward also came. He spent Thanksgiving with his family, then flew into Denver late that night and stayed until Sunday. Eric hadn't been here when he came in July; he wanted to meet Rosa's other brother.

That visit meant a lot. Mothers are always concerned

that their kids marry well. Both Robert and Marguerite had found jewels, spouses who loved the Lord, with true servant hearts and a desire to truly be part of our weird family. It looked like Rosa might have found one, too. It at least showed she was looking for the right kind of man, even if Ward turned out not to be the one. Courtney didn't expect to see Rosa's wedding, but she was pretty sure Rosa was on track to marry well. That was something else to add to her list of thanksgivings!

30 November 2021 (Tuesday p.m.)

Dear All

Today Courtney walked a little bit with a cane, without the walker. She also went up a complete flight of stairs. In both cases, she had assistance available if needed but did not need it. It did leave her very, very tired, though. The last two days she walked all the way around the block using the walker, which was also tiring, but very good progress.

Our next MRI is next Thursday. If it shows any significant tumor growth, Courtney will be out of the clinical trial. We've not observed any symptoms that would indicate any significant growth but we'll find out what the MRI shows on the following Monday.

Tomorrow is a long treatment day in Denver for us, as Courtney receives two different cancer medications. We saw Pete and his wife again yesterday, he is still doing really, really well—well enough to brag on his wife's pie! I declared myself skeptical and in need of evidence. :) It's fun to see the way God brings friends into your life through even difficult circumstances—not just Pete and his wife, but the researchers and the nurses in the treatment center.

> One year ago today was the first time I saw Courtney cry after her diagnosis. I'd been telling her that many friends had said it didn't seem fair that cancer had come to her. She was really, really upset by that, because the only fair thing would be for God to send us to Hell because of our sin. She told me that I needed to bring my computer the next day to help her write a letter. That letter went out on 1 December last year. Many of you will remember it but some weren't receiving updates back then, so I've copied the update from 1 December last year below.
>
> Thank you for your prayers!
> Justin

I did attach Courtney's letter (see chapter 3) to the end of that email, but I won't repeat it here.

From a pastor I've never met, in Kentucky, USA
What tremendous Honor our GOD deserves. THANK YOU SO MUCH for sending these.

> 4 December 2021 (Saturday p.m.)
>
> Dear All
> A friend asked if there was anything Courtney would add, after this last year, to the letter she sent a year ago. Here's some of her thoughts.
> "Cancer has been a lot harder the last couple of months. It's no picnic and it hits you in a lot of different ways. But I don't think God owes me anything. He's already given me so much more than I deserved or had any right to expect. Here I am, doing well, after a year.
> "I learned again this year that God is good, and

that He is loving. If something comes into your life, He has a loving reason for allowing it. The thing that really stands out for me is my seizure in April. It had such a huge impact on my quality of life, and when you apparently have a limited number of months, that matters so much. I just thought it was a bad thing to happen. But it changed the schedule on which they did MRIs, and as a result the fact that the tumor was growing rapidly was caught earlier than it would have been. I don't think I would be here today if it hadn't been for that seizure. So God really did have a loving reason for it, even though it seemed terrible at the time."

Eric returned to Eastern Europe yesterday (Friday) morning. Our dear friends who were supposed to arrive yesterday had to cancel because of illness, so that they didn't bring something unpleasant for Courtney. And yesterday we learned that Alyssa may have been exposed to COVID, so we banished her to Robert and Manda's house as an extra precaution. That means it's just Courtney and me here, and I'm still on a 10-pound lifting restriction after my operation. But Courtney is doing better and better with her strength and balance, and we're being really careful.

Thursday, with the physical therapist, Courtney did 2 full flights of stairs, up and down, and walked quite a bit, with the cane only for assistance. Later that day she went around the block with the walker again, her third day in a row doing so. That didn't happen today because there's no one here who can make sure she is safe with it, but Courtney's been tired today anyway, so perhaps a rest day is a good thing.

It was one year ago yesterday that we were told that one of the surgeons in Edinburgh wanted

> to "try some sort of operation." Up until that day, I was in doubt whether Courtney would see 2021. This Thursday, on the one-year anniversary of her operation, Courtney has her MRI to find out if the tumor has continued to grow or not, whether the triple treatment the doctor tried has had the effect he hoped for. We're at peace with whatever God sends us.
>
> Thank you for praying for us!
> Justin

The next morning, Courtney walked into church with just a cane, holding onto my arm. She might have been just a wee bit proud of that! The wheelchair was there, just in case, and after church we used it. She was too tired for me to agree to taking any more chances.

The next day, Monday, I thought I was seeing an increase in confusion a couple times, but her walking was still improving. On Wednesday, we went around the block without cane, wheelchair, or walker, for the first time since the infections got bad! Courtney wasn't quite independent (she was holding tight to my arm), but it was a huge accomplishment.

Courtney often said things that showed she thought her time was short. She was confused more and knew it. She knew the tumor was affecting her emotion control. She couldn't do anything about most of that—but she could work on her exercises. She could show that Christians, given life by the Almighty, shouldn't give up lightly. It may not seem much to do for Christ, but if she could honor Him by working hard to be able to walk around the block, she would do it. To succeed was a wonderful victory for her—and a victory some of our neighbors still remember.

Chapter 26

The Hardest Chapter

I couldn't figure out what to call this chapter. It was the hardest on which to reflect and the hardest to write, because it was the most difficult time Courtney faced. I finally gave up on having a "good" name, wimped out, and called it "The Hardest Chapter."

On Wednesday, we had walked around the block, but I'd noticed more confusion the last couple days. On Thursday (9 December, the anniversary of the operation), we went to Denver for Courtney's MRI.

During the drive, she asked, "Are those mountains or clouds over there?" Both her vision and memory were struggling—we'd driven that road many times, and there were no mountains in that direction. She also said other things that showed she was just forgetting things or not thinking clearly.

Thursday evening, I wrote to our kids—

The last 4–5 days make me think the tumor is growing again. First, Mom's distance vision has worsened. That could be macular degeneration, or it could be the tumor in the occipital lobe, but I'm guessing the latter. Second, there's been more confusion the last few days.

I'm almost sure she'll be out of the trial on Monday.

She sees the optometrist tomorrow about her eyes and we'll find out if it is her macular degeneration or not. That still won't tell us anything really either way.

That night was the worst in weeks. Vertigo hit hard, and every time Courtney moved, the room spun and she was sick to her stomach. She was so sick Friday that we rescheduled the optometrist appointment.

Friday around noon, to our kids—
Just to let you know, Mom had a bad night last night, she's still having vertigo and nausea. It, of course, could be some kind of virus but it's things a brain tumor could do. She's just staying in bed so far today.

Later, our credit card company called about a charge on Courtney's card, asking about a charge from Singapore for $69. She had not ordered anything for that amount, and nothing from Singapore. She had spent $90, though. They said there was no $90 charge, thanked us, canceled her card, and ordered a new one for her.

After the call, I asked what she ordered, and she reluctantly said, "A TENS machine." I said, "You have one," and she said, "It was for you. It's a combination neck massager and TENS machine, because you have so much trouble with your neck sometimes."

We looked it up—it was a Singapore company. Courtney broke down and cried. She was always so careful online but now had ordered from Asia without knowing it, giving her name, address, and credit card without checking the company. It was totally out of character.

Courtney cried, "You have to check *everything* now. I can't buy anything, not even a present for you, without your permission now." I was supposedly a loving husband, a pastor, but I could find no words to comfort. Maybe we aren't always supposed to have words, maybe we need to feel our own inadequacy at times, but I failed when my wife needed comfort. It was probably good for my soul, but my heart hurt then and still hurts. My analytical computer-programmer mind says that's silly because she's not hurting now, but it's still the way it is. Sometimes an analytical mind is clueless.

For months, we'd been joking about Courtney's "campaign" to bankrupt me. If she'd buy something online, even if just a bag of dog food, one of us would joke about it. That joke was gone for good now.

The next day, Saturday, the vertigo eased some, and Courtney was able to walk a little bit with the walker. She was still very, very down.

This was the first email update that Courtney didn't even want to read or hear. She said, "Just send it; it's okay."

11 December 2021 (Saturday p.m.)

Dear All

The last couple days have been pretty bumpy. On Wednesday, Courtney was able to walk all the way around the block without her walker, just holding onto my arm. But yesterday and today have been rough. She's been very weak, she's had vertigo and some nausea, and a couple other things going on. It could be that she picked up a virus somewhere, but the symptoms she's having could also be caused by tumor growth. If so, we'll find out on Monday, when we get the results of Thursday's MRI. The Lord knows and has known all along, so we're in the right hands.

Courtney is able to get around today with the walker and a little bit of help, not as good as Wednesday and Thursday but better than yesterday! We're doing fine, though tired, and I'm still finding it slow and hard to shake off the effects of my operation. Alyssa is home again so we have help if we need it. We hope Courtney can make it to church tomorrow (that wouldn't have happened if church had been yesterday).

As it's the eleventh of the month, I read Proverbs 11 this morning. Verse 18 says, "The wicked worketh a deceitful work: but to him that soweth righteousness shall be a sure reward." Please pray that we will be faithful in sowing righteousness as we travel this journey the Lord has given us.

A year ago today, two days after Courtney's operation, I got a call to ask if we were ready because she might come home the next day. She didn't make it home until two days later. At this point, I still didn't know what the impacts of the operation would be, whether Courtney's memory or personality would be destroyed, or whether she would be crippled by the operation. I certainly expected the ramifications to be far worse than they were. It's been quite a year.

Thank you for your prayers!
Justin

It was another rough night. Courtney woke up three or four times. The last time, around 3:30 a.m., I helped her to the bathroom and got her some water, and as she settled back in and I headed for bed, she asked for yogurt. As I returned, she stood up to take it. By the time I kept her from a hard fall, yogurt was everywhere.

I got Courtney back to the bed, made her promise to stay there, and grabbed another yogurt. I sat beside her until it was gone, tucked her into bed, turned off most of the lights, and cleaned up. By the time I was back in bed, Courtney was sleeping like a baby.

I lay down, shaking with rage. I wasn't mad at Courtney; she was trying to help me. I told myself I wasn't mad at God; I was mad at the situation. It's really the same thing, of course, because God allowed the situation, but I wasn't thinking clearly enough to recognize that. I think He allowed it just so I could see my own selfishness.

Suddenly, a thought sprang up: *Who do you think you are?* I suppose, really, I was angry because I thought I deserved better, but I was a sinner deserving nothing but God's wrath. In love He had saved me, and if He wanted me to serve by cleaning up yogurt in the middle of the night, well, I'd been bought with a price (1 Corinthians 6:20), and He gets to choose what He knows to be best. He had every right to assign me yogurt service, and His reasons were certainly good even if I didn't know them.

It was all I could do to keep from laughing out loud at myself. What an idiot! I should have quit crying over spilled milk when I was two, and the difference between spilled milk and spilled yogurt doesn't go far!

The next day, in a private conversation with our pastor, he said, "You are doing really well with it." After my silly anger, this was not my preferred day to hear that comment! I told him, "I'm good at writing emails, but that doesn't mean I'm always doing as well as the emails sound," and shared with him about the night before. But by God's grace, my stupid and sinful moments were rare. He sustained me through some really difficult days.

Monday, we headed for Denver for our appointment with Dr. Diamond for the MRI results. I knew the tumor must have grown, and that we'd be out of the clinical trial. There would probably be no more cancer treatment. I thought Courtney was sleeping, as usual, on the drive, but suddenly she said, "If I'm out of the trial, it will be a relief. It will mean I'm dying soon and can go to heaven, and I won't have to put up with this anymore."

It was the first time she ever said that. I said, "The credit card really hurt you." She said sadly, "It's the final loss of independence. I can't go anywhere without your help; I can't eat; I can't even go to the bathroom without your help. And now I can't even buy you a present without your help. I can't do anything!" The super-spiritual response "You can pray" wasn't going to cut it. She *knew* she could pray, but that wasn't what she was talking about. She hated being a burden instead of a help.

There was only one thing to say: that helping her was okay with me. I also reminded her of what I'd said more than a year ago: "If it ever gets too hard, if you get too tired of fighting, it's okay with me. I will be okay." I offered to call and say we weren't coming and wanted to stop the treatment. I could turn around to go home or go see Robert and Manda and their Cuteness Roarers.

Courtney didn't want that. She would see it through. If there was anything she could do to help with the trial, she would do it.

When we saw Dr. Diamond a little bit later, the news was as expected. Felicia was there as well. I think she already knew. The tumor had grown extensively, and Courtney was out of the clinical trial. He laid out options for us. We could move to palliative care only, and we might have two to four months (but her tumor was very aggressive). Or we could pursue a Phase 1 trial at another hospital.

I think we honored the Lord by taking the news the way true Christians should. Courtney cried at one point, when she asked which course Dr. Diamond recommended, but we thanked him for telling us. It was, of course, difficult for him too, and for everyone else. We then went up to the treatment center to thank the staff, and to see Pete and Eve and tell them. That was tough too. They all really, really loved Courtney.

Later, Felicia called with difficult news. Courtney was not eligible for the trials Dr. Diamond had mentioned, or any others in Colorado. She offered to check other glioblastoma trials around the country. There was no reason Felicia should have done that except kindness.

13 December 2021 (Monday p.m.)

Dear All

Today's MRI results showed that Courtney has substantive growth in the main tumor and both secondary tumors. The vertigo that she began experiencing Friday is apparently consistent with what the doctor saw on the scan. There is also increased swelling.

The growth exceeds the limits of the clinical trial. It is clear that the treatment is not working for Courtney as hoped, and the ethical oversight will not permit them to keep using experimental medicines (which can have unknown side effects) on someone for whom it is not working. So, Courtney is not receiving the treatment anymore, which I believe to be good and right. We're glad that Courtney's participation helped them learn more about which strains of glioblastoma respond well to the treatment and which ones don't. We helped them learn that they have to monitor platelet counts closely with this medicine, and that the infection risk is higher than previously thought. Given some of the other results, I do think this medicine will eventually be approved for the treatment of at least some glioblastomas, though maybe not Courtney's kind, so learning more about possible side effects is a real blessing.

For Courtney, we think the treatment did slow the growth of the tumor considerably. It's now five months since she was told she would live four months, or maybe six. She's still walking, still able to communicate, to think, to make decisions. She's still COURTNEY. Though the treatment hasn't worked as well as hoped, it's still better than we expected last summer.

One year ago today, I brought Courtney home from the Royal Infirmary Edinburgh after her operation. We were told to expect 12–18 months, and that the median survival was 14 months. After the pathology report came through, we were told it would be at the shorter end of that because Courtney's tumor is the "wrong strain."

There may be other clinical trials available to Courtney, but none in Colorado. One of the researchers is looking into this for us (though it isn't really her job to do that—so many people have been so kind to us). We will need wisdom as to whether to pursue this. We know the Lord can use experimental medicines, but whether that's what He has next for us or not, I do not know. Our doctor has only palliative care to offer us now.

I believe the Lord gave us the grace to honor Him today, first with the doctor and the researcher. Then we went up to the treatment center to see Pete and his wife, and to thank the nursing staff and tell them goodbye. There were some tears up there, they've grown to love Courtney and will miss her.

We so wish everyone had the same assurance of faith that we have. How devastating it must be to face situations like this without the Lord!

Thank you for your prayers.
Justin

Later that day, after I wrote that email, we were talking about a clinical trial in North Carolina and if it was practical to go there. Courtney said, "Why don't you call your mom and ask her? She's got a lot of wisdom."

I told her, as gently as I could, "Courtney, Mom is gone. She passed away in July." She remembered, of course, once I told her, but this was the hardest blow of all, and the most I saw her cry. It was more than just grief all over again. Not only could she not do anything to help, now she felt like she couldn't even give me useful advice.

Courtney's whole life had been spent helping me. We'd raised six godly kids because she helped me. God used us to start a church because of her help. She wasn't just grieving the loss of a beloved mother-in-law; she was grieving the change from being a help to being a burden.

We received many kind and encouraging emails after

sending that update. No one really knew what Courtney had experienced the last few days, what she was really going through, but their love was appreciated anyway.

The next day, I responded to one pastor friend—
I have had some tough trials in my life, usually brought on by my own sin and/or foolishness, but none that compared to this. Sometimes I stand back and look at myself and say, "How are you doing so well? I know what you are. This is impossible."

No doubt it helps that I've steeped myself in the Scriptures for many, many years. I've been trying to renew my mind to bring my thoughts and feelings and actions into conformity to Scripture for decades.

I was saved at 4 but when I was 24 I had my 2 Chronicles 32:31 moment and learned what was really in my heart. It was then I really began to internalize that the flesh had to be mortified and renewed. No doubt that's part of why the Lord has given such grace. I've done some things to avail myself of His grace. But it's still grace, not me. I know you know what I mean.

It's Courtney that amazes me. Honestly this is brutally difficult for me but it's a walk in the park compared to what she's going through. But she's still trusting the Lord.

Got to run. Thanks for your friendship.

I guess it should be said here that before long, my present arrived, exactly as Courtney had ordered, not from a fraudulent website at all. It was just over ninety Singapore dollars, which worked out to sixty-nine US dollars. If Courtney had realized it was in Singapore, she would have known to check the exchange rate and recognized the amount.

That gift is still in my drawer, the box still unopened.

It was bought in love, and I will open it and appreciate it—but I'm not ready, not yet. It all hurt Courtney so much, and so it still hurts me. God has been so very good to me, and I won't quit praising Him for His goodness, but my loving Father in His wisdom chose to leave me with some hurts, and I'm still learning to live with them.

Chapter 27

Well with Our Souls

♪

Our God did not leave us without encouragement through the griefs. The email inbox was full, and people found other ways to help and lift us.

From a dear friend in Scotland

Have been thinking of you all and praying as we were waiting on the results of the MRI.

However the Lord leads in the coming days, I know you have the grace you need and the deep peace of God in your hearts. Your faith in your caring and loving Saviour has remained constant through it all.

In the days ahead He will continue to supply you with comfort, assurance, and hope.

May His presence bless and keep you.

From a close college friend

Still praying for comfort, encouragement, and blessing for you and Courtney. Thank you for your transparent modelling of how to walk toward probable death patiently. These emails may communicate your greatest work of ministry.

A neighbor brought a ham and a bag of cookies. The ham and cookies were nice, but the kindness was priceless. So many neighbors helped and encouraged us; I can't possibly remember them all. Courtney said, as before, "The whole neighborhood is cheering me on." Perhaps her courage, cheerfulness, and determination were part of it. But people are made in God's image, and often situations like ours bring out an innate kindness that comes from Him.

This gift meant much because we were "out of sight, out of mind," as Courtney couldn't walk anymore. Colorado winter was here, and all were preparing for Christmas—yet this couple thought of us. It's fun to think that none of the other neighbors know who did this, but I know and, better yet, God knows.

The biggest encouragement was having Courtney's sister Myra come for several days. Courtney's balance and strength were significantly worse, so they were limited in what they could do together, but they still had some really fun times.

In November, Eric had brought some special chocolates home. Despite her historic disdain for chocolate, Courtney lost track and ate more than her "fair" share. When she realized that, she felt horrible and ordered more online so others could have plenty (this was when she was still trying to bankrupt me!). I had her order double so we could take some to Denver to give the nurses and staff.

On our last trip up, we had taken home-baked treats our kids had made, but we forgot the chocolates, so we had *loads* of extra chocolates. Myra hadn't had any, so Courtney said they should have some with a tea party.

Preparations proceeded apace. Tea was made and taken to the bedroom. I was working and minding my own business but went in the bedroom for something, walking in to see my wife with perhaps a dozen individually wrapped chocolates lined up. Her sister had just as many. They both had one of each kind, and Courtney obviously meant to eat *all* of hers.

When we married, I had to promise not to let her get fat. She was always careful, always slashing the sugar in our diet, but now her battle cry was "Life is short! Eat dessert first!" I could understand, but chocolates? That many? Courtney? My remonstrations fell on deaf ears. Her evil sister encouraged it, too! Nobody listened, and I left them to their "tea" party. My blood sugar levels surely went up just by being in the same house as such gluttony! Worse, this despicable event is the memory my sister-in-law seems to always bring up!

On Saturday, I went to the jeweler for Courtney's Christmas present. By now, things were moving so quickly that I wondered if we even had a month. What does one get a wife for Christmas when she has just weeks before heaven? I chose a ruby necklace. It was her birthstone, but it had a more important meaning.

At the jeweler's, I broke down and cried, and then, of course, I had to explain to the lady why I was crying. I felt guilty; it wasn't the nicest run-up to Christmas for that lady. I cried after Mom's funeral, but this was my first total meltdown since before Courtney's operation a year earlier. I knew she would probably only wear the gift two or three times, and she would call it a totally frivolous expense. It was still the best present I ever gave her.

In this book, I've described many things that didn't go out in our emails. In this next email, I pulled back the curtain a wee bit. People saw Courtney as a shining example of faith, and she was. I thought they should know it was coming from a place of hurt, too. Since she wasn't vetting emails anymore, I could get away with it.

19 December 2021 (Sunday p.m.)

Dear All

Courtney made it to church today. Just in case anyone doubted, I've included two pictures! She's wearing her Christmas present, a ruby necklace. I gave it to her last night so she could wear it if she was able to make it today.

I told her it's her Proverbs 31 necklace.

Proverbs 31:10 *Who can find a virtuous woman? for her price is far above rubies.*

(Now you can tell this is a Justin email, not a collaboration with Courtney like usual! :) She'd make me take that last bit out.)

It was a wonderful service. A man and his wife got baptized today. God saved him from a life of horrible sin. It was very hard for Courtney to make it to church, but she was so glad she did. I don't know if she'll manage to get to church again, however. The things that you would do in five seconds as you are getting ready to go to church may take her 5–10 minutes, and pain and fatigue kick in, too.

Late-stage glioblastoma is tough. There are memory blockages, emotional trauma, and just the fact that one's body quits working as it is supposed to. There's embarrassment and frustration and annoyance and heartaches, a loss of freedom and independence. There are tears over not getting to see grandchildren grow up, and tears over renewed griefs that were forgotten and that hurt again when remembered. There's the heartache of having been your husband's trusted counselor for years and suddenly finding that you just gave him nonsensical advice. There are regrets over the things you didn't get done. There are minor and major discomforts and feeling guilty over being a burden. And on top of it all, there's the awareness that with all of that, you're nothing special, that lots of people suffer, and sometimes a lot worse than you have it, and so you feel bad about feeling bad. And then you hear from someone else with glioblastoma and realize that for them, it's completely different because it all depends on what part of the brain is under attack.

It's clear to us that, though the medical and research communities are trying very hard to help people with glioblastoma, they can do little for us now except try to help Courtney be more comfortable. There aren't any trials left that Courtney could get into that would make sense. I am reminded of 2 Samuel 24 when David said, "Let us fall now into the hand of the LORD." Only if God somehow stops the tumors will this stop. We know we've been in His hand all along, of course. That which He gives, we accept gratefully. He already blasted through the timelines the doctors gave us last November, and the timeline they gave us in July.

Courtney had a fall Thursday. No serious injuries, though the rib she injured previously is quite sore again. We are grateful for God's protection, but we're now on full-scale fall alert and being very, very careful. We pretty much have someone with her full time now so that she doesn't forget and get up by herself. Courtney's balance has rapidly worsened in the last week and a half and she is physically much weaker. She is still able to use the walker, but only with help now.

Just under two weeks ago, Courtney began to have vision problems. She's seen the optometrist and he says it is her macular degeneration having worsened in one eye, not the tumor. He said the stress she's gone through (infection, fall, medication reaction, cancer) has probably triggered this. But it's encouraging to know that her other eye is stable and that this isn't the tumor, which would probably only get worse and worse.

One of our neighbors came by with a ham and a bag of cookies they'd made for us the night before. He said that his wife "made the ones that look good, I made the ones that look bad." :) Both kinds taste good (as did the ham)! But I might be in danger of turning into a big bag of sugar or something with all the sweets coming my way!

Courtney's sister came down for a few days to help out. So often, in heartaches, there are at least some little blessings that come with them. There's an empty place since our Lord took Miles Home, but it does mean Myra can be here, and we are thankful for that.

We go to Denver tomorrow for a medication that is supposed to help keep the brain swelling down and help hold back some of the tumor symptoms for a while. We'll be going up again 2 weeks later. It does mean we'll probably get to see Pete and his wife, as well as the staff at the treatment center, and probably at least one of our researchers. I know many of you are praying for Pete. Please continue to do so, they've promised to keep me posted on how he's doing.

Early this week, Katherine flies in from Wisconsin, and Neil and Charlotte bring their parents (Edward and Marguerite) from Utah. Rosa arrives later in the week. We've been getting up more Christmas decorations in preparation for grandchildren to be here.

I told our pastor a week ago that it's easy to write

good emails. It's hard to live it day by day, hour by hour. But Courtney has wanted God to use her cancer for good, and He's done that in our lives as well as in the lives of many other people. It's really true that He does give the grace and peace you need for the things He asks you to do. It's not always easy but the strength is there.

I suppose I should tell you that I'm pretty much recovered from my operation. I still have a little bit of discomfort and lots of fatigue but it's manageable. It seems strange to think that 200 years ago I'd have undoubtedly had a burst appendix and died, and here I am writing long emails.

I'm not sure there's any way I can express how grateful we are for your prayers and notes of love and encouragement. May God bless you.

Justin

From a pastor in Wales

We continue to keep you in our prayers here in North Wales. Your journey is so hard but that light that you want to shine through your cancer journey is shining so brightly we can see it here in Wales.

Life was easier now. Courtney knew heaven was hers soon, and she was content. All those hurts were only this life, after all. The necklace helped too. She never thought of herself as a "virtuous woman." She knew her Lord had cleansed and forgiven her, but she would never have claimed that description. I intentionally gave it to her with Myra and Alyssa present because I wanted her to hear it from me *and* in front of others.

Courtney already had peace about her eternal destiny—but it seemed to give her peace about all the things she was having to leave undone as a wife, mother, and grandmother. It was almost as if my giving her a "Proverbs 31" necklace told her that all of that was okay. She was okay with God, okay with me, and okay with all her family.

Of course, I knew none of that in advance. I don't know how I got the idea, being largely clueless about all things "woman." I think our Lord dropped it in my mind to be a comfort and encouragement to Courtney. It continues to be that for me, too.

The fact that our kids (except Eric) were all arriving also lifted Courtney. Physically, things were getting tougher, and she was sleeping more, but it was wonderful to have everyone home. When a one-year-old and three-year-old are in the house, the focus changes, anyway. There wasn't too much "Roaring" because "Nana needs to rest," but they made up the difference with enough "Cuteness" to still qualify as "The Cuteness Roarers."

We got up enough Christmas lights, inside and outside, to be fun for Neil and Charlotte, and for Winston, Daffodil, and Duncan when they came over (I'm not sure little Miles was really noticing the lights yet). And there were Christmas ornaments. Through our marriage, we'd collected ornaments from places we visited or to remind us of special events. There were many great memories associated with those ornaments that we'd bring out every year.

A year earlier (soon after her operation), Courtney had helped get those ornaments out, even put some on the tree, and helped put them away. She was saying goodbye to them, reliving the memories—she might not be around to see them again. Yet here she was, and we were thankful. She couldn't help this year, but she could see them on the tree. It was a reminder, not just of all those old memories but of God's goodness to us through the last year.

Christmas arrived, and so did illness. Our celebration was quite limited because Robert and Manda had sickness at their house. Mostly, we just deferred until Monday. Flights were changed, and everyone would be able to be here Monday.

Courtney wanted to go to church on Sunday, and we got up early to get her ready, but she was just too tired. I got her breakfast early, and then she needed a nap. After a while, I got her up and dressed, and then she just needed a nap again. She slept most of the day, probably about twenty hours that day, and church didn't happen.

The next day, we went to Robert and Manda's for Christmas. Courtney wasn't walking—we used the wheelchair—and we had to carry her up some stairs to get her in the house, but we had plenty of help.

On our trip to Yellowstone, Courtney had been very focused on choosing presents for the Roarers. Neil always liked Nana's Yellowstone blanket, so we got one just like it for him and another for Duncan, the two partners in crime. They lay down in front of the fireplace and covered up with their blankets to take a nap together. There was no sleep happening, but they were having fun!

Courtney had purchased play makeup for Daffodil, something she never would have done for our daughters. Being a Nana has its privileges; you can give frivolous and irresponsible gifts to the kids that you'd never give as a parent! I think our kids mostly got neglected by us for presents this Christmas, but the grandkids made out like bandits.

Courtney napped some and we didn't stay late, but it was a good and blessed day. The next day, she slept almost all day.

28 December 2021 (Tuesday p.m.)

Dear All

The palliative care nurse came today and said based on what she's seen over the last month, the tumor is growing very rapidly. She said we should be considering hospice care very soon, as she does not think Courtney has much time left. The tumor is obviously creating more pressure on different parts of the brain. She warned that Courtney may not be able to communicate much longer.

Courtney is still completely coherent. I asked her a little while ago, since she might not be able to answer it later, if there's anything she'd like to say to you all. She said to tell you, "I'm still in good spirits. God is still good and loving. I know where I'm going." The only thing bothering her is when she thinks I'm trying to do something to make her feel better about dying, she tells me to cut it out. :) I don't think I've seen her faith waver once through all this, though she says she hasn't always been as joyful as she should be.

She's been telling me today all the songs she'd like for her funeral. I've heard about most of these before. I've told her that a funeral is not an all-day concert, and she must prioritize. :)

We celebrated Christmas yesterday because family members had colds, so we decided it was best to avoid exposing Courtney. It was a little bit different from the usual Christmas, obviously. But the fact remains that God became a man specifically so He could die for our sins and rise from the dead. As He rose, so shall His followers. Christmas might have been significantly impacted by Courtney's condition, but the true Christmas story of the coming of Jesus is the answer to her condition, the only real answer. Because He came, one day there will be no more sickness, no more death, and God shall wipe away all tears from the eyes of His children. This world has no real answers to sickness and death—but the Answer came to this world 2,000 years ago. He waits to give more time to those who don't know Him yet to come to Him. If that means we have to go through this so that more people will be in Heaven someday, it's a small price to pay.

Another bit of sad news today—Pete's tumor also is growing significantly, and he also is out of the clinical trial Courtney was in. It looks like he will be able to get into another trial, a Phase 1 trial, in Denver, and they plan on doing that. Courtney wasn't eligible for that trial. Pete says he'll keep on fighting until God takes him Home.

Other than a sore rib from her fall, Courtney is not having any pain. She has grown more and more weak, and can barely stand, even with help. It's frustrating for her what she can't do but she's now sleeping around 20 hours a day so that mitigates the frustration. She still does forget that she can't get out of bed by herself, so she continues to be a fall risk and we have to be with her all the time. That's frustrating to her, too. But she's not really suffering, for which we are thankful. The worst is that she's always been one to serve others and now she feels a burden, that's hard on her.

Rosa left last night. Edward and Marguerite have

decided to extend their stay until Sunday afternoon. Katherine has extended until the 9th. Eric's plans are still uncertain.

Thank you for your prayers! May the Lord be glorified in us! I will try to keep you posted as I am able.

Justin

From a pastor's wife in central Scotland
I know I haven't responded much at all to your emails but want you to know that I have read every one and also shared with some others. I have truly appreciated you sharing all that you have and please know that we have kept Courtney in our prayers both individually and as a church. What a journey it has been for her and her sweet testimony throughout it all has truly been a blessing, encouragement and an inspiration!! I praise the Lord that she is in God's hands and praise Him also for her unwavering faith. Please give her my love and I send her a hug!!

I knew Courtney would be in Glory soon, but Grace kept shining in so many ways. She had always feared "life's final war with pain," and there was no real pain. Family was with her, and though she was sleeping a lot, she was alert and able to talk with them. Everything was peaceful. There was no fear, no fighting, just peace. We had been through some painful times, but we had come through, and it was well with our souls.

Chapter 28

Into the New Year

Courtney was regularly sleeping twenty hours a day or more. She couldn't get up at all, and we always used the wheelchair now. No one thought we had long. Edward and Marguerite extended their stay to January 2, Katherine longer.

Rosa had gone back to Virginia after Christmas for work but was returning for New Year's. Courtney asked about Ward. Rosa's initial response made it clear (to me, at least) that he wasn't coming, and then Rosa asked, "Would you like him to come?" Courtney said yes, so he came also. (That racked up some Dad-approval points!) Eric, of course, couldn't be home because of ministry responsibilities, but everyone else was with us, and Courtney's sister Myra came too.

I didn't know what to do about New Year's Day. Courtney was sleeping so much. With all here (including the Roarers), sleeping would be hard—but I wasn't sure we could get her to Robert and Manda's, or how she would do there if we did. We decided to have everyone come here, and it was great. Courtney was delighted, thrilled to see Myra again, and thankful Ward had come. She was awake most of the day in "my" recliner.

At Thanksgiving, as if to prove Mom was still

smarter (even with a brain tumor), Courtney had won the family game of Scattergories. She was too tired to even try anything like that at New Year's, but she did dish out a "zinger" or two when someone gave the opportunity! She might be tired, but she was still sharp and having fun!

Instead of a game, we ended up watching *Fiddler on the Roof.* Courtney always found the song "Do You Love Me?" emotional, but other than squeezing my hand a little tighter, she seemed okay. I found it hard to listen to several of the songs.

Swiftly had flown the years, "laden with happiness and tears." We had so much happiness, so much for which to be thankful. Our six children were adults serving the Lord, and five were with us. The one away wasn't missing; he was serving elsewhere, that's all. Our kids had married wonderfully, and we had six lovely grandchildren. Our little ones had all grown to follow the Lord, bringing so much happiness—but tears were so very present. Unlike the movie wedding, I knew the mother would be missing from our next family wedding.

Still, it was a blessed day. The Cuteness Roarers, always an adorable gift from God, were even more so when all together. There was lots of food, lots of fun, and just the joy of a gathered family. Most were leaving the next day, but that was because they all had God-honoring lives to lead elsewhere, and that was part of the blessing.

Courtney wore her ruby necklace, but it weighed on her in another way. She had gathered our daughters and Manda back in Scotland to divide her special pieces of jewelry, but now there was another piece. She kept saying, "It has real meaning. I have to decide."

That evening, heading for bed, she said, "I'm giving it to Marguerite. She is becoming the wife and mother she should be."

The next morning, Courtney just couldn't make church. We got her ready, but then she slept and slept. She regretted that, but I didn't. I loved her commitment, but she needed the rest.

Rosa and Ward left after church for Virginia. Later Edward and Marguerite left with their little ones, but first, Courtney asked for Marguerite to come to our room and said, "The ruby necklace. I want Rosa to have it." After they left, I asked why she changed her mind, and she said, "Marguerite doesn't need it. She's already on the way. I want it to be a reminder for Rosa. Tell her when you give it to her."

2 January 2022 (Sunday p.m.)

Dear All

This glioblastoma journey started in 2020, and we weren't even promised we'd see 2021, but we're now in 2022. It will truly take a miracle of the Lord if Courtney's part of the story is to see 2023. But what the Lord will do with it in the lives of others may go on, and on, for many years. Perhaps even the lives of some who are reading this will be impacted by Courtney's faith.

Courtney really wanted to go to church today but it just didn't work. She got up before 7 so there'd be plenty of time to get ready. But her legs weren't working at all, and by the time she was halfway through breakfast, she was exhausted. We got her dressed and ready and back into bed to rest, in the hopes she might wake up feeling well enough to go—

and she slept until after 1. It was a long day yesterday, so it may have just been fatigue from that, or the tumor effects may have gone to another level again. I think if yesterday had been Sunday, she'd have been in church, she had a pretty good day, but not today. The Lord knows why.

As much as Courtney has been sleeping, she perhaps wouldn't have got much out of a church service today, but of course, the main reason we go is not to "get something" but to honor the Lord who loved us enough to die for us. It's not for ME that I should go, but for HIM, as well as to encourage and challenge others. Of course, He knows and understands and loves us when our bodies let us down, but our hearts should be toward Him so much that we have that determination to be there and honor Him whenever it is at all possible. I don't know if Courtney will ever make it to church again, until she joins the church in Heaven—but I'm pretty sure her conscience is clear on this point, and having watched her this past year, I'd have a hard time missing church lightly! Many in our church have been challenged by her example, and perhaps some of you reading these updates have as well.

We go to Denver again tomorrow morning for her fortnightly treatment. This may be the last one, but Courtney is determined to get at least this one more treatment, in the hopes of holding back the tumor and brain swelling enough for Eric to get home to see her in a couple weeks. We've been encouraged to start hospice care, but Courtney doesn't want to do that yet.

All our kids but Eric were here for New Year's, as well as Courtney's sister Myra who came down from Denver. Rosa and her friend Ward came out from Virginia for the weekend and left this afternoon. Edward, Marguerite, and the kids extended their visit longer than expected but left today as well. Their plans for another visit are undetermined. Katherine has extended her visit and is still here. Our friends Deacon and Christine may be coming this week as well. We've had so much help, from family and church family, friends and neighbors.

Courtney is sleeping a lot, but not all of her sleep is restful and certainly not for me. I've been very, very tired recently. Alyssa is taking a leave of absence from work which should help me get some naps, at least.

Things aren't getting easier, not that we expected them to be. The Bible tells us to "Set your affection on things above, not on things on the earth." That's one of the blessings of cancer, it makes you love earth less and Heaven more. Courtney is far more ready to go there than she was when this started. So am I, even if I don't get to go as soon as she does. So many of the things of this earth that used to seem important, you can see right through them now, and that's a good thing.

Thank you for praying for us!
Justin

Monday morning, we prepared to go to Denver for treatment. Courtney didn't want home hospice care because it would have precluded this last treatment. She wanted it for a better chance to see Eric again—he couldn't travel before mid-January at the earliest. But she just didn't have the energy and finally said, "I don't want to go. I don't think I can."

Courtney had fought hard, doing all she could. She didn't want her service to the Lord to end early because she'd neglected exercise or not eaten right. She didn't want to limit her usefulness as a clinical trial participant by being irresponsible, lazy, or undisciplined. But now the fight was over, and she was on the Home stretch for Glory. The Lord would take her when He would take her, and she was okay with that. If she saw Eric again, that was well, and if not, he was where God wanted him to serve, and she was content.

I knew our pastor was busy, but I was keeping him informed.

Tuesday morning, I wrote—
This whole thing just drives home for me, and I keep thinking it and probably saying it too much, we're only here to serve. The Lord could have just taken us Home as soon as we got saved. He's kept us here to serve Him, so we'd better serve Him. So even though my service right now is right here, I know there's more and different service to come. I've been thinking about that more as it appears the end of this phase is getting closer.

Three times that day, each time when moving Courtney from her bed to the wheelchair or back, she appeared to have decerebrate posturing (a kind of seizure). It happened again the next day. It was a relief to get her into the hospital bed so we could just raise it for her to eat, and we didn't have to get her out of bed.

We weren't having any more issues with pain. There had been a couple days with minor headaches or neck pain, but a couple Tylenol each time sorted it. That was truly a blessing from the Lord, but the seizures left Courtney even more tired.

5 January 2022 (Wednesday p.m.)

Dear All

Three times yesterday, and again today, Courtney experienced what we believe to be seizures. It's hard to be sure because of her overall condition, which has deteriorated significantly since Saturday.

We were unable to make it to Denver for treatment on Monday and have now moved to hospice care. We now have a hospital bed for Courtney which means we don't have to get her up to get her a meal, we can just raise the bed. This is a blessing because we think that moving her may have been triggering seizures.

Courtney is still eating, still understanding when I ask her questions, but she talks little now except to answer questions, sleeps most of the time, and is very weak. She's not complaining of pain nor are there any indications of pain. She's not complaining of anything. The nurse today said that's one of the blessings of glioblastoma—often, as the end nears, pain is not as much of an issue for glioblastoma patients as it is for other types of cancer. There's a lot of the discomforts of being incapacitated but no pain. And because glioblastoma can move so quickly, if pain does start it likely won't be prolonged.

One of Courtney's favorite hymns has always been "Day by Day." That's where we are. We just go another day, with what the Lord sends our way. People seem surprised by that, but I think if you really believe in the Lord, what else would you do? Go against God when you need Him most? How silly would that be?

Thank you for your prayers during these difficult times.

Justin

The seizures really took a lot out of Courtney. With the hospital bed, it was easy to bring her to a sitting position to feed her, but for two days she barely spoke and hardly opened her eyes. It took a delivery of flowers from Neil to pop them open.

At age three, I suspect Neil didn't arrange for their delivery! But it was very important to him to send flowers to Nana, and he had done it before. Something he said made us suspect that he thought Nana ate the flowers, but if she wanted them for eating or anything else, he wanted her to have them! In any event, Nana certainly opened her eyes to see his flowers!

Throughout, we'd corresponded with a dear friend in Scotland, another missionary there. Her husband had been my good friend, and we buried him on a wet and windy day on a Scottish hillside after his brain tumor. I will never forget singing "It Is Well with My Soul" around his grave. She wrote, saying the hardest part was "not being able to go with them."

I replied—

I do find myself crying a lot more the last couple weeks.

That "not being able to go" isn't bothering me yet. It's like I know that the Lord has more for me to do here. I don't know what. Maybe something I couldn't have done with Courtney, and that's part of why He's taking her. But I just have this sense that it isn't my time yet, that He has another task for me first.

I was in continual contact with the researchers. Courtney wanted to give them anything that might be helpful. She was due a final checkup a month after her last experimental treatment, but it was now impossible to go. I said the sponsors could do a "brain harvest" after her death to examine her tumor, but they never took us up on that.

I asked about that checkup, and they suggested a Friday group call with Dr. Diamond. I expected questions about symptoms, Courtney's response to different things, etc. Instead, it was about how we were coping and what they could do for us. Dr. Diamond asked how often the hospice nurses came, wasn't happy with the answer, and promised to address it. It wasn't a "checkup" for research at all. It was kindness, to help and encourage us.

I asked for indicators of how much time we had. He said sleeping twenty hours a day often meant there was a week or less. She'd been doing that for almost two weeks! If Cheyne-Stokes breathing started, it might mean the brain stem was affected; it might even signal the last day.

Katherine extended her stay again. Marguerite arrived for the weekend. Our friends Deacon and Christine had asked if they should come (their visit before Christmas had been prevented by illness). I warned them Courtney might pass while they were here, but they decided to come and arrived on Friday; they only ever wanted to serve.

Our house was filling again, which seemed to give Courtney a lift. Perhaps the effect of the seizures was wearing off. In any event, our Lord gave us a good weekend. It was quiet and peaceful but good, and Christine put some wonderful food in front of us. We were very blessed. Courtney didn't feel like talking so she said little, but she listened and smiled.

9 January 2022 (Sunday p.m.)

Dear All

Courtney seems to have stabilized and perhaps even had a little bit of an upswing the last couple of days. I suspect that the seizures earlier this week took a toll on her and that she has now recovered a little. She completely stopped talking for two days and only opened her eyes a couple times in those days.

But yesterday, and even more today, she's opened her eyes more, spoken several times, nods her head sometimes when asked a question, and smiles if someone is joking/laughing in the room. Today, she listened to most of the broadcast of our Sunday School and church service.

Our friends, Deacon and Christine, arrived on Friday and Christine made some really good salmon which I thought would be soft enough for Courtney to eat. THAT was a winner, we might have to put Courtney on a diet! :) She's still taking plenty of foods and fluids. She had difficulty swallowing pills, so we've gone to alternative means to get her the medicines she needs, but it's not keeping her from getting nourishment. We've been told with a glioblastoma that appetite is not necessarily any indication of how long we have, but certainly she's not starving herself like some cancer patients do.

Courtney is still sleeping 20 hours or more a day

and doesn't leave her bed now for anything. She is still moving arms and legs, but they have no strength at all. Breathing is fine, oxygen levels are fine, no signs of infection. Other than occasional neck soreness/stiffness, she doesn't seem to be having any pain at all. I don't know if the neck problem is just because of being in bed all day or if it's being caused by pain/pressure in her head caused by the tumor. But at this point, at least, it certainly isn't severe.

Marguerite just left after flying in early Friday morning (a lady from church drove to Denver to pick her up, which was a blessing). Katherine has extended her stay again, until Thursday. My sister Kim arrives on Wednesday, and Deacon and Christine leave next Sunday.

It seems weird to put this in an email at this point, but I'd like to ask you to pray for wisdom as we plan Courtney's funeral. She got very bossy about this :), which songs she wants, what Bible verses she wanted me to speak on at her funeral, etc. But that left some things still needing to be organized/planned. She very, very much wants her funeral to honor the Lord who has loved her and will love her to the end. That became hugely important to her. She didn't want her cancer to be wasted, she wanted the Lord to use it for good, and now she doesn't want her funeral to be wasted. We're praying that the Lord will give wisdom in the rest of the planning and that His power and blessing will be on the service.

The girls made sure I got some good sleep last night, after two pretty rough nights in a row. I'm thankful for the Lord's protection from any serious injury or illness for me, and for a good recovery from my operation.

Please pray that we will finish this phase well, not by human evaluation, but in the eyes of the only One who really knows.

Thank you for your prayers.
Justin

It seemed as if Courtney was rushing down the Home stretch to Glory, but all was peaceful. God had blessed us abundantly, and as Courtney had written many months ago, the Comforting Presence is real. Our Father carried us, and the road did not seem grievous. The pain might come in waves when a song played on the movie, but God was still good.

Chapter 29

A Threefold Cord

On Friday, Dr. Diamond had told me that Cheyne-Stokes breathing might signal the last day, and on Monday it started. Courtney's breathing would pause, so you wondered if it had stopped, and then restart. It wasn't severe, and while she had almost entirely stopped speaking or opening her eyes now, she was still responding with smiles and movements and still eating almost normally.

On Monday also came tough news from Eric. Away for an important ministry commitment, while helping in that ministry, an accident left him with an injured knee and very sore (and probably cracked) ribs. We told Courtney but didn't tell her it put his ability to travel in jeopardy. Eric and I kept that to ourselves; it would have helped nothing to tell her.

Katherine and Alyssa, our oldest and youngest, were with us. Eric called every day, as did Rosa and Marguerite. Robert and Manda brought their little ones every day. Nana didn't talk or open her eyes, but Winston could wipe her forehead with a cool cloth, and she knew they were there. She still smiled at times, was still aware of us, and obviously enjoyed the calls. She always kissed me back when I kissed her. Once only, she rubbed her head as if with a headache, so we gave her Tylenol, but I don't know if she needed it. She never gave any other indication of pain.

On Tuesday, Deacon and Christine hit the local British fish and chips shop. Christine, being Scottish, knew what she wanted! It wasn't our local chippie in Scotland, but it was authentic enough to feel you were on the fish and chips side of the ocean! (This dear couple did so much for us. When they left, our basement chest freezer was full of easy-prep meals from Costco. I don't know who smuggled all that food into our house, but it wasn't me!)

Tuesday night was rough, and keeping the researchers informed, I wrote to Felicia—

Courtney is peaceful. Lots of rough breathing and some coughing the first part of the night. Even then, she wasn't acting as if she was distressed.

I read her some Scriptures and sang some hymns for about an hour and the coughing stopped and the breathing settled, and she slept from about 2 until 7. Don't know if it was the Scriptures or singing or whether she just wanted me to shut up :) but anyway she slept. Sleeping now. Breathing is irregular but not as much as last night.

Wednesday morning, Eric and I talked, and it was clear he wouldn't get home. Even if not injured, it didn't make sense. I explained to a pastor friend later that day.

He wrote—

We pray for you regularly and know that the Lord is your strength and shield.

It is such a blessing to hear that so many of the family and friends have been able to be with you all during this time. We pray that Eric will be able to get over soon.

As Courtney's homegoing draws closer, the Lord also draws closer. (I know I said that to the choir.) I love the truth that He is an ever-present help in time of trouble, and that He inclines His ear to our cry.

I replied—

Eric will not make it home until the funeral. Courtney is not opening her eyes or speaking, and she hears him and is aware of him on video calls. If he were to fly on Friday (earliest day practical, probably) it would mean no video calls on Friday and Saturday, and then he would be here and she would not open her eyes or speak but could hear him on Sunday, if she is still here. It would gain little and lose two days. We have always been glad he wanted to go serve the Lord there. Our parents lost a lot of what would have been precious times with us because the Lord sent us to Scotland. Now, it is our turn, and we are ok with it.

So much happened Wednesday. My sister Kim flew in from Louisiana. There was another spell of bad breathing. Courtney started to have an almost constant tremor in her right hand, and occasional strong tremors in her arms and legs, which I suspected were seizures. But I am sure the most important thing to Courtney was a conversation I had.

I was forced to consider a partial decision about the future. I couldn't wrap my head around it, so I called our pastor. His advice was clear and simple, so virtually identical to advice I'd given in the past that I thought, *Duh. How could I be so stupid?*

Then, he said it was too soon to discuss, but if I was

looking ahead, there was something to consider. He had thoughts about what role I might have in the church going forward. We had never told him, but it grieved Courtney that I was out of the ministry "because of her," "on the shelf" and not active in ministry. Though he didn't know all that, the Lord laid it on his heart to talk to me about returning to more active ministry when she could still be happy about it.

As soon as I got off the phone, I told Courtney, and she smiled and relaxed. I said I didn't know exactly what God had planned, but it was obvious He could put me to work one way or another. She knew that, of course, but I think the Lord caused that conversation to give yet another gift of peace, easing her heart and smoothing her road.

Thursday morning, Courtney's breathing worsened, and I told her sister Myra that I didn't know if this was the last day, but she should probably come. Myra drove from Denver, but by afternoon, Courtney was more stable. Our house was now pretty full, with Katherine and Alyssa, my sister Kim, Myra, and Deacon and Christine.

Thursday evening, Courtney's breathing worsened. We are "fearfully and wonderfully made," as the Psalmist said, and we rarely think about what a gift it is that God breathed into us the breath of life. We just breathe, without even thinking about it. But then, when a brain tumor starts to shut that down, it consumes the thoughts of everyone around.

Courtney was still conscious (she ate dinner and kissed me back when I kissed her), but she wasn't talking. We got her settled for the night, but her breathing kept me from sleeping. At 1:00 a.m. it changed for the worse, and I thought she might leave for Glory very soon.

What do you do when you think your wife's real life, the one in Heaven, is about to begin, leaving you behind? There's no manual to prepare you. Seminary theology classes don't cover it very well—as an academic subject, it probably wouldn't be popular with students.

All I could think was to let her know I was there, I loved her, and I was trusting the Lord. She wouldn't be alone on the Glory side, but she wasn't going to feel alone on this side either. I was sure, with the way her breathing was, she wasn't sleeping. As I had done with others in the past, I read Scripture and sang hymns until 5:00 a.m., when her breathing changed and worsened again, and I asked Katherine and Alyssa to join us. The Lord had helped her sing for years, but now that she could sing no more, He would help us do the singing for her.

It was a long day. There were changes in breathing, seizures, and other things, but even with all that, Courtney mostly rested peacefully. She spoke once, just after lunchtime, but no one understood what she said. Just before 4:00 p.m., when I kissed her, she kissed me back, but an hour later, she was no longer responding.

The breathing was so hard for her that I was asking the Lord to take her soon. Eventually all in the house were with us into the evening as it was clear He was granting my request, and everyone joined in to sing my sweetheart into Heaven. The last hymn was "I Am His and He Is Mine." I know she breathed at least twice during it, but I think she passed during the first verse. "Loved with everlasting love . . ."

14 January 2022 (Friday p.m.)

Dear All

Courtney was promoted to Glory just after 7 p.m. our time this evening. We had a good long time of singing hymns and reading Scripture this morning when it looked like she might be going to Heaven imminently. Things stabilized but then late this afternoon it was clear the time was short, and we again sang and read Scripture. Our daughters Katherine and Alyssa, my sister Kim, Courtney's sister Myra, and our friends Deacon and Christine all joined us.

I do not think Courtney was having any significant pain, but she was having seizures and breathing became very difficult for her today. I was thankful to the Lord for taking her to Himself and bringing all of that to an end. I know she thought I loved her but now she is learning what love really is from the One who loves perfectly and everlastingly.

I'm sitting here now in our bedroom, next to the hospital bed that they brought in for her. Courtney's body is lying here motionless, and she is not here. And yet, as I look over at her body, I find that the physical resurrection matters more than it ever did to me before. I know that in the resurrection we won't be married. I know that God could take our spirits to Heaven without a physical resurrection, and He could have made it absolutely wonderful for us.

But no, God chose that there will be a physical resurrection, and as I look at Courtney's face, it strikes me—death can't win. God was never going to let death win. That's at least part of the reason why, when Jesus comes back, she will rise from the dead. Death can only kill the body, but it can certainly do that. But the Bible tells us death is an enemy, and one to be defeated. God won't let it win. We shall rise.

Today's long day really began at about 1 a.m. this morning. That's when Courtney's breathing first made me think today was her Home-going Day. I read her some Scripture and sang some hymns, until around 5 when I woke up Katherine and Alyssa. The first Scripture I read her in the night last night:

1 Corinthians 15:51 *Behold, I shew you a mystery; We shall not all sleep, but we shall all be changed,*

1 Corinthians 15:52 *In a moment, in the twinkling of an eye, at the last trump: for the trumpet shall sound, and the dead shall be raised incorruptible, and we shall be changed.*

1 Corinthians 15:53 *For this corruptible must put on incorruption, and this mortal must put on immortality.*

1 Corinthians 15:54 *So when this corruptible shall have put on incorruption, and this mortal shall have put on immortality, then shall be brought to pass the saying that is written, Death is swallowed up in victory.*

1 Corinthians 15:55 *O death, where is thy sting? O grave, where is thy victory?*

1 Corinthians 15:56 *The sting of death is sin; and the strength of sin is the law.*

1 Corinthians 15:57 *But thanks be to God, which giveth us the victory through our Lord Jesus Christ.*

1 Corinthians 15:58 *Therefore, my beloved brethren, be ye stedfast, unmoveable, always abounding in the work of the Lord, forasmuch as ye know that your labour is not in vain in the Lord.*

Yes, the resurrection is coming. Death will certainly be defeated. The victory is ours through our Lord Jesus Christ.

Thank you for traveling this journey with us. Courtney's funeral is unlikely to take place until early February, tentatively the 4th. I will send another update with funeral information when it is known for sure. Our family would be honored to have any of you with us, especially in person but also online, if necessary.

Justin

And so, I was "alone." Of course, the Lord would never leave me, so I would never be alone. Family and friends were kind. My phone rang and my inbox was full—but Courtney was no longer with me, nor would she be ever again. The thought of Ecclesiastes 4 is still with me:

> Ecclesiastes 4:9 *Two are better than one; because they have a good reward for their labour.*
>
> Ecclesiastes 4:10 *For if they fall, the one will lift up his fellow: but woe to him that is alone when he falleth; for he hath not another to help him up.*
>
> Ecclesiastes 4:11 *Again, if two lie together, then they have heat: but how can one be warm alone?*
>
> Ecclesiastes 4:12 *And if one prevail against him, two shall withstand him; and a threefold cord is not quickly broken.*

"Two are better than one." How many millions of bereaved spouses, down through the centuries, have remembered that verse, with both thankfulness for the blessed years and sorrow for the one-ness they now must face? There was nothing special about me—I was just one of millions upon millions—but still the reality was fully mine: "Two are better than one."

For so many years it was true. The Lord had given us to each other and fit us for each other. When I was weak, Courtney was strong, and when she was weak, I was strong. "A threefold cord is not quickly broken"—but often through the years of ministry, the only Third Strand we had was the Lord. How strong is your cord, though, when interwoven with the Lord!

Now, if there was to be a threefold cord, the Lord would have to be two of the three strands. How strange to think that *should* make me stronger than before—when I feel so weak.

Courtney was concerned about me from the very first, so long ago, when I had told her the diagnosis, and she smiled and said, "Are you okay?" So often she asked if I was okay. Many cancer patients turn inward, but she turned me-ward, even more than before. In one conversation, talking about how concerned she was about me, I had admitted it would be very hard. I said, "You are being heroic, but only for a little while, and then you are going to go to heaven and be with the Lord. And I will be stuck here, having to go on, and on, and on, honoring the Lord anyway. I'm not sure I'm up to it. I can do heroic for a while, but I don't think I can handle it long term."

Now, that time had arrived. I wasn't up to it. My strand of the cord was weaker than ever, Courtney's strand gone forever, but the Lord's loving arms were there. I was devastated, but I knew it was okay. He might teach me to feel weakness, but He would never leave me nor forsake me. Courtney might be gone to Glory, but God's Grace was still present.

Chapter 30

Courtney's Farewell Service

The day after Courtney went Home, the messages poured in, many from people I'd never met or heard from previously. People were sharing our emails with their Bible class, sharing them with their entire church. It is strange that it didn't seem strange. I kept hearing, "You will never know the impact Courtney has had."

I wrote to Joy and Felicia. I didn't know if it would help the clinical trial research at all—I thought probably not—but just in case, I described (as best I could) all I had observed.

Courtney thought a "funeral" was morbid rather than joyful. "Celebration of Life" seemed trite, and besides, she wanted it to be about the Lord, not about her. We decided on a "Farewell Service."

Katherine and my sister Kim worked on a video for the Farewell Service. On most visits to English churches, we heard John Rutter's "For the Beauty of the Earth," and Courtney loved it. It represented treasured memories of our trips south to England. They mixed pictures of my beautiful wife with pictures of beautiful scenery to fit the words.

They finished the video Sunday afternoon, and I couldn't watch it without crying. I watched again, and again. I knew if it made me cry at the start of the service,

I would cry all the way through and be unable to speak. I tortured myself for three weeks, watching it ten or more times a day, to get used to it so I could watch it when the service came.

Soon, Myra, Kim, and Katherine were gone, and not long after Deacon and Christine. It was just Alyssa and me now—for a while, until the week of the Farewell Service.

In the remaining emails, I've removed some of the service details.

20 January 2022 (Thursday p.m.)

"Courtney Martin Update—Funeral Arrangements"

Dear All

Funeral service is at 10 a.m. on February 4th at Colorado Springs Baptist Church, 5410 E. Woodmen Road, Colorado Springs. Courtney said I'm supposed to preach and told me what I'm supposed to preach on. Bossy. :)

We would be honored to have any of you come from wherever, but it will take some doing to get "longest journey" recognition, since Eric is coming, and one person is coming from Scotland!

I have been asked to compile these emails into a booklet. I am not sure whether to do that or not, but enough people have suggested it that I thought I would just acknowledge the suggestion here, and I will let you know in a future update whether I intend to do so or not.

I wanted to mention Pete. I spoke to his wife yesterday. He's possibly going into one of two trials in Denver, or possibly into one in Houston. He is still feeling pretty well. His wife expressed trust in God for their today and their eternal destiny. Please continue to keep them in your prayers, which she specifically requested.

Finally, here's the last hymn we sang to Courtney, as she was taken to Glory. The singing wasn't as good here as when she got to Heaven's side, of course. But the song was still a good one:

Loved with everlasting love,
Led by grace that love to know;
Spirit breathing from above,
Thou hast taught me it is so!
O this full and perfect peace!
O this transport all divine!
In a love which cannot cease,
I am His, and He is mine.

His forever, only His;
Who the Lord and me shall part?
Ah, with what a rest of bliss
Christ can fill the loving heart!
Heav'n and earth may fade and flee,
Firstborn light in gloom decline;
But while God and I shall be,
I am His, and He is mine.

["I Am His and He Is Mine," Wade Robinson, 1890]

The following email, sent the next day, included specific suggestions for contributions in lieu of flowers. (Not everyone followed this request, and we had a bit of a flower problem by the time the service was over!)

21 January 2022 (Friday p.m.)

"Courtney Martin—Donation Information"

Dear All

Soon after Courtney was diagnosed, before we even knew she'd be able to have an operation, a church of which we weren't a member did something to help us with food for our family who were coming in.

Courtney was upset. She said, "We're becoming takers instead of givers!" So she got my sermon
(1) if no one is willing to receive, no one gets to give
(2) Galatians 6:2 ("Bear ye one another's burdens, and so fulfil the law of Christ") is in the same chapter as 6:5 ("For every man shall bear his own burden") and
(3) there comes a time to receive. I won that argument because she was in the hospital and there wasn't anything she could do about it! :)

But the donation thing is still strange for our family. We've always felt like God has been so good to us that we should be the ones who are giving. That said, we know some want to do something, and a big show of flowers is not consistent with who we are. The alternatives below, however, are consistent with who we are.

We wanted a brain cancer research organization that actually does research, rather than just paying salaries and lobbying. The doctor supervising Courtney's clinical trial recommended a couple, one of which I'd already looked at.

I have known ______ for almost 20 years, during which our church in Scotland supported him and his family. His ministry (in a European city) helps with drug and other addictions. NOTE: This is not a US charity, so contributions are not US tax-deductible. I strongly endorse this ministry.

You may also make US tax-deductible contributions that will instead go to supporting the needs of ________ and his family. Again, I strongly recommend this man and his ministry.

For those in the UK and elsewhere outside the US, I can't make a particular recommendation for a cancer charity. Many are merely lobbying organizations, unfortunately, and I've not done the research to find out.

For all, anywhere, if you have a good local church of which you are a member, giving there is always something I'd endorse, and if you choose to give to your church in memory of Courtney, that would be a great thing as well. If you aren't a member of a good local church, try to find one!

Thank you,
Justin

Preparations continued. We'd made no arrangements before Courtney's passing except to choose a funeral services company, so while we had planned the service, there were many details to iron out. Courtney's life verse was Jeremiah 29:11, and I told her I needed to include the two following verses. My message was ready, but I kept going over it.

> Jeremiah 29:11 *For I know the thoughts that I think toward you, saith the Lord, thoughts of peace, and not of evil, to give you an expected end.*
>
> Jeremiah 29:12 *Then shall ye call upon me, and ye shall go and pray unto me, and I will hearken unto you.*

Jeremiah 29:13 *And ye shall seek me, and find me, when ye shall search for me with all your heart.*

Courtney's favorite hymn was "Wake, Awake, for Night Is Flying." It wasn't well known, so she decided that rather than ask the congregation, our family should sing it. I told her if she thought I would be able to sing that song at her service, the tumor had addled her brain! Our kids agreed to sing but asked for friends from the church to sing too, so if they started crying, someone else could carry it.

Friends were recruited to "help in case the kids started crying." One, not realizing it was adult "kids," said, "How am I supposed to help their kids if they start crying?" When she understood that the need was to sing on if they stopped because they were crying, she said, "I'm going to be crying, too!" On the day, more than one person had tear-laden eyes.

Everything came together, and I sent out another email a week before the service.

29 January 2022 (Saturday p.m.)

"Service Link and Other Stuff"

Dear All

Stuff About the Funeral:
[edited]

Other Stuff:
Courtney's Dad has COVID, and we are not sure whether he will be able to make it.

Courtney's dear friend in our church has COVID.

Rosa's boyfriend has COVID and she was exposed. So far, she's testing negative.

Our dear friend is coming from Scotland, but her son has COVID, so if she catches it, she probably can't come.

Eric has three broken ribs and has an uncomfortable long flight. His Saturday flight was canceled so he is now flying on Sunday. Maybe the Lord knew he needed an extra day of rest before flying.

I saw my doctor today and he told me he has a patient going through a similar situation and really struggling with it. I told him if he wanted to invite his patient to Courtney's funeral, we'd be honored to have him, it's open to all. He assured me he was going to do exactly that. I could tell that my doctor really, really wanted to come too, but he can't. Please pray that if this man does come, he will find the peace that only God can give through Jesus Christ.

For Those Wondering How I'm Doing:

I'm fine, mostly. But occasionally, the emptiness of the house or the inability to ask Courtney what she thinks about something hits me. Or a picture. It doesn't seem real. And I suppose, it really isn't. This life is just a shadow of what real life will be like if the Bible means anything at all. But this life used to seem real, and now it doesn't. It's not that I'm distraught by that. Of course, it bothers me sometimes. But mainly it's just very, very strange.

I suppose it is compounded by the fact that for months, my life has been wrapped around taking care of Courtney and now that's gone. I have a million things to do, so no time for anything, but none of them involve helping her out of bed into the wheelchair, or getting her lunch, or getting her toothbrush for her, or helping her roll over in bed, or shifting her when she slides too close to the edge of the bed, or any of that. And it still feels like I ought to be doing those things. I'm still waking up 5 or 6 times a night to help her, but now there's nothing to do except go back to sleep or lie in bed with my mind spinning about those million things to do.

I'm not complaining, at all. I know that this transition is good, and that God has a great purpose in it. I'm already seeing Him do some really good things through it all, and even if I couldn't see, there would be few things stupider than complaining. It wouldn't help anything and would dishonor God. I've stayed the course this far without taking that turn and I'm not going to do it now. But it all just does seem very strange to me. Mostly, I'm excited to see what God has next, even if my life feels strange now.

All of that probably only makes sense to those who've gone through this, and maybe not even to all of them. At this point, if Courtney were here, she'd say, "You're rambling. You should probably get rid of those last three paragraphs, but at least, don't go further." :) So, I'll stop.

I'll probably send one more email before the funeral.

Thank you for your prayers!
Justin

The day came. Horrible weather stopped many flights, so many people didn't make it. Our friend from Scotland caught COVID and couldn't come, nor could

Courtney's parents, but all our kids and grandkids were there, and people came from around the United States. Courtney would never have believed she was so loved.

I was told one family brought their children (who had never been to a funeral before). They wanted the children's first one to be a God-honoring one, and they were sure that was what this would be. That would have really pleased Courtney.

The Farewell Service was as wished. Our daughters handled the piano. Courtney's coffin came in to "Highland Cathedral" on the bagpipes. Our pastor said it was not a "Celebration of Life" but a celebration of what God had done in Courtney's life. Scriptures were read; we had music that honored our God; and I spoke on Courtney's verses. At the graveside, we sang "It Is Well with My Soul," and our pastor led a brief service.

As I knelt beside the coffin, I couldn't pray; I just cried. (Now, I think the tears *were* a prayer.) Then, three-year-old Duncan came and patted his Papa on the back, which reminded me, "I still need to serve." I would never pretend I wasn't grieving—but I would try, at least, not to grieve in ways that would interfere with serving others.

We returned to the church for lunch. People were so kind, and new friends and old had tears in their eyes at times. Then, friends and family gathered at our house for food, talking, and hymns. Finally, some left and others bedded down for the night. I didn't sleep much, but I could still be thankful for God's blessing on the day. The next day, I wrote the following email.

5 February 2022 (Saturday p.m.)

"Courtney Martin's Farewell Service"

Dear All

Courtney's Farewell Service in the church was recorded and is now available online. (We don't have a recording of the graveside service.) I thank you for your prayers.

We would be very glad to have you download it if you want and/or share it with others, if you think it would be profitable to them. Many people said the service was a real blessing, so if you find it so, please feel free to share with others.

I have discussed with my kids the suggestion that we turn these emails into a book, and we do think this is something the Lord would have us do. Lord willing, I'll have more on this for you next week, but I believe it's about time to wind down these emails. Thank you again for your prayers and for sharing this with us.

Justin

Chapter 31

No Good Thing Withheld

♪

8 February 2022 (Tuesday p.m., four days after the Farewell Service)

"Courtney Martin 'Final' Update and Book Info"

Dear All

This is sort of my final update. However, we do intend, Lord willing, to proceed with the book project and my company has kindly agreed to leave this email list open until the book is finished, so there should be one more email when that happens.

The Funeral:
I believe God was honored in the funeral, and so, apparently, do many others, as I keep hearing from people. I believe it had a positive impact on both Christians and unbelievers alike. I am very grateful for God's goodness and help in preparation and in all that was done. So many people helped us to honor Courtney's wishes, but even more, to honor our God.

The Book:
[edited out—if you've read this far, you don't need to read about the book in an email!]

How Is Justin?:

Previously, in the death of loved ones, I've found the grief is harder after the funeral. In this case, I think it was harder before the funeral. Grief is always untrustworthy though; it seems to me that you never know how and when it will hit you. But I think that the preparation for the funeral involved several things that stirred the grief and it helps to have that done.

Sleep is still iffy for me. I have noticed that pretty consistently when I have mentioned sleep in these emails, I sleep better that night. Sometimes we wonder if we are really asking God for the right thing, but there is so much in Scripture on rest and sleep that indicates it is God-honoring and I don't think we should ever hesitate to ask God for that. I believe that when I have mentioned it, more people have prayed for it, and God has blessed that for me, and it belongs on my "remember to pray for" list for others.

I'm going to be busy for a while with getting all the legalities/accounts sorted out.

There are people I need to see, some people who couldn't make it to the funeral, some people who didn't get to see Courtney this last year. So, while I can't possibly see everyone, I am going to be traveling for a few weeks, Lord willing, to see some of those people, and also to visit Mom's grave, since I missed her funeral. I've not really worked since the start of the year, so I'll be taking my computer and working at least some while on the road, and I'll be driving a lot, praying a lot, thinking a lot.

I have many questions about what God intends me to do going forward, and few answers. I know I am supposed to serve Him, but in exactly what ways I do not know. So, I'm seeking wisdom on that.

I'm not sure there's much else to say about me that hasn't been said about Courtney and me over the last 14 months. "No good thing will he withhold from them that walk uprightly." If I remain true, "walk uprightly," everything that is really good will come my way. That seems odd coming from a man who just lost something really, really good, who buried his wife (and a wife like Courtney), but I don't doubt it. My future is bright, whatever shape God gives it. I can't believe the pain will ever be gone but it's part of what He is using to refine me. As Courtney said in her letter 14 months ago, "I'm okay, I'm better than okay." She's a lot more okay than I am now, she's in Glory. But I'm okay, too, and I don't see that changing. God is faithful even—in fact, especially—when I'm weak. If He loved me enough to send His Son to die for my sins so that I could have eternal life in Glory with Him, I'm pretty sure He loves me enough to lovingly direct my steps for the years I have left on this earth. He'll give Grace and Glory.

Thank you again for all your prayers. I've come to love many of you as you've corresponded even if I frequently haven't been able to take the time to respond. May the Lord richly reward you for your encouragements and other ways of helping during this time.

And more than anything, if you don't have the peace and joy God has given us through the trials, I pray that you'll come to know Him as Courtney and I have, that the same peace and joy can be yours. It's real, and I think those who have been reading for the last 14 months know that. And you can have it, too. Please, if you don't have it, and you want it, hit "reply"

> and let's talk. I can't give you that peace and joy but I know where you can get it.
>
> Justin

And how is Justin now? Since so many people keep asking, perhaps my readers will care to know. Perhaps my experiences will ring a bell with some or help prepare others who are facing similar life upheavals.

I still believe everything I wrote in that final email. It is as true, and as real in my heart, as it was then. I've learned a lot more about grief, and a lot more about myself. I'm much further down the road of learning to live as newly single than when I wrote last February.

I have experienced Valentine's Day, Mother's Day, and Father's Day without Courtney. I've gone through our anniversary, through my birthday and Courtney's. I've known the thrill of helping someone come to know the Lord Jesus Christ as his Savior, the excitement of seeing others take huge steps forward in their faith, and the grief of not sharing those joys with my wife.

I now know that I really do have emotions. I thought I was 95 percent computer-brain/robot, but there really is some human being lurking inside me, maybe even 50 percent! I know what it is like to have the Lord take me through painful weeks, my emotions always near the surface.

I learned that my Lord had loving reasons for it all. I had to really feel pain, to feel like an utter emotional basket case. Without it, I would not really be able to "comfort them which are in any trouble, by the comfort wherewith we ourselves are comforted of God" (2 Corinthians 1:4). I now know by experience what it is to have someone describe his pain to me and truly be able to say, "I know, it was like that for me too."

Six months after Courtney's passing, I learned what it is like to walk out of church crying when one of her favorite hymns comes up. I think this is ridiculous. Millions of people lose their spouses. Millions heal enough that they don't have to walk out of a service to cry after six months. Clearly, it is not ridiculous to the Lord. He must have reasons for me to be so emotionally vulnerable, and I accept that.

I've learned how to rejoice that my son has found a godly wife even though I don't get to rejoice with his mother. Eric married a lovely Christian girl in the land where he serves—I can share this with my other kids, with friends and Christian family, but not with Courtney.

I was driving home to write the chapter on Courtney's passing when Ward called to say he had a ring for Rosa and to ask my blessing. I don't get to share that joy with Rosa's mother, but it cannot be a coincidence that he called right then. It was as if the Lord was saying, "I know, I am here; I've given you a joy to help you through this, but also a sorrow with this joy. Always remember you need Me." I suspect most joys, for the rest of my life, will have a bittersweet tinge, a tinge intended to teach me to love heaven more.

Two more Cuteness Roarers are on the way. Courtney didn't get to see the others grow up, but she at least got to enjoy them for a while. Not these two—but how can I be anything but thankful?

Despite the heartaches and the "tinges," I still have far more for which to thank God than to regret, not just in my sure hope of heaven but also in the joys of this life. I don't have to try to face life with a smile; it comes naturally, because there is so much reason to smile. If I have to find a corner to cry sometimes, I will, but it isn't hard to return to life with a smile.

That doesn't mean losing my "helpmeet" has been easy. I was always rather "hopeless at life." A few things, by the grace of God, I can do rather well, but beyond that, I'm clueless. I teased Courtney that she was afraid I would "dress like a dork," but I mostly manage by remembering which coat and tie she used to match with which shirt when choosing Sunday clothes.

I bought a shirt, all by myself, for the first time since college. I wore it in public and didn't notice anyone laughing, which makes me quite proud. I really can use the washer and dryer (though Alyssa usually handles that). I am super-careful to avoid stains because I don't know what stain remover works for what kind of stain. I will learn eventually, but always before, such things were left to the expert.

I am still "bad at life." In a ministry situation I forgot Memorial Day, so I failed to honor those who have given so much. Courtney knew I was "hopeless at life" and would remind me of such things, but she is not here. I spent years training my brain to be Scottish, and in Scotland, instead of Memorial Day in May, we have Remembrance Day in November. The one who would have helped me transition back to the United States is not here.

I have mostly not killed Courtney's plants that she chose so carefully, and I have mostly killed the weeds. I have kept our bedroom from becoming a disaster except for all my stuff piled on one table in the corner. I am thankful that I believe the rapture comes first, because if Courtney came back in the resurrection before the Lord took me in the rapture, I'm afraid I'd be in a lot of trouble over that table!

Being a widower has not magically endowed me with the good sense to lie down and rest for a wee bit after overdoing it. That is a "hopeless at life" situation where Courtney's input is sorely missed. I have not yet killed myself by either poisoning or eating a heart–attack-inducing diet, but if left entirely to my own devices, it might not end well.

I am now more efficient on one thing. Making the bed in the morning is silly—you just fold the sheets back again at night to get into bed, so what's the point? Why wives do not accept my logical and efficient approach, I do not know—but some silly people think this is further evidence that I'm not good at life. Courtney was one of those people! But she is not here, and I can be as efficient as I like in leaving the bed unmade without worrying whether it means I'm bad at life! (This paragraph is also my escape clause in case my kids try to match me up with a bride I don't like. I can just show her this paragraph, problem averted!)

In these "hopeless at life" situations, I've been learning just what a gift I was given for the years of our marriage and learning more and more what God meant that His "strength is made perfect in weakness." I've learned that I should not pray for strength but rather for the right kind of weakness in each situation, the kind of weakness that will make His strength perfect for that situation.

I've also learned some things about God's hidden graciousness. There were ways He helped us that we didn't even realize at the time. It may sound strange, but in struggling with hay fever through this Colorado summer, I've found it a source of great thanksgiving. Last summer, I didn't even think hay fever was a thing here. I had no trouble at all. Now, knowing what it is really like, I look back to last summer and see a special provision of God's grace. Last year, caring for Courtney, I couldn't have done everything if hay fever had been sapping my energy, and our Lord protected me. Each annoying sneeze now reminds me of God's grace last summer and makes me wonder how many other graces He sent our way that I have completely missed.

Psalm 84:11 is still true. "For the LORD God is a sun and shield: the LORD will give grace and glory: no good thing will he withhold from them that walk uprightly." God is our sun and our shield. He certainly has given and still gives Grace and Glory. And if those are true, so also is the last part—"no good thing" will He withhold from me if I walk with Him. I do not know which good things will come my way, but I know that His plan is best.

I will always be grateful that, when we left Scotland, the Lord dropped us into Colorado Springs Baptist Church. We didn't have to search through the many churches in the city; the Lord put us, on the very first Sunday, in a place that would love us wonderfully and where I could go on serving Him. That's certainly one of the good things He has given.

I suspect some who read this book may have similar experiences to what I wrote about or will be facing them soon. You enter into "not two, but one" territory, not really knowing what it will be like. I'm sure it is different for everyone, but the joy of the Lord is still there, still available, whatever shape your life-as-one may take.

This book has been hard to write at times. It has brought back memories that were already receding, sometimes with much more pain than I felt at the time. It has undoubtedly been good for me to do, but I wouldn't have done it if I hadn't hoped it would help others facing "life turned upside down" trials.

In that spirit of helping others, I'd like to answer a question I'm often asked: "How did you do it? How did you and Courtney go through it with a joyful spirit, trusting the Lord?"

1. It wasn't us.

There was nothing special about us. We had given our lives to the Lord, had built our lives around His Word and His service, but so also have many others who yet have really struggled when the heart-wrenching trials hit. We weren't any better Christians than millions of others.

God brought us through it in the way He did. For reasons best known to Him, He chose to touch our lives in this way, both to suffer this grief and loss and to be carried by Him through it.

2. It wasn't faith; it was peace.

People said, many times, "You have so much faith." I never agreed. Faith is something we exercise. This was different—this was peace that God gives.

"Faith is always the answer to the tension between doctrine and experience." So wrote Michael Barrett, my seminary Hebrew professor (*Beginning at Moses* [Greenville, SC: Ambassador-Emerald International], 3). Pastor Paul Brown in Green Bay, Wisconsin, quoted it in a sermon I heard in February. Doctrine (what God says) and what we feel or experience can seem to disagree—when that happens, faith is the answer. We trust God that His Word is true.

As I pondered it, it struck me that faith and peace differ. Faith answers that tension, but peace is when God removes it. Sometimes, God steps in and makes us really feel that the truths of His Word are true. He brings our feelings and experience into line with doctrine, and there is no tension.

Talking to Pastor Brown after his sermon, he said, rightly, that peace comes as a result of faith. That is certainly true, but I'm convinced it is only part of the story.

3. Perhaps there's a reason God gave peace.

I think God gave peace, in our case at least, because we weren't even thinking about trusting Him. We were thinking about honoring Him.

From the first morning (when I reminded myself I live to serve the Lord), from the meeting (later that day) with the doctor on his rounds when we smiled in the face of a horrible diagnosis, we wanted to represent Christ and honor Him.

Our pastor recently said, "There's peace and power in doing what God wants you to do and has authorized." God wanted us to honor Him, to testify of His goodness, of His love, joy, and peace. When we set out to do that, seeing cancer as a chance to honor and praise Him, He gave power and peace.

It's a small but important difference in the way we think. When we remind ourselves to trust God, we continually remind ourselves of the difficulty of doing so. We may even magnify the problems in our own mind. When instead we set our minds to honor God, problem becomes opportunity.

You can grit your teeth and determinedly say, "I'm going to trust God, even though it is really, really hard."

Or, you can smile and say, "There are opportunities. Lord, help me to see them and take them!" The former is wonderful, but the latter is, I believe, even better.

4. We trusted Romans 8:26.

It says that "we know not what we should pray for as we ought: but the Spirit itself maketh intercession for us."

We avoided the stress of feeling we must figure out the right things for which to pray. We knew to pray for strength to stay true. You ask the Lord to help you sing and praise Him, for opportunities to tell others of His goodness, for wisdom, for all the things the Bible clearly says to request.

But what about praying for sleep? Perhaps He had a purpose for us to be tired the next day. What about praying that we could make it to church? Maybe He had a purpose in keeping us home . . .

We just relaxed in our Father's love and didn't stress out. If we thought it was good to pray for something, we did. We knew if we got it "wrong," the Spirit would intercede.

We asked for healing, miraculously or through treatment. We asked for Courtney to walk again after her fall. The Lord gave us something medical professionals thought wouldn't happen. We asked for much that we didn't know the Lord's will. Some things He gave as we asked, and others the Spirit interceded when we clearly didn't know how we ought to have prayed. It was peaceful. We could go to our Father like little children.

Those things helped. But, of course, none of that matters if you don't have a relationship of trust with God. Pastor Brown was right. Peace starts with trust, and God won't give peace to those that don't trust Him.

It all flows out of a right relationship with Him. If you don't have that, whether facing a life crisis right now or not, start at ground zero and get it right. It's never *too* late to get right with God, but if you leave it until you are in the crisis, things will be a lot tougher. Sort it now. If this is you, please see Appendix A.

Chapter 32

Elijah Clouds

♪

It is hard to know how to end this book because, you see, the story hasn't ended.

God gave us eight children (two went to heaven before birth and are with Courtney). The six still here are walking with the Lord. Her influence lives on. Can her story be over when her children are still serving the Lord, teaching their children to know Him, and encouraging others to follow Him?

A church exists in Scotland because Courtney was willing to (as I call it) "stare at the wall." She left behind friends and family to go to Scotland. If I made a hospital visit (or prepared a sermon) in the evening, she was alone. If I did those things during the day, I worked into the evening, and Courtney was left to "stare at the wall" alone. She had many lonely evenings with "a wall to stare at" as company.

Some people seem impressed that I worked two jobs, one to pay the bills and another in ministry. Courtney never wanted me to talk about it, but her sacrifice was greater. Our story, Courtney's story, cannot be over while the church for which she gave so much still exists and is proclaiming the Word of God.

People will be in heaven through Courtney's service to the Lord. The only Person who can put a value on that is the One who priced it in His blood shed at the cross. Only He can end their story, for He holds their times in His hand. If their story is not over, Courtney's cannot be, so how do I end this book?

I decided to close with some "Elijah Clouds."

In 1 Kings 18, Israel had left the Lord to follow idols. God sent a great drought to help them see their need of Him, then sent Elijah to call them back to Himself. A great challenge was issued on Mount Carmel, and in the end, the people said, "The Lord, he is the God."

Afterward, Elijah prayed for rain, and his servant saw "a little cloud out of the sea, like a man's hand." Only God knew it was the early sign of a great blessing, the long-awaited rain. To others, it may have appeared just like an empty cloud that had often been seen before.

When we moved to Colorado, Courtney watched for the little clouds over the mountains. She would say, "There's an Elijah Cloud!" We didn't know if it would come to nothing or if the rain would come in later to water the plants and break the heat of the summer days. An Elijah Cloud was an early (albeit uncertain) sign that a blessing might be coming.

Some Elijah Clouds came through Courtney's cancer. I don't know what God will bring out of them, but they remind me that God worked in us and through us. Perhaps some have become, or will become, "showers of blessing," but that rests with the Father.

I have kept these short and changed enough details (in some cases substantially) to protect the privacy of individuals, but the essence of the account is accurate.

Elijah Cloud: Shaaf said, "Pray for me."

I chose the name Shaaf (Arabic, "one who gives health") for a nurse who helped care for Courtney. One day,

Courtney told me, "I've been talking to Shaaf about the Lord for an hour." Soon, Shaaf came in and said to me, "You are different from anyone in my religion. They would not respond as you do."

We talked for half an hour, and then Shaaf asked about a Bible. I brought one the next time. Shaaf's words the last time we met were, "Pray for me." Perhaps Shaaf has found that the Lord Jesus Christ can give peace and joy like He gave us. For us, Shaaf was an Elijah Cloud, a reminder that God was working and could do great and wonderful things.

Elijah Cloud: "My cousin is talking about God."
Someone wrote, "My cousin has been reading your updates. He is talking about God. Maybe he will trust Jesus!" To think that someone might come to know Jesus and be in heaven forever!

Elijah Cloud: "I'm thinking about the ministry."
Someone wrote that Courtney's faithfulness had challenged him about serving the Lord. He wondered if God wanted him to become a pastor. Someone else is thinking about missions.

Elijah Cloud: "I wish I had done better."
A pastor wrote that when he lost a loved one to cancer, he had not been as he should have been. Our story made him determined that the next time, he would honor Christ.

Elijah Cloud: A neighbor told a neighbor.
A neighbor told another neighbor, who told another neighbor, who told me, "Courtney was a real Christian. I don't believe exactly like they do, but you could tell it

was real. Justin, too. That's what Christians should be."

Elijah Cloud: A friend (in the Middle East) of a friend.
"I have read all your emails. My faith teaches we cannot be sure of heaven, but I think that is wrong and Courtney must be there. I am sorry for your loss."

Elijah Cloud: "I will never forget."
Often I read, "I will never forget these emails. I want to be like this when trials come."

Elijah Cloud: "More than you'll ever know."
People said God used us to "touch more lives" than we would ever know, to "encourage more people" than we would ever know, to "help me more" than we would ever know.

Elijah Cloud: "I learn so much about faith."
A medical professional told Courtney, "I learn so much about faith from you. I will not forget. I have seen religious people, but I have not seen this."

Elijah Cloud: "Your family is different."
A medical professional, at the first hospital, said, "Your family is different. We all see it. People do not smile when they are told they have a glioblastoma. You bring light onto our ward. We will do everything we can for you."

What will come of these Elijah Clouds? Will they fade into nothing? Perhaps some will, perhaps many. Maybe someone will go to heaven as a result of Courtney's cancer, but maybe not. Perhaps no one will carry through and be more faithful, more committed to the Lord. Maybe the emotional responses were simply that, emotions. Or (just possibly) God will bring many abundant blessings into many lives as a result.

It doesn't matter what God does with the Elijah Clouds. They look like victory to me. We were "cast down, but not destroyed" (2 Corinthians 4:9), bruised, but not conquered. We won. We did not beat cancer—Courtney's body is dead and awaiting the resurrection—but neither did cancer beat us. We accomplished what we set out to do.

Jesus said, "Let your light so shine before men, that they may see your good works, and glorify your Father which is in heaven" (Matthew 5:16). We succeeded. We let our light shine. People saw a difference, and we told them why it was there, and they glorified our heavenly Father. That is why there were Elijah Clouds.

Jesus didn't say what God would do when our lights shine; He just set us a goal. Courtney and I weren't perfect, not even close. I've told of some of our weaknesses, but there were other things too. They are with our Lord, and He covered it at the cross. None of them change this—we went through cancer with Christ, and the Elijah Clouds show that, by His grace and through the peace He gave, we did let our light shine.

We may have failed in a lot of things, but in that one thing at least, we conquered. The story may not be over, but I am content. God still helps me sing, and by His Grace, I will go on serving and praising until I also can't sing anymore and He takes me to Glory. "But until then, my heart will go on singing" of the One who loved me and died for me.

Appendix A

Getting Right with God

A Systemic Problem

To solve a problem, we usually need to first understand it. Many people think their problem with God is in the wrong things they do (what the Bible calls "sins"). They are focused on symptoms, rather than the real problem.

If medicine had solved Courtney's symptoms (headaches, fatigue, confusion, and balance troubles), it wouldn't have saved her life. The only way to do that was to stop the tumor growth. Another operation might have left her paralyzed, blind, and unable to speak—and solved nothing, because glioblastoma spreads, sending tendrils throughout the brain. It is a systemic problem needing either a miracle or a new treatment to kill it everywhere.

Our *Own-Way* Problem

The problem in our relationship with God is also systemic. The Bible describes it this way: *"All we like sheep have gone astray; we have turned every one to his* ***own way****"* (Isaiah 53:6).

Our problem is not what we do while going our ***own way***. It is that we have chosen our ***own way***. The wrong things we do, while following our own proud, selfish, greedy, and/or lustful way, are mere symptoms.

Someone else may have more ***own-way*** symptoms than us, may do more things wrong, but some people who had more symptoms than Courtney are still alive. As with cancer, the vital question is not how many ***own-way*** symptoms we have, but whether the problem is cured.

Neither you nor a doctor can cure a glioblastoma, and neither you nor a pastor nor anyone else can cure your ***own-way*** problem. You might fight off or control a symptom, but others will pop up. It takes a miracle. It is going to take God—so we need God's solution. We find it in the Bible.

The Bible Says We All Have an *Own-Way* Problem

Isaiah 53:6 says, *"We have turned every one to his **own way**."* God calls it "sin." Romans 3:23 says, *"For all have sinned, and come short of the glory of God." All* includes you as well as me. Just as medical problems need a true diagnosis from someone who knows about it, spiritual problems need God's diagnosis—that there is a problem, it is me, and it is systemic.

The problem is serious. God says it leads to death: *"For the wages of sin is death"* (Romans 6:23). Ignoring cancer, or pretending it is minor, doesn't help—nor can pretending that sin is minor protect us from the payment that must be made.

The usual things people do to try to get right with God aren't His way. Religious actions, or trying to be moral, will fail. God calls them "dead works" and says repenting (turning) from them is foundational: *"the foundation of repentance from dead works"* (Hebrews 6:1).

Just as treating cancer with aspirin may cover some symptoms, religious actions and self-reform might cover some problems—but the systemic problem remains.

God's Plan, a Gift of Love

God always has the best ideas, and His plan for solving our problem is better than anything we'd have invented. He made the way to a right relationship with Him by giving a gift of love. He sent His only Son to die to pay those "wages of sin." John 3:16 says, *"For God so loved the world, that he* ***gave*** *his only begotten Son, that whosoever believeth in him should not perish, but have everlasting life."*

"For the wages of sin is death; but the ***gift*** *of God is eternal life through Jesus Christ our Lord"* (Romans 6:23). The Bible says Jesus *"bare our sins in his own body"* (1 Peter 2:24) so we could have eternal life in righteousness. He took our sins on Himself and died to pay those "wages" so we could be forgiven. This solves our ***own-way*** problem, replacing our sin with His righteousness, and it solves it forever, so we'll be with Him eternally in heaven.

"But God commendeth his love toward us, in that, while we were yet sinners, Christ died for us" (Romans 5:8). Jesus Christ's death for us was a demonstration of love. But God didn't just say, "Look at My love; here's how it works." It is more as if He said, "See how wonderful My love is; won't you receive it?"

So, If Jesus Died for Me, What Now?

It comes down to belief. John 3:16 says this is for *"whosoever believeth in him."* We need to believe God's diagnosis of our ***own-way***/sin problem. We need to believe Him about how serious it is, and the payment/wages/penalty it brings. We need to believe Jesus died to take care of it and to give us a gift of love, a gift of a restored relationship.

We need to believe God when He says it is a gift, and that "dead works" is not the way. Ephesians 2:8-9 says, *"For by grace are ye saved through faith; and that not* *of yourselves: it is the **gift** of God: Not of works, lest any man should boast."*

What About Repentance?

We need to repent—but some people misunderstand. We don't need to repent of every sin—we'd forget more than half! Imagine arriving at heaven, and God saying, "Sorry, you forgot to repent of a couple sins; you're out!" What kind of a gift would that be?

Remember the real problem—that *"we have turned every one to his own way."* We don't need a cure of the symptoms, but of our ***own-way*** problem. We need to repent of being a ***my-own-way*** person and decide we need to live God's way—but it is still a gift! We don't reform, changing from a ***my-own-way*** person to a ***God's-way*** person. That's impossible, just like curing ourselves from glioblastoma is impossible. It is a gift because God does the work of changing us!

Repentance is accepting what God says about it all—how bad our ***own-way*** problem is, what it does to our relationship with Him, and ultimately, the solution. It means no "dead works" (doing good things) solution, or any other solution besides God's. We accept what God says about our need for change and accept His gift of love that changes us. That is enough because the miracle of changing us is His job, not ours.

We can't get right with God if we don't want to be changed, for the problem in the relationship is us, not God. We also can't get right with Him by changing ourselves, because self-cure, just like with glioblastoma, is impossible. You have to trust God to do it.

If you are a ***my-way*** person and want God to change you, I'd love to hear from you. Maybe we could meet, or I could find someone near you to help you understand

God's way to get right with Him. I can be contacted through info@csbaptist.org or through my website at www.HeHelpedUsSing.com.

Okay—but I Knew That

Perhaps someone reading this has believed, has repented, has trusted God. You know you have eternal life. Jesus died for you, and God forgave you—but you messed up. You let sin in your life that shouldn't be there. You trashed your relationship with God. If cancer (or something like it) came along, you know you wouldn't have peace. You might even be thinking, *I deserve something like that, and I'd just have to say, "What did you expect?"*

For that person, I have one verse: *"If we confess our sins, he is faithful and just to forgive us our sins, and to cleanse us from all unrighteousness"* (1 John 1:9). I want to break it down for you.

- **A condition**, "if we confess our sins." God doesn't want us to water it down; He wants us to describe it as He does. Don't say you were "economical with the truth"; call it lying. Don't call adultery "a fling." He wants honesty.

- **A quality**, "He is faithful." That means you can count on Him. God put His reputation on the line. He is dependable, so if we confess, He will forgive.

- **Another quality**, "He is just." If Jesus died to pay for our sins, then the only just thing for God to do, when we repent, is to forgive. It would be unjust to hold us accountable for confessed sins for which Jesus has paid. God is just, so He will forgive.

- **A promise,** "to forgive us our sins, and to cleanse us from all unrighteousness." He completely takes away everything messing up our relationship with Him.

It's simple—unless we are too proud to be honest with God. Confess, and He makes it right. He loved you enough to send Jesus to die for you, so He won't make it hard to get things right.

You don't want to hit life-with-cancer (or something like it) with a messed-up relationship with your God. If you need help, talk to your pastor. If that's not possible, I can be reached through info@csbaptist.org or www.HeHelpedUsSing.com.

Appendix B

Symptom List

Courtney told Dr. Diamond, who was overseeing the research in Denver, that she had found cancer easier than expected. However, as the following list shows, "easier" is relative. This is a list of some of the symptoms Courtney was experiencing when she entered the clinical trial.

As I said in chapter 19, I include this for cancer patients who may read this to say, "Yes, us too." We knew we were more fortunate than many, but there's still a "fellowship of cancer patients," and "Yes, us too" is worth saying sometimes.

Physical Things:

- Spider veins in legs
- Small bruises on legs
- Very slow wound healing
- Little red dots on legs and stomach
- Dark stripe on thumbnail
- Feet and ankles swelling
- Trembling hands
- Frequent waking up at night
- Significant fatigue
- Occasional headaches
- Digestive tract difficulties

- Pins and needles in feet
- General muscle weakness
- Balance troubles
- A "sticky" feeling in her teeth, like she couldn't really get them clean
- Transient headaches with elevation changes
- Muscles spasms in feet
- Troubles with depth perception
- Difficulty assessing the distance and speed of moving vehicles (feels very insecure crossing streets on foot)
- Vision not as sharp as before

Cognitive Things:

- Occasional and minor logical lapses
- Sporadic memory loss
- Struggles to track the passing of time, sometimes forgets the day
- Difficulty with making plans
- Difficulty controlling emotions; tears at strange times for no apparent reason
- Everything is just slower
- Difficulty with multitasking
- Damaged spatial awareness (For instance, she didn't always notice that she was blocking the aisle in a grocery store, or she stood in front of an elevator waiting for it to open and seemed unaware she was blocking the way of people coming out.)
- Difficulty with directions
- Occasional difficulty with verbalizing thoughts in a logical and clear manner even when the thoughts are entirely logical and clear